Beyond the Cloister

BEYOND THE CLOISTER

CATHOLIC ENGLISHWOMEN
AND EARLY MODERN
LITERARY CULTURE

JENNA LAY

PENN

UNIVERSITY OF PENNSYLVANIA PRESS

PHILADELPHIA

Published by
University of Pennsylvania Press
Philadelphia, Pennsylvania 19104-4112
www.upenn.edu/pennpress

Printed in the United States of America on acid-free paper
1 3 5 7 9 10 8 6 4 2

Library of Congress Cataloging-in-Publication Data
ISBN 978-0-8122-4838-8

In memory of my grandmother,
Edna Livingston Duggan

CONTENTS

NOTE ON SPELLING AND PUNCTUATION

When my analysis depends upon early printed texts or manuscript materials, I have preserved original spelling, punctuation, and capitalization, with the exception of *i/j*, *u/v*, and long *s*. I have silently expanded obsolete abbreviations and contractions.

Introduction.
Gender, Religion,
and English Literary History

Tell all the truth but tell it slant –
Success in Circuit lies
—Emily Dickinson

This book traces a circuitous path through English literary history and the process of canon formation—a path by which Shakespeare's sister takes a detour en route to the suicide Virginia Woolf depicted as her likely fate, converts to Catholicism, travels beyond the seas, joins a convent, and writes devotional poems that imaginatively rebuild her brother's bare ruined choirs. But we needn't create our own fictions to glimpse how it would be possible to read literary history differently by recognizing Catholic women's ongoing participation in it, as both subjects and objects of literary representation. Their stories are woven into the fabric of early modern literature and poetic theory, and we find them in both the texts that exclude them and those that foreground their authority and agency. Recent scholarly work has demonstrated that nuns and other Catholic women wrote in a range of genres and for multiple audiences;[1] I show how their writings offer a fresh perspective on English literary history, enhancing our understanding of the available contexts for canonical literature and the conversations of which that literature was a part. By excavating conflicted engagements with Catholic femininity in early modern poems and plays, the following chapters enable a more nuanced interpretation of how confessional and gender identities are woven into the poetics of erasure undergirding the English literary canon.[2]

The exceptional work of feminist literary critics over the last three decades has done much to draw attention to the significance of female authorship in the early modern period, and the writings of Protestant women of a wide range of social positions and sectarian affiliations have been the subject of multiple monographs.[3] But Catholic women's influence on mainstream literary culture beyond the sphere of the Stuart court has yet to receive such sustained attention.[4] To create a more complete picture of English literary history, we must ask how nuns and recusant women who were not central to England's courtly life shaped its literary culture. I demonstrate that these female authors, whom we might imagine to be marginal figures because of their gender, religion, and social position, are centrally important to an enriched analysis of how literature works in the early modern period and how our own critical perspectives have been shaped by the texts at the heart of our canon that have rendered a more expansive literary history illegible. Rather than taking either conformist Protestant ideology or pamphlet literature at its word, I query the formal effects of Catholic women evident in a wide range of literary texts, thereby illuminating the fraught relationship of gender and religious change to canon formation.

By reading the revelatory works of Catholic women alongside well-known authors who were both formally and thematically engaged with similar literary, religious, and political issues, this book proposes a reassessment of the relationship between canonical literature and its intertexts. Building on the foundational work of scholars of both early modern English Catholicism and women's writing, I show how the literary strategies of men and women of various and shifting confessional identities contributed to the exclusion of Catholic women from the main narratives of English literary history. While the monastic associations of characters like Christopher Marlowe's Hero and William Shakespeare's Isabella demonstrate that contemporary authors were aware of the continued relevance of nuns and recusants, such representations do not directly respond to the texts produced by those women. As a result, it is easy to imagine them writing only for themselves and one another: images of nuns quietly confined to their monastic cells and rendered inconsequential through exile spring to mind. But it is the contention of this book that the writings of post-Reformation Catholic Englishwomen profoundly engage with early modern literature. Through their incursions into contemporary literary culture, Catholic women offered alternatives not only to their country's religious settlement but also to the forms and genres that helped to define and support that settlement. The exclusion of nuns and recusant women from literary history thus results not from an absence but from their contemporaries' routine denials of both their presence and their relevance. In writing, compiling, and authorizing manuscripts and printed books that rejected limited or pejorative representations of their religious practices and identities, Catholic women offered their own texts as alternatives to those that cast them as relics or renegades rather than writers—texts that eventually solidified into our own canon.

As this brief summary suggests, the following chapters explore questions at the intersection of the turn to religion, historical formalism, and feminist criticism.[5] Such an approach may not seem intuitive, given that early work in historical (or new) formalism was relatively silent on matters of gender: feminist scholarship on early modern literature was identified as "most conspicuous in its absence" in the introduction to one influential edited collection.[6] But reading women's writing for form is essential, and I follow Sasha Roberts in believing that "if we neglect early modern women's interest in questions of literary form, we fail to do justice to their work as readers and writers."[7] I would add, though, that our approach to form must be attuned to the complexities of identity in the early modern period: as many critics have shown, "woman" is no more a homogeneous category than "Catholic," and the texts I examine reveal as many instructive differences as they do provocative commonalities, even when authors share both gender and confessional identity. So, too, we need a capacious understanding of form. Many recent critics have recognized that "poetic form is a site for experimentation and engagement," but a narrow focus on poetry would obscure the fact that Catholic women's formal experimentation in a variety of genres offered sites for engagement in broader religious, political, and literary networks.[8] And it is a central claim of this book that attention to form can reveal not only the literary sophistication and interventions of these women but also their effects on their contemporaries. Rather than simply identifying representations of nuns or recusants, I show how ideas about Catholic women got under the skin of early modern authors and into their texts. By recognizing both how Catholic women were relevant to the uses of form in early modern literature and how they responded to and adapted those forms, we can see that our canon has always been more expansive and inclusive—even in its deliberate exclusions—than it has seemed to be.

Many works that seem to have little to do with Catholicism, much less the politics and poetics of Catholic women, reveal a submerged attention to competing voices and literary histories in their very omissions and their unacknowledged intertexts. George Puttenham's *The Art of English Poesy* is one such text. Scholars have traced how *The Art* constructs a literary culture focused on the Elizabethan court despite Puttenham's marginal position in relationship to that court,[9] but his concomitant exclusion of Catholic women from the production and reception of poetic forms has not provoked critical comment, perhaps because such an exclusion is neither unique nor surprising: we expect nuns and recusants to be absent from the texts that helped to define early modern poetic practice. Yet archival materials hinting at both the devotional practices of Puttenham's wife and his potential connection with an English nun named Mary Champney suggest the importance of competing perspectives on early modern culture that his text obfuscates in glancing references to Mary Stuart and to his own extratextual predilections. Champney's narrative survives in an anonymous manuscript—part hagiography, part romance—documenting her life and death. While the gaps in Puttenham's self-consciously foundational text of early modern poetic and rhetorical theory cannot be filled by this manuscript's depiction of Champney's self-consciously literary practice of religious devotion and political resistance, together these seemingly unrelated late sixteenth-century texts reveal a process of erasure that is simultaneously historical and literary: we have lost the connective tissue that would enable a firm archival link between Mary Champneys and Mary Champney, the first raped by Puttenham and the second an English nun in exile, but that loss is written into the poetic theories and literary forms of the early modern period. Puttenham's *The Art of English Poesy* thus offers an extreme example of a routine erasure. His focus on Queen Elizabeth as an exceptional case works to exclude other women from the making of literary history,[10] but the possible historical connection of Puttenham and Champney—and the alternative to a life of abandonment available to Champneys on the continent—suggests that we should not simply read this omission in terms of gender but also in terms of confessional identity and social position.

*   *   *

In *The Art of English Poesy*, George Puttenham represents himself as courtier, poet, and literary historian, documenting a burgeoning national poetic tradition from the inside. By writing about poetry in terms of the court and the monarch, Puttenham helped shape both the creation of the early modern canon and its perception as the product of a distinctly Elizabethan—and therefore Protestant—culture. From the frontispiece image of Elizabeth and its inscription *A colei / Che se stessa rassomiglia / & non altrui* ("To her who resembles herself and no other") to the final supplication of her favor, *The Art* revolves around the queen: her patronage, her status, and her poetry are figured as the center of Puttenham's treatment of English literature.[11] But Puttenham's own relationship to court and queen was never what he desired it to be, and an attentive reading of *The Art*'s politics hints at the very literary histories Puttenham refuses to name.

The logic of early modern political theory structures Puttenham's textual invocations of Elizabeth, which cast her as the fulfillment of his opening declaration that "A poet is as much to say as a maker" (93). As England's queen, she is necessarily the "most excellent poet" of her time, for she "by [her] princely purse, favors, and countenance, mak[es] in manner what [she] list, the poor man rich, the lewd well learned, the coward courageous, and vile both noble and valiant" (95). This is a neat inversion: if a poet is a maker "by way of resemblance" with God's creative power, so too must England's monarch, who most resembles God in her political power, be a poet (93). Praise of Elizabeth's poetic skill thus does not depend upon her poetic production: she is the culmination of Puttenham's genealogy of English poets at the end of Book 1 not because of what she has written but because of who she is.

> But last in recital and first in degree is the Queen, our Sovereign
> Lady, whose learned, delicate, noble muse easily surmounteth all
> the rest that have written before her time or since, for sense,
> sweetness, and subtlety, be it in ode, elegy, epigram, or any other
> kind of poem heroic or lyric, wherein it shall please her Majesty to
> employ her pen, even by as much odds as her own excellent estate
> and degree exceedeth all the rest of her most humble vassals. (151)

In a grammatical sleight of hand, Puttenham transforms the list of forms that Elizabeth has mastered (she "easily surmounteth all the rest that have written") into a conditional through the modal verb "shall": if she were to write in these forms, then her poems would necessarily surpass all others, just as she herself surpasses her subjects.

While she was not as prolific as Puttenham suggests in Book 1 of *The Art*, Elizabeth was indeed a poet, and her verse exemplifies the analogy between political power and literary significance that underlies both Puttenham's bid for patronage and his creation of an exclusive and exclusionary English literary tradition. His choice of Elizabeth's "The Doubt of Future Foes" as the exemplar for "the last and principal figure of our poetical ornament," *exergasia* or, as Puttenham defines it, "the Gorgeous," reveals this interrelationship between literature and politics, while hinting at those silenced by Puttenham's focus on the Protestant monarch and her court (333).[12] By claiming that there is "none example in English meter so well maintaining this figure as that ditty of her Majesty's own making," Puttenham analogizes the figure that he defines as "the most beautiful and gorgeous of all others" and Elizabeth, "the most beautiful, or rather beauty, of queens" (334). In this analogy, the aesthetic appeal of poetry is both a sign and a function of social status and political power. Puttenham thus neglects an evaluation of the poem's formal qualities in favor of an explanation of its political occasion: "our Sovereign Lady, perceiving how by the Sc. Q. residence within this realm at so great liberty and ease . . . bred secret factions among her people. . . . writeth this ditty most sweet and sententious, not hiding from all such aspiring minds the danger of their ambition and disloyalty" (334). "The Doubt of Future Foes" may be "sweet and sententious," but its political message is what makes it so: the value of poetry lies in its political authority. As Puttenham explains, the threat that Elizabeth's poem inscribes "afterward fell out most truly by the exemplary chastisement of sundry persons, who, in favor of the said Sc. Q. declining from her Majesty, sought to interrupt the quiet of the realm by many evil and undutiful practices" (334). Poems make politics, just as Puttenham's *The Art of English Poesy* makes a literary culture in which Mary, Queen of Scots, cannot be named in full, much less acknowledged as a poet in her own right or as just one of many nonconformist women resistant to Elizabeth's sovereignty.[13]

By elevating his own status as poetic authority through repeated invocations of Elizabeth, Puttenham transforms a bid for financial patronage into a political agenda that silences dissenting literary traditions, especially those developed by women other than the queen. He locates himself as a central figure in English poetics—as historian, critic, rhetorician, and poet—at the same time that he positions Elizabeth as the culmination of an English literary history that helped shape modern understandings of Protestant poetics.[14] But recent archival discoveries have revealed that this maker of English literary history was not what *The Art of English Poesy* made him seem to be. He was no court favorite; on the contrary, "the historical documents suggest that his public reputation was, in the eyes of most established courtiers, mainly a spectacle of disgrace."[15] For the purposes of this Introduction, it is unnecessary to detail the lawsuits, excommunications, assaults, and imprisonments that characterized Puttenham's life.[16] But his violent history with women is worth pause, especially considering how it may illuminate *The Art*'s erasure of Catholic women from English literary culture.

As a result of his spousal abuse and frequent adultery, Puttenham's advantageous match to the Lady Elizabeth Windsor—ten years his senior, twice widowed, and likely a practicing Catholic—is well documented in the legal record.[17] Lady Windsor initiated divorce proceedings in the ecclesiastical Court of Arches in 1575, and seventeen witnesses were deposed to support her case. We thus have a paper trail on Puttenham depicting not simply an adulterer but a sexual predator who seduced or attacked numerous young women: Izarde Cawley, Mary Champneys, and Elizabeth Johnsonne, among others, are named as victims of rape, abuse, kidnapping, and imprisonment at his hands.[18] Lady Windsor hoped to "seperatte [her] selfe from the company of soe evell a man," and urged the court not to give "creditt to his gloryous and paynted speache whose custome is all supreme aucthoritie and ordynarye civil governement as a mockarye to use."[19] Her fear of Puttenham's "gloryous and paynted speache" suggests a long history of rhetorical embellishment that would eventually culminate in *The Art*'s portrait of an author at the center of court culture. Puttenham's treatise thus offers a rhetorical practice that matches its theory: in writing, he obscures his own violent sexual history behind a rhetorically compelling text. So, too, he theorizes a poetic tradition that not only effaces women's writing but quite literally drowns out their voices.

The relationship of historical life, writing practice, and poetic theory throws into stark relief the relish with which Puttenham describes the epithalamium, especially the possible violence of the initial sexual encounter between bride and groom. By praising the continental neo-Latin tradition of authors such as Johannes Secundus and narrating the progress of folk epithalamia, Puttenham emphasizes the aggressive and erotic elements of the genre—the very elements that seventeenth-century English poets would soon repress.[20] The wedding song, he explains, must be "very loud and shrill, to the intent there might no noise be heard out of the bedchamber by the screaking and outcry of the young damsel feeling the first forces of her stiff and rigorous young man, she being as all virgins tender and weak, and inexpert in those manner of affairs" (139). For Puttenham, the first sexual encounter is an "amorous battle," followed swiftly by "second assaults" (140), and poetry is an essential part of this ritual of sexual violence: the wedding song drowns out the voice of a woman who is lucky to "escape with so little danger of her person" (141). She is nonetheless physically transformed: "the bride must within few hours arise and apparel herself, no more as a virgin but as a wife . . . very demurely and stately to be seen and acknowledged of her parents and kinfolk whether she were the same woman or a changeling, or dead or alive, or maimed by any accident nocturnal" (140–41). Puttenham thus depicts a literary culture in which women are bodies to be acted upon, marked, and read by others, and one in which the transformation from virgin to wife is a violent and inevitable alteration of the self. Yet the epithalamium in Puttenham's telling is also a form that acknowledges and is predicated on the existence of women's resistant voices, even as it elides the possibility that they may remain virgins or choose a life without marriage. The unnamed objects of the epithalamium are not silent: instead, their words are submerged within the very poetic tradition that Puttenham celebrates for its exclusion of them. Here and elsewhere, *The Art* alludes to the poetic significance of those whose words it refuses to include—not only a Scottish Queen but also virgins and resistant wives.

Unlike the brides whose cries are muffled by a song, Lady Windsor's divorce proceedings enable her to tell her own story and record the stories of others abused by Puttenham. These narratives offer an anticipatory rebuke to Puttenham's description of the epithalamium and its social function, particularly in their attention to the relationship between pleasing rhetoric and violent physicality. In his attack on Mary Champneys, a "waitinge gentlewoman of [Lady Windsor's] beinge of tender yeres," Puttenham

> to wynne his ungodly purpose . . . firste practized with faire wordes and rewardes who neverthelesse resisted the same with a verie godly mynde disposed ^But sith he cold not so wynne her he did dayly^ [illegible] so beate her from tyme to tyme in suche sorte that the maiden shold wax wery of her Service / After which practize he the said George assaulted the said maiden in moste wicked Maner and therewithall shewed her what thraldome and miserye she shold sustayne [illegible] and therefore the next way was to assente unto him in his Carnall Desires / And that then she shold lyve in the estate of a gentlewoman in greate quietnes and in no lesse wealeth and felicitie. . . . after that he begote her with child and caried her to Andiwrappe in Flanders beyoynd the Sease where she was delivered of ~~child who is yet lyvinge~~ and lefte her in there in grete misery as it can be Proved.[21]

The deposition suggests two cultures at odds: Puttenham's desire "to Wynne his ungodly purpose" clashes with her "verie godly mynde." As a result, he abandons his initial seduction, modeled on the "faire wordes and rewardes" of rhetorical manuals and love lyrics, and instead "dayly so beate her." He turns from glorious and painted speeches to physical assaults, from rhetoric to violence, and thus substantiates the implicit—and sometimes quite explicit—associations that would later appear in *The Art*, in which a lady who "was a little perverse and not disposed to reform herself by hearing reason" must have reason "beat into [her] ignorant head" by "the well-spoken and eloquent man" (225).[22] In response to Champneys's coerced consent, Puttenham promises that she will live like a gentlewoman, but this life of "quietnes" and "felicitie" instead mutates into a life of exile on the continent: Puttenham took the pregnant Champneys to Antwerp and abandoned her there.

Champneys was not Puttenham's only, last, or even most pitiable victim, and her brief story is simply one of the many pieces of evidence Lady Windsor marshaled to support her case for divorce. But I would suggest a literary afterlife for this young woman, an alternative to what Woolf imagined for Shakespeare's sister and Puttenham imagined for brides on their wedding nights, in the manuscript life of an early modern English nun. The historical link between these two women is speculative and circumstantial—a coincidence of names, dates, and locations that may or may not point to a shared life—but exploring it suggests the importance of being attuned to the omissions that have erased Catholic women from English literary history and the texts written by and about nuns and recusant women that were essential to that history. Steven W. May has suggested that "Puttenham's *Art*, stripped of its bogus connections with the court, now deserves a thorough reassessment of its actual, and still significant, place in literary history."[23] But I would suggest that the fabrications and exaggerations at the heart of Puttenham's treatise have always been essential to *The Art*'s "actual . . . place in literary history." Puttenham mythologized not only himself and his relationship to the court but also early modern England and its literature as that literature was being written. The unsavory life that lies behind the courtly work was just one of the many historical narratives that his project obscured through its choice of emphasis. In *The Art*, Puttenham "constructed his identity—for himself, for his readers, and for us. For himself especially, such an identity might help displace that other, decidedly historical one."[24] At the same time, he was one of many authors who constructed an identity for English literature that helped to displace another, decidedly historical one. His biography illuminates the relationship between these two literary histories: one centered on a Protestant Queen as the principal maker within a nonetheless masculine poetic culture, and the other written through, against, and by women whose religious beliefs, geographical positions, and social standing have relegated them to the footnotes of literary criticism—or, as Puttenham might describe them, "perverse" women "not disposed to reform" themselves. To recognize the latter, we must acknowledge both the silences at the heart of canonical literature and the revelations of the archive, which together enable a more nuanced understanding of how literary responses to Catholic Englishwomen and their own remarkable literary practice offered alternatives to the nascent narratives of Protestant England.

*   *   *

By losing an "s" and shifting from legal depositions to manuscript life, Mary Champneys transforms into Mary Champney,[25] who "professed at Messaghen not farre from Antwerpe" with the English Bridgettine nuns of Syon in 1569, at twenty-one.[26] Such a transformation—impregnated and abandoned woman turned bride of Christ—may seem unlikely, yet *The Life and Good End of Sister Marie*, an anonymous manuscript focused on Mary Champney's life as a nun, reveals a number of striking parallels between the two young women.[27] Both hold the position of "waytinge gentlewoman" and "goe over the sea" to Antwerp (2v). Champney is soon "tempted with a marveilous longinge desire to returne again into Englande, thinkinge every daye a yeare, untill shee might so doe" (2v)—a feeling akin to Champneys's "grete misery" at being left on the continent. Their chronologies offer similar overlaps: Champneys's pregnancy occurred sometime after September 1564,[28] and her trip could have taken place in either 1565/1566 or 1567.[29] Champney spent enough time in the Antwerp area prior to her profession in 1569 to seek counsel from the Jesuits and participate "in further conference of with some of the good Nunnes about Antwerpe" (3r).[30] These two women also had employers with Catholic tendencies: there is evidence to suggest that Lady Windsor was a Catholic, including the "copes, vestments, mass books, and other religious contraband" found in the home she shared with Puttenham in 1569.[31] While this would not necessarily determine the doctrinal allegiance of her waiting woman, the home was a powerful devotional space for nonconformists, and Catholic women worked to maintain and expand their faith through the religious education of children and servants. Mary Champneys, who resisted Puttenham with "a verie godly mynde disposed" thus may have had a formative experience like that of Mary Champney, who served "one of good worshippe" and was drawn from a young age to the religious life (2v).[32]

The circumstances connecting Mary Champneys to Mary Champney may not have an "actual . . . place in literary history," yet allowing for the possibility that they are the same woman does offer a fresh perspective on that history. *The Life and Good End of Sister Marie* reveals that the literary culture constructed by Puttenham in *The Art* was contested in the lived practice of early modern nuns, for whom literary forms and figures did not serve as signs of royal or patriarchal authority but instead structured modes of political resistance and patterns of devotion. The rhetorical and literary skill that Puttenham located at the heart of the Elizabethan court was just as much in evidence in the nomadic book cultures supported by the English convents in exile, and, when read in relationship to *The Art*, texts like Champney's manuscript life compellingly critique a poetic culture predicated on female silence.

Champney is the dynamic and articulate literary subject at the center of a text that draws heavily on hagiography and romance in its rejection of the ascendancy of a heroic narrative of English Protestantism. She was one of a number of Bridgettines to travel back into England when war in the Low Countries threatened the convent in the late 1570s. A group of young nuns left the dangers of life on the continent only to face a difficult journey across the channel and possible imprisonment in England, where they worked to secure patronage for the convent and support the Catholic cause through missionary activities.[33] Champney died in England in 1580, and *The Life* was written in the same year. It details her calling to the Bridgettine order, the perils of her travels, and her good death. Mary Champney's life, according to the anonymous author of the manuscript, was "well worthie to be written for the memorye of so rare a virgin, raysed upp of god in the middest of a stiff-necked nation" (2r). To a modern reader, this virgin does seem like a rarity: a pious yet outspoken early modern English nun who leaves her monastic enclosure, narrowly avoids the seduction of an English captain in the Low Countries, and inspires her countrymen in England through "the light of her good example" (2r). But the manuscript also makes clear that Champney was not alone: she was one of many women whose "good examples of their virtue since their coming over had donne more good to their Cowntrye by gods sweete disposinge, then ever their tarryinge in Machlin had bene able" (15r).[34] As scholars such as Ann M. Hutchison and Claire Walker have argued, the individual circumstances of Champney's death in an English recusant household exemplified and advanced the collective work of these early modern nuns: her deathbed demeanor inspired one of her countrymen to provide the order with printed devotional books and money for the profession of new sisters, and the account of her life was likely written in order to garner additional material and political support for the English convents in exile.[35]

To achieve these pragmatic ends, *The Life and Good End of Sister Marie* adapts a hagiographical pattern to post-Reformation Catholicism in order to offer a model for other English Catholics.[36] Yet the text's didacticism does not foreclose attention to questions of form. Instead, its didactic purpose depends upon narrative structures that undercut linear progressions—from birth to death, virgin to wife, Catholic to Protestant.[37] While the manuscript begins with a brief reference to Champney's birth and life before the convent, it turns almost immediately to the visions that anticipated her profession, along with a description of her eventual entrance into the convent and adjustment to religious life. Champney's vows serve as the true beginning of the narrative, but the author self-consciously disrupts the expected linear progression with a first-person interjection: "Well I must yet retire backe agayne from entringe into discription of her deathe: to declare first a little more of some poyntes of her life: But first I will compare the manner of her extraordinarye callinge . . . unto the like callinge of an other sister of the same house, which died also in England since their cominge over" (5r). In other words, the central focus of the narrative is nominally Champney's death, and yet the author repeatedly jumps forward and backward in time, anticipating and sometimes describing deathbed scenes in juxtaposition with details drawn from Champney's life. This fragmented structure is further disrupted by a brief narrative of the life and death of a second nun, Anne Stapleton. Stapleton's "like callinge" appears immediately after the story of Champney's initial profession, and it echoes both the beginning and ending of the latter's life, though not the narrative structure of *The Life*. Like Champney, Stapleton has a prophetic dream in which God prompts her to lead a religious life, and she eventually dies "also in Englande verie blessedlie" (5v). This brief interjection, which shows precisely how unremarkable Champney is, precedes a catalogue of her remarkable qualities and the incidents that exemplify them: "meeknes in spirit," "devocyon in gods service," "workes of penance," and "abstinence of diett" (6r–7r). And yet even these vignettes from Champney's life in the convent, ostensibly offered as evidence of her incomparable devotion, are in fact examples of "straighte keepinge of her rule" (6v). Champney thus demonstrates the commonalities of those women who endured exile for their faith even as she is singled out for her individual expression of communal characteristics.

Stapleton's story is one of a number of narrative discontinuities in *The Life* that together underscore the tensions in writing the life of a young woman who does not actually seem all that unusual: Champney's life in the convent is echoed in the obituaries of countless other early modern nuns.[38] Even her trip to England is distinguished primarily by her death, in contrast to the varied experiences of some of her companions. Elizabeth Sander, for example, endured imprisonment by English authorities and eventually found her way back to the Syon community, where she recorded her own narrative in a letter that eventually appeared in multiple printed editions.[39] To make Champney's story seem exceptional, the author of the manuscript life borrows not simply the tropes of hagiography (visions, a calling to monastic life, an exemplary death) but also the elements of a romance, most notably in the nuns' journey to England. After "holye gospellers" invade other convents in the area, a regiment of English soldiers offers, "ether of pollecye or of curtesie," to escort members of the Syon community back to England (9r). The interpretive problem that accompanies this offer—is this a political maneuver or a courteous gesture?—shapes an encounter between Champney and one of the English captains that serves as a rebuke to the political and cultural values of English Protestantism under Queen Elizabeth.

In this remarkable passage of the manuscript, the captain practices with fair words and rewards, much like Puttenham with the other Mary Champneys: he claims "she shoulde not lacke for golde nor pearls, if shee would be his dearlinge" (9v). But she rejects his attempted sexual seduction and (probably specious) offer of marriage, and the author's omniscient narration allows us to imagine a voice for Puttenham's Champneys and an alternative to *The Art*'s violent image of married love:

Say you so sir (quoth shee) well cease these filthie speeches to me, wayinge my profession made (saithe shee) at your perill, well knowinge, as you will perchaunce to your payne, if you tempte god to farre, whose Spowse by solempe vowe I am professed & consecrated, though most unworthie of the honor: beholde here my weddinge ringe (quoth shee) which I weare, wherewith I am alredye wedded to my lorde & Savioure to live & die his trewe handmaide in holie chastitie for any temptinge or threatninge in

> this worlde, As for golde & coyne (quoth shee) I renownced the
> towchinge of it by my profession, which my harte is to keepe &
> continewe in my cloyster, and therefore I weighe it as chaffe. (9v)

Champney proclaims her marriage to Christ, reminding her Protestant interlocutor that his virgin queen is not the only woman devoted to chastity
outside marriage. Her response simultaneously rejects the language of
seduction—transformed here into nothing more than "filthie speeches"—
and the captain's religious politics, which he makes explicit in the suggestion
that she might live like the "Princes of Orenge, which had ben a Nune" (9v).
This reference to William I's third wife, Charlotte of Bourbon, who abandoned her vows in 1572, provokes Champney to condemn the transition from
Catholic to Protestant as vehemently as that from virgin to wife: "As for the
paynted princes of Orenge, whome I shoulde be in such credit with, I detest
her, as accursed of god, for slaunder which she hath broughte to religion:
Such an other Nunne (quoth shee) belike as Luther was a frier" (9v). She
compares both Charlotte of Bourbon and Luther to Judas, suggesting that
their apostasy is no more a reflection on her religious life than Judas's be-
trayal of the other apostles.

This dramatic encounter suggests that *The Life and Good End of Sister
Marie* is a text with literary aspirations as well as religious and political
goals—but Champney is no virgin martyr or Lucrece. Rather than providing
English Catholics with a foundational transgression against which they
could position themselves and a ruined body upon which they could rebuild
their religion in England,[40] Champney's narrative reveals her rhetorical skills
and raises the possibility that Catholic women might change perceptions of
both their sex and their faith through individual oral arguments and written
testimonies. Her "wise and vehement speeches," underscored by the author's
repeated use of "quoth she," leave the captain "so astonyed that he little
thoughte to have founde such a Paragon, perceavinge nowe, and so it was told
him by his counsellors, that all his labor aboute his purpose with her, or with
any of the rest of that spirit woulde be but lost" (10r). The rhetorical skills of an
English nun triumph over the persuasive capabilities of her countryman
fighting on behalf of the Protestant forces in the Low Countries. Champney
is simultaneously "such a Paragon" and one of many potential nuns "of that
spirit" who could prove equally effective in a battle of wits and faith. These
women would not allow themselves to be corrupted or converted by the
Englishmen in the Low Countries who were fighting to advance interna-

tional Protestantism. Instead, they engaged religious controversy on their own terms in manuscripts and printed books that recorded their educational and missionary activities as well as the details of life within their enclosures.

The possibility that Mary Champney, Bridgittine nun and early modern virago, is the same Mary Champneys who gave birth to George Puttenham's illegitimate child and was left in misery on the continent is tantalizingly inconclusive. But this onomastic coincidence nonetheless suggests that competing narratives of—and alternate perspectives on—English literary history may be reconstructed with careful attention to manuscripts, local record offices, and continental archives. Literary criticism is still overwhelmingly influenced by late Elizabethan, male-authored Protestant narratives of the development of English literature and its relationship to early modern social, political, and religious change: the representations of *The Art* have entered and possessed our minds, making it difficult for us to recognize the influence of Catholic women on a significant chapter in the history of English literature. Yet Champney's encounter with the captain suggests that counter narratives are possible: that not every woman is a bride and/or a victim, and that texts by and about Catholic women—the poems of the Scottish Queen, the legal documents of Puttenham's wife, the manuscripts of early modern nuns—offer alternatives to a literary history that attempts to efface them. This book shows that uncovering the forgotten texts of Catholic women can help us learn new things about even well-known canonical literature by authors such as Marlowe, Shakespeare, Donne, and Marvell—and thus enable us to remake our understanding of English literary history.

*   *   *

The defining narratives of early modern England, fashioned by sixteenth- and seventeenth-century authors and reified by later histories, cast nuns as the relics of an unenlightened past and equate Catholic femininity with the dangerous charms of the Whore of Babylon.[41] In recent decades, as historians and literary critics have uncovered the myriad ways that Catholicism continued to matter in post-Reformation England, nuns and recusant women have been recognized for their role in maintaining Catholic religious practice,[42] and manuscript recovery work has revealed a remarkable and still growing body of texts associated with the early modern English convents.[43] Yet these manuscripts and printed books have not yet led to a holistic reassessment of

crucial decades in the development of English literary history—decades
that overlapped with the establishment of new English cloisters on the
continent—or of the texts and authors foundational to our contemporary
canon. While Catholic women helped to craft a language for religious and
political concepts such as obedience and chastity and to shape England's literary culture in the decades following the dissolution of the monasteries, the
significance of women such as Margaret Clitherow, butcher's wife and martyr,
and Winefrid Thimelby, Augustinian prioress and letter writer, was effaced in
their own time and has been mostly forgotten in ours.

England's religion was far from settled even in the final years of Elizabeth's reign, and at various moments it was possible to imagine a Catholic
future for the state, its ruler, and its subjects.[44] At the same time, doctrinal
affiliation had grown increasingly complex: both English Catholicism and
English Protestantism were marked by internal debates regarding liturgical
practice, the space of worship, and political allegiance, to name just a few of
the questions central to the shaping of confessional identities in sixteenth-
and seventeenth-century Europe.[45] Thus, I use terms like "Protestant" and
"Catholic" flexibly, attending to internal divisions when they are relevant to
my analysis: when, for example, debates over church attendance and religious
conformity shape the representation of a committed recusant like Clitherow,
or when the conflicts among religious orders regarding monastic spiritual
direction rise to the surface in Gertrude More's theorization of obedience.
I am especially interested in the conflicted stances taken by Protestant writers
with a range of confessional identities and political affiliations—men and
women who struggled to define themselves, and their period, as different
from that which came before, and who did so, in part, through depictions
of Catholic women as historic relics, superstitious ascetics, or hypocritical
Machiavels, all but the last of which faced almost inevitable rehabilitation in
a Protestant marriage relationship. But Catholic women resisted any easy
demarcation between a Catholic, medieval past and a Protestant, reformed
present in both their religious practice and their print and manuscript books,
and their diverse engagements with English literary culture offer evidence of
the complexities of early modern religious politics.

The English Reformation produced a localized Catholicism that provided women with opportunities and authority not always available to their
counterparts in Italy and Spain: since priests and Jesuits were outlawed and,
when caught, subject to potential torture and execution, women hid priests,
facilitated mass, and took responsibility for the religious education of their

children, servants, and neighbors.[46] Parliament, meanwhile, had difficulty addressing the threat posed by Catholic women who managed to evade the anti-Catholic statutes because of their positions as wives: under coverture, married women could not control property and were difficult to penalize economically, and the state hesitated to punish husbands (many of whom were at least nominally Protestant) for their wives' crimes. Thus, contrary to the tenacious notion that Protestantism liberated women from the strictures of a hierarchical and oppressive church—releasing them from the prison of the convent into loving, companionate marriages—the politically subversive choice to be Catholic in England after the Reformation could provide women with opportunities for political, religious, and literary expression that were not necessarily available to their Protestant counterparts or their coreligionists in other countries. As a result, I argue that the traditional literary critical focus on Protestant women, whether conformist or sectarian, should be supplemented with an equivalent acknowledgment of the wide variety of Catholic women who were significant to the literary culture of early modern England.

At the same time that recusant women drew political attention at home, English convents were flourishing abroad. The early seventeenth century saw the establishment of dozens of monastic communities for English women on the continent, including both enclosed, contemplative cloisters and unenclosed orders modeled on the Jesuits.[47] Starting in 1598, with the first new English foundation in Brussels, a renewed interest in female monasticism prompted a surge in professions—an uptick that was evident elsewhere in the post-Tridentine church as well, but is all the more remarkable given England's restrictions on travel beyond the seas and the financial and emotional difficulties involved in enduring exile for one's faith.[48] These two aspects of the practice and perception of female Catholicism in England—on the one hand, the importance of female recusancy to maintaining the faith and, on the other, the popularity and surprising visibility of the English cloisters—provide the central orientation for this book. I thus focus primarily on the 1590s until the 1660s: decades during which women associated with Catholic devotional practice outside the traditional corridors of religious and political power were nonetheless influential in the imaginative construction of English literature.[49]

In order to demonstrate Catholic women's significance to early modern literary history, the following chapters cumulatively address three perspectives on the making of English literature. First, my Introduction and Chapter 1 explore Catholic women as objects of representation or erasure. I analyze texts written about nuns and recusant women, such as Mary Champney and Margaret Clitherow, and canonical works that express or repress figurations of Catholic femininity in order to show how writing about Catholic women not only reveals literary historical erasures but also demonstrates that even as Catholic women's interventions were written out of the canon, their significance was registered formally in the fabric of canonical literary texts. Second, Chapters 2 and 3 explore nuns as authors, revealing their literary and political interventions through detailed close readings that show how their texts demonstrate a rigorous engagement with the very issues and questions that canonical texts represent as preventing their contributions. The monastic writings I analyze here are complex texts that do more than demonstrate nuns' political engagement or offer clarifying context for well-known plays, and I show how reading them (rather than simply recovering them) offers fresh insights for scholars of early modern literature. Finally, in Chapter 4 and the Epilogue, I trace an alternative genealogy of English literary history, asking what we might discover if Catholic women were positioned at the center of the tradition rather than on the margins. How, for example, does reading certain strands of seventeenth-century poetry—first focusing on a particular family's recusant and monastic literary community and then on a particular genre—help reveal both the possibility of a more flexible and fluid canon and also the literary interventions that helped to solidify the canon as we know it, erasing Catholic women's contributions and their significance as literary agents?

Chapter 1 explores the relationship between virgin bodies and narrative insufficiency in the final decades of Queen Elizabeth's reign, from Edmund Spenser's *The Faerie Queene* and Christopher Marlowe's *Hero and Leander* to William Shakespeare's *Measure for Measure*. The twinned threats of female recusancy and revivified monasticism resulted in a crisis of representation centered on female virginity: in Spenser's and Marlowe's unfinished poems of the 1590s, female virginity is simultaneously already lost and not yet relinquished, consummation is ambiguous or preordained, and marriage or death is always just over the horizon of the poem's narrative telos. Bringing together materialist feminist criticism and formalist literary readings, I reveal the suggestive relationship between incomplete narrative structures and vows of virginity. While many scholars have interrogated discourses of chastity in relationship to Elizabeth, I show how Spenser's conflicted representations of virginity and marriage in *The Faerie Queene* demonstrate formal ruptures that point to a broader crisis of representation, which suggests that Elizabeth's use of her virgin status as a sign of royal power did not simply supplant virginity's close association with Catholic religious devotion. Instead, the increasing social and political importance of recusant women in the wake of Margaret Clitherow's 1586 execution offered a bridge between monastic vowed virginity and the burgeoning post-Reformation ideal of married chastity. These heterogeneous materials—on the one hand, literary texts in which female virgins occasion textual disruptions and stalled narrative closure and, on the other, historical and legal accounts of recusant women's political status—ground my reading of the notoriously difficult Isabella of *Measure for Measure*. The rhetorically powerful female virgins of *The Faerie Queene*, *Hero and Leander*, and *Measure for Measure* locate their social status in vows under near constant attack, whether on the battlefield, in the bedchamber, or at court. These literary depictions of virginity-in-crisis offer oblique responses to the political implications of female recusancy, and I conclude by demonstrating how Shakespeare's account of incomplete political reform and unresolved marital status in *Measure for Measure* exhibits formal effects that reveal the extent to which Catholic women were recognized actors on an international stage.

My first chapter traces the discourses associated with Catholic femininity that entered and shaped canonical English literature; Chapter 2 turns to physical objects associated with religious controversy and transformation, such as books and ruins, which Protestant playwrights and pamphleteers invoked in order to obscure Catholic women's contributions to literary culture. John Webster's portrait of women seduced and destroyed by the Catholic clerical hierarchy in *The Duchess of Malfi* is one of many English revenge tragedies that builds upon the language and imagery of anti-Catholic polemic in its portrait of a corrupt religious and political hierarchy. Yet I argue that *The Duchess of Malfi* not only evokes the standard imagery of Protestant propaganda; it also anticipates the specific textual concerns of pamphleteers writing in the ensuing decade, as the proposed Spanish Match prompted scrutiny of the English convents in exile. Webster's attention to the spiritual traces of the past and the material dangers of the present gives vivid life to the tenacious idea that Catholic women—and especially nuns—were at the mercy of priests and their poisonous books. Fears of a corrupt monastic book culture influenced pamphleteers such as Thomas Robinson, whose influential exposé of Syon Abbey, *The Anatomy of the English Nunnery at Lisbon*, imagined textual control at the root of sexual depravity. *The Anatomy* was one of the best known anti-Catholic pamphlets in early modern England, and it remains a popular resource for both historians and literary critics. This chapter thus addresses the persistence of pejorative representations of Catholic women and the book, despite the fact that the nuns of Syon participated in both print and manuscript culture throughout the sixteenth and seventeenth centuries. I identify how Robinson's rhetorical and representational strategies work to efface female contributions to monastic book culture, and examine the strategies used by members of the convent to refute his claims in a manuscript response written in the months following the first printing of his pamphlet. By examining this rare surviving example of direct female monastic engagement with Protestant propaganda, I shed light not only on the relationship between print and manuscript publication in the early modern period, but also offer a corrective to the idea that Catholic women were victims of, rather than participants in and shapers of, early modern book culture.

Building on this exploration of monastic book culture, Chapter 3 shows how nuns' devotional reading and writing functioned as a form of active political participation in post-Reformation religious conflicts. Members of the English Benedictine convents in Cambrai and Paris interrogated the status of women's political and religious obedience during a particularly fraught period of approximately thirty years—from the beginning of Charles I's reign to the aftermath of the English Civil War—when both Catholics and Puritans confronted the competing claims of temporal and spiritual authorities. Writers during this period drew on century-old debates over Henry VIII's royal supremacy, including nuns who modified earlier writings on the limits of political authority in reflections on their own religious practice. Most striking is Dame Gertrude More, one of the founding members at Cambrai and the great-great-granddaughter of Sir Thomas More, whose *The Spiritual Exercises* invoked her famous ancestor and his martyrdom in order to emphasize the link between a long tradition of English Catholic political resistance and her own community in exile. Gertrude More's defense of spiritual independence reveals that clerical authority did not produce unthinking obedience on the part of female monastics and that nuns remained central to the concept, the practice, and the subversion of obedience long after the Reformation. My analysis of More's devotional writing not only further undermines the limited representations of Catholic femininity created by authors such as Webster and Thomas Robinson, it also helps reveal the limits of allegory in the most overtly political play of the early seventeenth century, Thomas Middleton's *A Game at Chess*. The symbiotic relationship between

Protestant propaganda and the English stage outlined in my previous chapter also fueled Middleton's drama, a political allegory staged after marriage negotiations between Prince Charles and the Infanta Maria of Spain collapsed. Middleton borrowed extensively from Robinson, and yet the play's only nun—the Black Queen's Pawn—is a figure of surprising political efficacy who undermines both plot and allegory. In his pawns' plot, Middleton imagined what an autonomous nun might look like: a religious woman alienated from Catholic hierarchies and uninfluenced by conventional alliances. By reading More's theory of obedience alongside Middleton's play, I demonstrate how the concept of obedience offered a rich literary resource to both nuns and their political adversaries, provoking reflections on political authority and religious faith that ultimately collapse rigid doctrinal distinctions and the conventions associated with certain genres and literary forms.

Convention and poetic tradition are more directly explored and upended in Margaret Cavendish's *The Convent of Pleasure*, which incorporates both the pejorative and the celebratory strains of literature focused on female monasticism, and in the literary practice of a recusant Catholic community scattered throughout England and continental Europe. In my final chapter, I show how the manuscript poems and letters of the Aston, Fowler, and Thimelby families reveal the limits of Cavendish's depiction of female community as the impetus for intellectually engaged and generically heterogeneous literary production. Through these poems and letters, which draw upon the theory and practice of devotional verse expounded by Catholic poet and martyr Robert Southwell, as well as the secular poetry of John Donne, a more ambiguous poetic predecessor for committed recusants, I explore the particularities of English Catholic poetic practice in the mid-seventeenth century, when networks of readers and writers mixed strictly religious poetry and prose with a broad range of written materials, from pastoral poetry to love letters. Repositioning Catholic women at the center of the literary communities to which they were so essential reveals a more capacious literary history and helps to uncover the poetic interventions that contributed to the formation of our relatively narrow canon of early modern literature, including Andrew Marvell's striking dispossession of female monasticism in *Upon Appleton House*. While Marvell acknowledges that communities associated with the convent offered a space for literary production, he supplants a history of female community with the promise of exceptional Protestant individualism in his concluding portrait of the young Maria Fairfax and her future marriage. Cavendish's representation of the convent as a space for cultural production offers a more current vision of female community but it too is quite limited when compared to the prolific writings of her Catholic female contemporaries, whose texts reveal the remarkable generic and formal complexity of recusant literary culture. Nonetheless, even as Cavendish's utopian vision of convent life falls short of the dynamic devotional and literary practice of seventeenth-century English nuns and recusant women, *The Convent of Pleasure* demonstrates that Catholic women's literary engagements remained vital to the imaginative landscape of early modern England.

Yet the vibrant literary practices of Catholic women in post-Reformation England have largely disappeared from narratives of English literary history. My Epilogue explores this oversight through a brief survey of seventeenth-century Passion poems, which reveal a moment at which a broader understanding of that history was still possible. Through brief readings of perspective and subjectivity in the work of poets of different religious aesthetics and political affiliations, I analyze the formal strategies that contributed to a critical discourse in which Catholic women were exiled from English literature as supposedly foreign intrusions into post-Reformation Protestant poetics. To read Catholic women out of this tradition is, I argue, to create an English literary history much like John Milton's "The Passion": unsatisfying and incomplete. Catholic women's manuscripts and printed books necessitate a fresh look at early modern religious and literary culture, and this book demonstrates how their politically incendiary and rhetorically powerful lyrics, prayers, polemics, and hagiographical lives can reshape our understanding of both the canonical and noncanonical literature of sixteenth- and seventeenth-century England.

CHAPTER I

Fractured Discourse: Recusant Women and Forms of Virginity

Nuns and vowed virgins appear with surprising frequency in sixteenth- and seventeenth-century English literature, but they are nonetheless outnumbered by their Protestant counterparts—virgins whose narratives are structured around the expectation of marriage. The slow process of sixteenth-century religious reform stimulated a parallel reconfiguration of the imagery and ideology associated with Catholicism, and female chastity has long been the most visible and contested site in this competition for representation.[1] From the virgin warriors, virgin queens, fleeing virgins, and virgin shepherdesses of the *Arcadia* and *The Faerie Queene* to the chaste young women on their way to the altar (or, in the case of certain star-crossed lovers, the grave) in early modern drama, a marital telos informs and motivates literary representation. In the decades after the Elizabethan settlement, it became increasingly unusual to find women like Hero of *Hero and Leander* and Isabella of *Measure for Measure*, who conceptualize virginity as an earnest religious vow rather than a transitional phase that must culminate in marriage. These nuns—one a votaress of Venus, the other a future Catholic Poor Clare—demonstrate that the devotional markers associated with female virginity could never be completely subsumed under a Protestant ideology that repositioned chastity not within the female community of the convent but within a marital relationship. Yet both are lured away from their religious positions, into negotiations with men who urge them to abandon their vows and participate in a social system in which patriarchal control takes precedence over faith. These virgin characters thus simultaneously profess a devotional practice associated with the convent and occupy a political space reminiscent of the married recusant women who refused to participate in church services and drew increased government scrutiny in late sixteenth-century England.

Hero and Isabella have inspired endless critical consternation, in part because they do not fit neatly into Protestant England, ancient Sestos, or Catholic Vienna. Together with Queen Elizabeth, that most famous of perpetual virgins in sixteenth-century England, they take on a surfeit of meanings associated with female virginity: they are rhetorically powerful, yet their gendered bodies are vulnerable; they are self-possessed, yet the objects of male desire; they are motivated by religious and political convictions, yet restricted by a patriarchal culture. In a period of ongoing religious reform, virginity offered a complex discursive field for authors interested in the conflict between patriarchal ideologies and social practice, and thus pointed not only to convent and queen but also to the recusant women whose outlawed faith enabled active political resistance and underscored the fact that marriage held its own ambiguities in early modern England.[2] In the last half of the sixteenth century, when English female monasticism had yet to be revived on the continent, recusant women put pressure on the social and ideological reconfigurations that accompanied the English Reformations through their unique position on the margins of Catholic religious hierarchies and English law. Their political significance is amply represented in the historical record—in legislation, court records, letters, and manuscript lives—and this chapter demonstrates how their complicated relationship to the patriarchal state contributed to the multiple and sometimes competing significations that female virginity bears in early modern literature. Just as Elizabeth's iconography as Virgin Queen was not a simple appropriation of the cult of the Virgin Mary, the vowed virgins of post-Reformation English literature did not offer straightforward representations of female monasticism.[3] Instead, authors engaged the political dimensions of female chastity in their representations of vowed virgins, creating characters whose dramatic and poetic disruptions formally expressed the social and political disruptions of a broad range of early modern Catholic Englishwomen.

The virgins and nuns imagined by Edmund Spenser, Christopher Marlowe, George Chapman, and William Shakespeare offer a complex map of the relationship between literary form and ideological content in canonical early modern literature. In disparate texts marked by narrative insufficiency or deferral—poems left unfinished or completed by another author; a play that ends with an unanswered question and the promise of further explication—virginity functions as both a social position and a discursive concept under near constant attack.[4] Queen Elizabeth's marital politics offer one touchstone for these late sixteenth- and early seventeenth-century explorations of virginity, and Spenser's fragmented representation of the Virgin Queen serves as a foundation for my reading of the formal effects precipitated by conflicting ideologies of chastity and marriage in his contemporaries' representations of women associated with Catholic devotional practice and religious politics. As Kathleen Coyne Kelly and Marina Leslie have argued, "Elizabeth as the cynosure of the age has created a focus but also a blind spot in the study of the poetics of virginity in the Renaissance."[5] Both focus and blind spot are evident in *The Faerie Queene*, which exposes the ambiguities at the heart of late sixteenth-century celebrations of married chastity even as it resolutely turns away from the representation of vowed female virgins. Instead, the poem explores multiple facets of the queen's chastity through Spenser's diffuse representational strategy: Elizabeth is everywhere and nowhere. She is Gloriana, the unreachable virgin queen; Britomart, the desiring virgin knight; and Belphoebe, the quick-tempered virgin huntress—amidst a host of other virgin characters, flattering and not.[6] At the same time that he creates this fractured mirror of chastity for his queen, Spenser offers the promise of marriage at the end of his epic poem, in a narrative strategy that puts pressure on the marital telos through a constant process of deferral, as both consummation and social recognition are delayed for almost all of the poem's prospective married couples. Spenser seems almost constitutionally incapable of representing married life in *The Faerie Queene*, though the marital relationship remains imaginatively significant to his characters. The narrative ruptures that occur when, for example, the Red Cross Knight postpones his marriage to Una or Merlin prophesies but barely describes the future of Britomart and Artegall are, I argue, products of a representational crisis surrounding female virginity in post-Reformation England that extended beyond "the body and the iconography of a queen" to women of diverse religious affiliations and social positions.[7]

The effects of these discourses of late Elizabethan virginity and marriage are evident in Marlowe's unfinished *Hero and Leander* and Chapman's moralizing continuation of it. Beginning in 1598, when Marlowe's poem was printed with the suggestive "desunt nonnulla" at the end of its final line, readers have felt compelled to supply what they imagined to be lacking in

Hero, Venus's nun. She has been called "equivocal and equivocating"—a suggestive choice of words, considering the Catholic connotations of her devotional status—"both a naive virgin serving the goddess of the household and of love and a prostitute whose chief interests are carnal."[8] Marlowe's Hero is paradoxical and troubling: she is a virgin, yet she is dedicated to the goddess of love; she is a nun, yet she is not bound by rules of enclosure; she is a woman, yet she performs the duties of a priest. George Chapman attempted to transform the inconsistencies of Marlowe's poem and its heroine into material for allegory, and his remarkable depiction of the goddess Ceremony in competition with Venus for control over the lovers' relationship explicitly positions Hero outside an appropriate social order. The two parts of *Hero and Leander* thus make visible the conceptual and social transformations created by the Protestant Reformation, the exile of English nuns, and Elizabeth's status as the Virgin Queen. When read in its entirety, as Chapman imagined it after Marlowe's death, the poem underscores the evolving and precarious position of Catholic women in late Elizabethan England and reveals the literary significance of contemporary debates over female recusancy and marital coverture addressed in manuscripts such as John Mush's "A True Report of the Life and Martyrdom of Mrs. Margaret Clitherow," a hagiographical account of an executed recusant woman written by her priest.

By 1604, when Shakespeare's *Measure for Measure* was first performed, the revival of English female monasticism had begun, and parliamentary efforts to control recusant women remained largely ineffectual. As a result, whether they joined convents on the continent or married in England, Catholic women in the early years of the seventeenth century were able to maintain a certain degree of religious freedom. Shakespeare's depiction of Isabella as a defiant virgin agitating for governmental change in a play that ends with many marriages but little resolution thus points to a turning point in English conceptions of Catholic femininity, when a burgeoning interest in monasticism on the part of English Catholic women aggravated, rather than alleviated, concerns over female recusancy. *Measure for Measure* registers Isabella's significance through chiastic formulations that recall the mirroring and fragmentation of *The Faerie Queene* but reveal that Queen Elizabeth's virginity was not alone in exerting a shaping influence on early modern literature. Together, the texts I examine in this chapter demonstrate that in addition to being objects of representation in poems and plays of the post-Reformation period, Catholic women's social positions, sexual choices, and political efficacy were essential to the formal and narrative structures explored by canonical English authors.

"But Yet the End Is Not": Virginity and Narrative Teleology

The Faerie Queene encompasses multiple understandings of virginity, including the iconic virginity of England's queen and the continued imaginative influence of its ruined cloisters, yet Spenser does not allow for the possibility of female virginity as the product of an eternal religious vow. Instead, he positions his female characters as participants in a courtly culture for which marriage is the presumptive endpoint. This expectation is most conspicuous at moments when Spenser alludes to female monasticism only to implicitly reject it. In the House of Holiness, which looks suspiciously like a convent, virgin maidens practice "godly exercise."[9] Yet this house, "renowmd throughout the world for sacred lore, / And pure vnspotted life," is unlike a monastery in one significant respect: its inhabitants are mothers and wives (1.10.3.2–3). Spenser reveals their participation in a Protestant spiritual and social economy through an instructive sleight of hand, as he leads his readers to believe that the two eldest daughters of the house may be nuns. "Most sober, chast, and wise, / *Fidelia* and *Speranza* virgins were," and, as such, they seem to fit into the Catholic imaginary that Spenser has already invoked through their mother Cælia's "bidding of her bedes" (4.5–6, 3.8).[10] But he immediately reverses course: "*Fidelia* and *Speranza* virgins were / Though spousd, yet wanting wedlocks solemnize" (4.6–7). The uncertainty created by this series of reversals—they are virgins, then married, then married but for the ceremony—raises the possibility of female monasticism at the same time that Spenser denies perpetual virginity a place in this most religious household.

Instead of lifelong celibacy, *The Faerie Queene*'s female virgins occupy a transitional space positioned between an understanding of chastity as "abstinence from *all* sexual intercourse" and "purity from *unlawful* sexual intercourse."[11] They have entered a Protestant narrative of chastity, in which women no longer have an institutionally supported alternative to marriage—but their marriages remain beyond the poem's narrative horizon. Spenser embraces a devotional ideal of vowed virginity in only one instance, and then only for men: priests in the temple of Isis "by the vow of their religion / They tied were to stedfast chastity / And continence of life, that all forgon, / They mote the better tend to their deuotion" (5.7.9.6–9).[12] Celibate monasticism is possible for religious men, but, in this mirror of Elizabethan England, it is not an option for women.[13] In what follows, I will demonstrate how the multiple virginities—and multiple deferred marriages—of *The Faerie Queene* reveal the fractures in a social system that simultaneously elevated married chastity, celebrated powerful virginity, and denied women a religious vocation.

Spenser suggests that Elizabeth made every facet of female virginity her own, leaving him with no basis for the representation of chaste women who did not fit within England's post-Reformation religious and political system.[14] By the last decade of her reign, iconography associated with England's Virgin Queen proliferated in literary and visual representations, and Elizabeth's youthful intimation that "it might please almighty God to continue me still in this mind to live out of the state of marriage" had resulted in the seeming paradox of a Protestant monarch dedicated to perpetual virginity.[15] Critical scrutiny has focused not simply on the queen's choice to live and die a virgin but on the similarities between her representation and that of the Virgin Mary, leading many scholars to interrogate discourses of virginity in early modern England as part of an Elizabethan appropriation of Marian iconography and Catholic devotional materials.[16] Recent work has questioned this narrative of substitution and suggested that, rather than replacing the Virgin Mary, Elizabeth "functioned as an icon of Protestant reform and England's newly imagined identity."[17] Indeed, like England's religious settlement, Elizabeth's virgin status remained under near-constant scrutiny, especially during the first twenty years of her reign.[18] While she imagined a monument raised in commemoration of her rule in 1559—"in the end this shall be for me sufficient: that a marble stone shall declare that a queen, having reigned such a time, lived and died a virgin"—it would be many years before this statement could be viewed retrospectively as a kind of prophecy.[19] Elizabeth's early preference for an unmarried life was a savvy political maneuver, one that enabled her to avoid the inevitable questions of how a queen would negotiate the internal contradictions of a patriarchal system in which the ideology of marriage necessitated female submission. But it was also one of many ways that virginity came to be redefined for English Protestants: even as the queen adopted a rhetoric of perpetual virginity, she positioned herself as an object of courtly desire and remained at least conjecturally open to a future marriage.

Virginity was essential to both courtly and literary figurations of Elizabeth's power, though the queen maintained the possibility that she might eventually conform to a Protestant ideal of married chastity. Theodora A.

Jankowski has argued that "Elizabeth used the cultural 'fact' that there was no profession, no place for adult women virgins in the early modern sex/gender system to stress how unlike other women she was, as well as how unlike other rulers."[20] The Virgin Queen's exceptional status, in other words, depended in part on the religious and cultural shifts that accompanied the Protestant Reformation: if nuns had remained a significant presence in England, Elizabeth's vow to remain unmarried until "it may please God to incline my heart to another kind of life" would have carried devotional rather than political implications.[21] Just a few years after Queen Mary had restored Catholicism and attempted to revive English monasticism, Elizabeth's accession meant both the perpetual exile of England's remaining nuns and a significant shift in the early modern religious, political, and literary representation of virginity.

In the years following the dissolution of the monasteries, English nuns had largely disappeared. While some former monastics remained in England, their diminished social positions and meager pensions led to lives of poverty outside the cloister walls.[22] A number of women traveled to the continent to join religious orders, individually and in groups, but exile in foreign monasteries prevented them from fully participating in sixteenth-century English religious and political life.[23] When Mary took the throne, the renewal of monastic foundations briefly became possible: in 1557, members of Syon Abbey—the only convent to survive the dissolution intact—returned to England after exile on the continent and were "restored" to their "former happy foundation and monastery of Syon."[24] But their restoration was short-lived, and, with Mary's death, they "were once again cast into the sea of their previous sorrow and tribulation, and expelled from their monastery and from all their first hope and consolation."[25] This second exile coincided, on the one hand, with Elizabeth's attempt to position herself as a politically self-contained virgin for whom marriage was not essential and, on the other, with a significant reconfiguration of the relative social status of marriage and vowed virginity in humanist thought on both sides of the doctrinal divide.[26] Protestant writers were especially eager to valorize female chastity within marital relationships; virginity, in their tracts, became a "transitional phase" to be supplanted in every woman's life by chaste married sexuality.[27] The complexity of religious life in early modern England, however, prevented such cultural constructions from solidifying. Thus, while I find Jankowski's argument regarding Elizabeth's self-representation and "the cultural 'fact' that there was no profession, no place for adult women virgins" useful as starting point in 1559, when

Elizabeth offered herself as a uniquely Protestant and exceptionally powerful virgin at precisely the moment nuns were forced to leave England, this chapter will question both the validity and the relevance of that "cultural 'fact'" in the later years of Elizabeth's reign, when literary representations of vowed virginity reflected on the unsettled status of chastity and religion in post-Reformation England.

In the proem to Book 3 of the 1590 *Faerie Queene*, Spenser suggests that his depiction of chastity is superfluous, since Elizabeth already provides the best example of "that fairest vertue" (3.proem.1.2). "Sith it is shrined in my Soueraines brest, / And form'd so liuely in each perfect part, / That to all Ladies, which haue it profest, / Need but behold the pourtraict of her hart, / If pourtrayd it might be by any liuing art" (1.5–9). Chastity lodges like a relic enshrined in the reliquary of Elizabeth's breast, in a devotional image that is swiftly overtaken by a series of conditionals and reversals that recall those initiated by Fidelia and Speranza in the House of Holiness. Instead of worshipping Elizabeth's chastity directly, women should look at the portrait of her heart, if such an artistic reproduction is even possible. Spenser asks whether art is sufficient to represent the virtue most prominently associated with the queen, says no, and then says yes. Sculptors and painters "may not least part expresse" and even poets will not dare to try "for fear through want of words her excellence to marre" (2.1, 9). Yet Spenser's "lucklesse lot doth me constraine / Hereto perforce," and he asks Elizabeth's pardon "sith that choicest wit / Cannot your glorious pourtraict figure plaine / That I in colourd showes may shadow it" (3.4–5, 6–8). Allegory, in the form of "colourd showes," is an unsatisfying solution to an intractable problem, for here and in the first line of the proem ("It falls me here to write of Chastity"), Spenser implies that he *must* write of chastity, and that he must do so here, in the final book of his 1590 *Faerie Queene*.

As the virtue "farre above the rest" (1.2), it makes sense that chastity would serve as a culmination, and yet Book 3 is only a temporary endpoint. Both the title page, which advertises "*The Faerie Queene*. Disposed into twelve books, *Fashioning* XII. Morall vertues," and the letter to Ralegh printed at the end of the poem promise twelve books—twenty-four if the moral virtues are "well accepted" and Spenser frames "the other part of polliticke vertues."[28] Chastity is only a temporary conclusion, for both his poem and his characters. Rather than perpetual, vowed virgins, Spenser depicts women who participate in a culture of courtly love and whose narratives incorporate a future transition from premarital virginity to married chastity. But that transition seldom occurs within the poem: just as readers will never reach the forecasted end of *The Faerie Queene*, which was left unfinished at Spenser's death, chastity offers the promise of a conclusion that is never fully realized. This indeterminacy manifests in the history of *The Faerie Queene*'s print publication: while the 1590 version of Book 3 concludes with the reunion of the chaste Amoret with Scudamour, the 1596 version replaces this gesture toward marital and sexual union with renewed separation and deferral. In 1590, Amoret and Scudamour embrace while Britomart witnesses their love and "to her selfe oft wisht like happiness, / In vaine she wisht, that fate n'ould let her yet possesse" (3.12.46.8–9). Even though Spenser's knight of chastity has not "yet" found Artegall, her own future husband, the final stanzas of the 1590 Book 3 suggest that marriage is the inevitable conclusion for both Amoret and Britomart. And yet, as Jessica C. Murphy notes, "we have only Merlin's prophecy to rely on if we are to think that Britomart will marry Artegall."[29] The 1596 *Faerie Queene* further complicates the possibility of marital resolution and suggests that even if Spenser had reached twelve or twenty-four books, he may have never fully resolved the representational difficulties of late Elizabethan female chastity.[30] In 1596, Scudamour leaves the House of Busirane before Britomart and Amoret emerge from it. Instead of an image of heterosexual union, Spenser concludes his revised book on chastity with the delays and digressions that characterize romance: Scudamour must now "wend at will" rather than standing still with Amoret "like two senceles stocks in long embracement" (1596, 3.12.45.9; 1590, 3.12.45.9).[31]

In Book 4, we learn that Spenser's deferral of Amoret and Scudamour's union replicates Busirane's earlier disruption of their wedding:

For that same vile Enchauntour Busyran,
The very selfe same day that she was wedded,
Amidst the bridale feast, whilest euery man
Surcharg'd with wine, were heedlesse and ill hedded,
All bent to mirth before the bride was bedded . . .
Conueyed quite away to liuing wight vnknowen. (4.1.3.1–9)

Rhyme calls the reader's attention to the expected progression from marriage vows to consummation and to Amoret's suspension between the two. She is kidnapped in the liminal space between being "wedded" and "bedded"— still a virgin and not yet a wife. By relating this interrupted marital history after he prolongs Amoret and Scudamour's separation in the revision of Book 3,

Spenser suggests that his own poetic project is not far removed from Busirane's rape and torture of Amoret.[32] The opening of Book 4 thus acknowledges both the violence of poetic representation and its fundamental limits: while he can fragment chastity into different characters, Spenser cannot fully reconcile its complexities and ambiguities.

What does Amoret's chastity signify, if she is both virgin and wife? The 1596 *Faerie Queene* leaves this question open, as virgins proliferate and the poem's few weddings do little to contain chastity's accretion of meanings. Book 4 features the metaphorical marriage of the Thames and Medway rivers, an extended poetic conceit that does not clarify the poem's treatment of either chastity or marriage. Rachel E. Hile argues that "Spenser's choice of a reluctant, proud bride and his focus on the wedding procession to the exclusion of the wedding itself suggest the possibility that he intends the Thames-Medway wedding to represent a concordant union, not an ideal of marriage based on the virtue of friendship."[33] But this focus on the wedding procession is not unusual for Spenser: the twelve stanzas dedicated to anticipation, preparation, and procession in *Epithalamion*—compared to the single stanza depicting the ceremony itself—reveal a similar hesitation surrounding the marriage service. Rather than indicating what type of union Spenser hopes to depict, the weddings in *The Faerie Queene* help reveal the narrative ruptures occasioned by conflicting ideologies of chastity and marriage in late Elizabethan England. While marriage was no longer a sacrament in the English church, chastity within marriage had at least conceptually surpassed the virtues of perpetual virginity. And yet Spenser struggles to represent a smooth transition from unmarried virginity to chaste wedlock. The wedding of Florimell and Marinell in Book 5 is especially notable in this respect, as the narrator acknowledges that he will not represent the wedding itself.

> To tell the glorie of the feast that day,
> The goodly seruice, the deuicefull sights,
> The bridegromes state, the brides most rich aray,
> The pride of Ladies, and the worth of knights,
> The royall banquets, and the rare delights
> Were worke fit for an Herauld, not for me. (5.3.3.1–6)

The bride, groom, guests, food, and, most important, the "goodly seruice" are here dismissed as material for a herald rather than a poet. Spenser suggests that such subjects would be digressive distractions from the true task at hand:

the advancement of virtue. "But for so much as to my lot here lights, / That with this present treatise doth agree, / True vertue to aduance, shall here recounted bee" (5.3.3.7–9). Even if "this present treatise" refers specifically to Book 5's focus on justice, readers may be surprised to learn that when "true vertue" is at stake the poem must turn its attention away from the spousal union.[34]

Marriage is nearly as impossible to represent as chastity, but for different reasons: rather than accruing meanings throughout the poem, it remains almost exclusively promissory. For many of Spenser's paired characters—Una and Redcrosse, Amoret and Scudamour, Britomart and Artegall, Arthur and Gloriana—a consummated marital relationship is at the poem's narrative horizon, always just out of reach and only visible in the prophetic mode. For Britomart, whose first sight of Artegall is of a "manly face" in a magic mirror, marriage is originally a spectral vision with an unknown object (3.2.24.4). The details of their union are communicated only through Merlin's prophecy, part of Spenser's chronicle history of Britain. The poem's characters look forward as the poet looks back, but Britomart's marriage is nearly invisible in both prospective and retrospective visions. She learns that "the man whom heauens haue ordaynd to bee / The spouse of *Britomart*, is *Arthegall*," but this identification of marital status does not produce a representation of marital practice (3.3.26.1–2). Instead, Merlin's syntax grows knotty as his narrative approaches Britomart and Artegall's life together. After explaining that Artegall is in Faeryland but not of it, he reveals that "from thence, him firmely bound with faithfull band, / To this his natiue soyle thou backe shalte bring, / Strongly to aide his countrey, to withstand / The powre of forrein Paynims, which inuade thy land" (3.3.27.6–9). The delay of the "thou" identifying Britomart makes the "faithfull band" that binds Artegall ambiguous: is it a marriage band or is he bound to his native soil?[35] Subsequent clauses ("strongly to aide," "to withstand") suggest that Britomart brings him home so that he may demonstrate his martial might rather than enjoy their marital union. The next stanza emphasizes military prowess on the part of both Britomart and Artegall: "long time ye both in armes shall beare great sway" (3.3.28.5). They are united on the battlefield, "till thy wombes burden thee from them do call, / And his last fate him from thee take away" (3.3.28.6–7). Pregnancy arises from the battlefield rather than the bedroom in a parallel construction that aligns Artegall's death with his child's birth. Spenser thus elides Britomart and Artegall's marriage in favor of their political and martial alliance, the outcome of which is dynastic rather than domestic.

As Jonathan Goldberg has argued, "there seems never to have been a domestic partnership. . . . This story seems less to support the seamless relationship between sexuality, marriage, and socio-political efficacy than to continue the problematization of these linkages."[36] Goldberg offers this reading in the interest of demonstrating that "marriage is not the only legitimate form of sexuality in *The Faerie Queene*, although it is a critical commonplace to say so."[37] I would add that this critical commonplace arises out of the poem's many representations of female chastity, which consistently point toward a marital future that rarely materializes. Marriage is a representational blank and an empty future in *The Faerie Queene*: an end that is not, to borrow Merlin's formulation of the post-Elizabethan future for England. He concludes his chronicle of Britomart and Artegall's dynastic legacy with Elizabeth, the "royall virgin" whose own uncertain dynastic legacy prompts Merlin's inconclusive "But yet the end is not" (3.3.49.6, 50.1). This syntactic deviation from Matthew 24:6—"but the end is not yet"—suggests not only that the end has not arrived but also that the end may not exist at all.[38] In Matthew 24, Christ foretells the end of the world for his disciples; Merlin's prophecy integrates this apocalyptic gesture but also suggests the failure of a narrative telos by way of the failure of Elizabeth's marital telos. The end does not exist, because Elizabeth has not married and produced an heir. This might suggest that "Elizabeth's choice of lifelong virgin chastity is so far from the virtue of chastity that she has cut off its lineage."[39] But I would instead argue that it points us to the ways that female virgins exert formal pressure on early modern literature, not simply as a result of Elizabeth's representational dominance and the exile of vowed virgins but also in response to the indeterminacy of post-Reformation chastity. Like the rewritten end of Book 3, the conclusion of Merlin's prophecy reveals that the ends of chastity are ultimately unknowable: while ideologically it may point toward marriage and children in late Elizabethan England, it can also signal political authority, perpetual religious devotion, or unions that do not conform to a simple patriarchal hierarchy.

"Dim and Darksome Coverture": Marriage, Recusancy, and Female Autonomy

Spenser's contemporaries built upon his representation of multiple virginities and marital deferral in order to explore the nonroyal associations of female chastity. The nuns of late sixteenth- and early seventeenth-century literature challenge the representational dominance of the Virgin Queen while also calling attention to the political significance of women during a period of ongoing religious reform. By considering the social and legal status of female virgins, authors such as Marlowe, Chapman, and Shakespeare offered veiled interventions into debates over England's Catholic women, particularly those married recusants whose legal position under coverture enabled them to avoid the full force of statutes requiring attendance at church services. As vowed (or nearly vowed) virgins, Hero and Isabella point toward Catholicism and the cloister while simultaneously participating in debates regarding female autonomy and choice, sexuality and marriage, and the role of the state in matters of conscience. While they are, in many ways, radically different characters in radically different texts, both resist entering a sexual or marital relationship that will necessitate abandoning their devotional practice, and their resistance carries narrative implications. As in *The Faerie Queene*, these virgins occasion formal disruptions, and Chapman's desire to provide narrative closure for *Hero and Leander* helps reveal how these literary effects relate to the political position of recusant women in early modern England. The troubling conclusion of Marlowe's poem, which offers a sexual culmination so fraught that most editors have altered the order of its lines, makes visible the fractures in a sex/gender system predicated on female submission. Like modern editors, Chapman attempted to smooth away Marlowe's rough edges, but in so doing drew attention to the legal and social implications of Hero's odd and paradoxical position as an unenclosed and sexually active nun.

In the final lines of Marlowe's *Hero and Leander*, the eponymous lovers engage in an ambiguous seduction: Hero simultaneously resists and encourages Leander's advances, leading to a sexual encounter that some critics read as mutual while others suggest rape.[40] A significant editorial emendation in most modern editions—the silent displacement of ten lines ("She trembling . . . the golden tree") from 763 to 785—has allowed readers to gloss over some of the more troubling metaphors Marlowe uses to describe the moment or moments when Leander takes Hero's virginity.[41] It is easy to imagine a joyous consummation as the narrator describes how Leander "like Theban *Hercules*, / Entred the orchard of *Th'esperides*. / Whose fruit none rightly can describe, but hee / That puls or shakes it from the golden tree" if these lines signal a final moment of bliss before Hero's postcoital reverie.[42] Instead, the 1598 poem positions Leander's entrance into the metaphorical garden before the narrator's violent description of "a bird, which in our hands we wring" and then jumps abruptly from the bird that "flutters with her wing" to Hero wishing "this night were never done."[43] This line, like Spenser's "but yet the end is not," simultaneously points in two directions that resist narrative closure: Hero may wish that the night could be never-ending—or that it had never happened.

The confusion that results from these abrupt reversals is, in large part, a product of the confusion that Hero herself inspires: does she desire Leander? Does she wish to have sex with him? To marry him? How does she interpret her vow to Venus? What would constitute a breaking of that vow? Leander's desire and intent are largely static: from the moment he is "enamourèd," he pleads with Hero to renounce her virginity, exchanging it for marriage and "the sweet society of men."[44] Hero, on the contrary, is nearly impossible to pin down. This is literally the case in the final seduction: "His hands he cast upon her like a snare; / She, overcome with shame and sallow fear, / Like chaste Diana when Actaeon spied her, / Being suddenly betrayed, dived down to hide her" (2.259–62). Instead of completing the trajectory of the Diana and Actaeon myth by turning against Leander, Hero hides under the covers. "With both her hands she made the bed a tent, / And in her own mind thought herself secure, / O'ercast with dim and darksome coverture" (2.264–66). This is one of many times that the expectations created by the poem are not fulfilled, but in this particular instance Marlowe's word choice and imagery also provide a key for understanding the frustration that Hero inspires in critics and readers.

Hero's protective covering is both material and mental: she hides under bedclothes and "in her own mind thought herself secure." Marlowe thus alerts his readers to the possibility that "coverture" may hold a variety of meanings for Hero. It is not simply that which literally covers (a quilt, clothing, a veil) but also that which figuratively protects or deceives (concealment, dissimulation).[45] Yet the covering seems to deceive Hero rather than any external observer: she only *thinks* herself secure under "dim and darksome coverture," perhaps because the term used to describe her refuge paradoxically conjures the social status that she wishes to avoid. Coverture, in its broadest legal definition, "is when a man & a woman ar maried together."[46] In religious discourse, Protestant writers and theologians went further in identifying how marriage could cover an individual's sins. John Harmar's translation of the *Sermons of M. John Calvine, upon the X Commandementes of the Lawe*, describes how "the coverture of marriage sanctifieth that which is polluted and unhallowed, it serveth to purge and make cleane that which in it selfe is filthie and uncleane."[47] Marriage, in other words, provides a means by which men and women can practice chastity even though humans are by nature corrupt and lustful: "albeit men bee incontinent: yet are they not ac-cused before God, nor brought before his throne of judgement, if so bee they keep them selves within the boundes of marriage."[48] The goddess Ceremony makes a similar argument regarding marriage and sexuality when she appears to Leander in Chapman's poem, and Marlowe's use of "coverture" suggests that the Protestant marriage system, which dominates Chapman's postcoital depiction of the lovers, also serves as an essential background for their initial encounters in Marlowe's poem.

But Hero's covering is individual, and it is meant to protect her from Leander rather than with him. While marriage as coverture provided spiri-tual protection for both partners, it also carried a more specific legal implica-tion for women: in early modern legal discourse, a woman under coverture was subject to her husband's authority—but she was also able, in certain in-stances, to evade the authority of the state under the cover of her marriage. Coverture in this final, unsettling scene of Marlowe's *Hero and Leander* thus raises questions that extend beyond the bedclothes that Hero pulls over her head or the consummation that she seeks to avoid. When she attempts to hide herself, Marlowe evokes the very legal and social system that Leander has urged her to enter—a system that held within itself the elements of its own subversion. The troubling ending of Marlowe's poem, which both Chap-man and later editors have felt the need to complete or correct, is largely a product of the ambivalent sexuality of his lovers, who seem not to know what they want or how to achieve that unknown desire. But it is also a product of the religious and political climate of late sixteenth-century England, where a woman who vowed virginity and invoked coverture as a protective shield would have called to mind the Catholic women whose marriages created a space for devotional practices that were the province of nuns before the Ref-ormation.

As penalties for male recusancy increased over the course of Elizabeth's reign, women became ever more important to the survival of English Ca-tholicism. Married women in particular were able to avoid the full force of the statutes because of their status under coverture. Legally, these women could not control their own property and were subject to their husbands.[49] Practically, this meant that it was almost impossible for the state to punish them: monetary fines would necessarily be imposed on their husbands, in effect punishing men for their wives' crimes. Parliament was reluctant to take this course, or to imprison married female recusants—thereby separating them from their families—for long periods. Some families were willing to exploit the legal situation: husbands attended English services, giving rise to the term "church papist," while wives maintained the Catholic faith at home.[50] In the wake of the Gunpowder Plot, "An Act for the better discovering and repressing of Popish Recusants" acknowledged that Catholics might feign conformity to the English church: "divers persons Popishly affected, doe neverthelesse, the better to *cover and hide* their false hearts, & with the more safety to attend the opportunitie to execute their mischievous desseignes, repaire sometimes to Church to escape the penaltie of the Lawes in that behalfe provided" (emphasis added).[51] But even this act of 1606, which instituted the Oath of Allegiance and attempted to control church papistry, avoided punishing married women or their husbands for actions associated with the wife's recusancy. It provided that "no person shall be charged or chargeable with any penalty or forfeiture by force of this Act, which shall happen for his wives offence, in not receiving the said Sacrament, during her marriage, nor that any woman shall be charged or chargeable with any penaltie or forfeiture by force of this Act, for any such offence of not receiving, which shall happen during her marriage."[52] Marital coverture denied women autonomy within the patriarchal household, but it could also serve as a protective shield from the power of the state for those women who made the politically subversive choice to be Catholic in England after the Reformation.

By the late sixteenth century, women had become visible and vocal members of the recusant community.[53] In a letter of 1576, Henry Hastings, the earl of Huntingdon and lord president of the Council of the North, simultaneously acknowledged the persistence of female Catholicism while dismissing its importance: "for those that are in thease matters most peavyse, so farr as I yet see, are in thys towne wemen, and in the cuntrye verrye meane men of Callynge."[54] As Huntingdon saw it, the threat of political rebellion was contained by the gender and class of those who were most "peevish" in their adherence to Catholicism. But as little as ten years later, Catholic women had become a force in local religious politics. In 1586, Margaret Clitherow, a York butcher's wife, was accused of sheltering priests and put to death when she refused to go to trial.[55] John Mush, Clitherow's priest, wrote a manuscript description of her life and death and, within a year, accounts of her martyrdom began to appear in continental books detailing the persecution of English Catholics.[56] Mush's "A True Report of the Life and Martyrdom of Mrs. Margaret Clitherow" was not simply a hagiography; it was also, as Anne Dillon points out in her definitive study of martyrdom after the Reformation, a "conduct book for recusants" since "recusancy was . . . perceived as itself an act of martyrdom."[57] The narrative of Clitherow's recusancy demonstrates one of the ways that sixteenth-century Catholic Englishwomen were represented: as individuals willing to take advantage of coverture and reconfigure its effective meanings and ideological associations. In what follows, I will demonstrate how Mush's representation of Clitherow can illuminate the sociopolitical issues that precipitate the startling shift in tone between Marlowe's ambiguous ending of *Hero and Leander*, written before his death in 1593, and Chapman's subsequent affirmation of state-sanctioned matrimony, printed with one of the two 1598 editions of Marlowe's poem.

Mush's Clitherow calls into question one of the ideological underpinnings of Protestant England: she refuses to acknowledge the patriarchal power of the state and yet professes her loyalty to her husband, John Clitherow, whose symbolic position as "her head" she affirms before her death.[58] Margaret Clitherow was a product of post-Reformation English Catholicism: she converted only after her marriage and, despite her change of faith, proclaimed herself "a true and a chaste wife to my husband, both in thought and deed" (407). In many respects, the Clitherows' marriage conforms to a companionate model of married chastity and thus fits comfortably into the ideological landscape of Elizabethan England. But this marriage creates the possibility of political subversion rather than serving as an ideal microcosm of the state. Clitherow's faith and her willingness to hide elements of her religious practice from her husband form the basis for her remarkable choice to disavow the government's ability to put her to trial. Mush establishes the foundation for her resistance early in his text, when Clitherow queries her priest regarding the limits of temporal authority. " 'May I not,' said she, 'receive priests and serve God as I have done, notwithstanding these new laws, without my husband's consent?' " (381). Clitherow blurs the boundary between the power of government ("these new laws") and the power of the domestic patriarch (her "husband's consent") and thus reveals how the relationship between Catholic wife and Protestant husband could be read as a metaphor for every recusant's relationship to England. While she accepts her husband's authority in worldly matters, taking care "in selling and buying her wares . . . to have the worth of them, as both her neighbours uttered the like, as also to satisfy her duty to her husband, which committed all to her trust and discretion," her interpretation of spiritual affairs encompasses far more than the Elizabethan government would allow, including the Catholic education of her children (399).[59] The individual circumstances of Clitherow's marriage demonstrate how ideological and legal frameworks meant to restrict women to the household and to certain prescribed roles could have very different practical results.

Margaret Clitherow's husband shields her from the full force of the laws against recusancy, and she correctly fears that his absence from their home will lead to her arrest. When he appears before the Council to explain their son's trip to the continent, which Margaret arranged "without the knowledge of her husband," "they deceitfully practised indeed, and sent forthwith the sheriffs of York, with divers other heretics, to search her house" (409, 410).[60] Both Clitherows are arrested when Catholic devotional materials and evidence of a priest are discovered in the search, but John is released when Margaret explains that she " 'could never yet get my husband in that good case that he were worthy to know or come in place where they were to serve God' "; he was not, in other words, "privy to her doings in keeping priests" (414). At the same time that Clitherow publicly reveals that she has kept her husband in the dark regarding her religious activities, she also " 'refuse[s] to be tried by the country,' " thus simultaneously diminishing her husband's authority in spiritual matters and dismissing the state's authority altogether (414).[61] Mush describes a series of encounters between Clitherow and government representatives, and, in every case, she openly questions the applicability of English law. When asked " 'Will you put yourself to the country, yea or no?' " she explains that she sees " 'no cause why I should do so in this matter: I refer my cause only to God and your own consciences. Do what you think good' " (416). According to Mush, her defiance prompts even a "Puritan preacher" to argue against " 'the Queen's law' " in favor of " 'God's law' " (416). As Christine Peters has argued of this moment, "concerns about the temporal authority trampling upon religious conscience were not limited to Catholics. The underlying arguments, because they concerned the higher obedience owed to God, were also shared by spokesmen for godly Protestants."[62] Clitherow undermines the ideological substructure of early modern England, which treated the monarch as a representative of God's divine authority, but in so doing she reveals the many fissures occasioned by the intersections of religion and politics, even as she positions herself outside the conceptual boundaries of English society—much as Hero will in Chapman's continuation of Marlowe's poem.

Many of the responses to Clitherow's refusal to go to trial reflect on her choice to stand apart from the legal system of early modern England, including those of her fellow Catholics. In conflating religious dissent with domestic upheaval and sexual deviance, these responses reveal the imaginative relationship between political resistance and social or cultural norms. Members of Clitherow's community repeatedly urged her to change her mind by invoking her duty to her family: "others also came to her at divers times, and said she died desperately, and had no care on her husband and children, but would spoil them, and make all people to exclaim against her" (426). The urgency of these interventions reveal the divisions among York's Catholics, who were by no means a unified or homogeneous group. As Peter Lake and Michael Questier have demonstrated, these divisions were part of a complex "struggle between different local claimants to or versions of what English Catholicism should be like—a struggle conducted in terms of a range of different responses to, on the one hand, the regime's demands for conformity and, on the other, to the no less totalizing claims of certain priests and lay people for a completely separatist recusancy."[63] Clitherow's response—that she loved her husband and had done her duty in raising her children to fear God—did little to convince her interlocutors that she was the "true and . . . chaste wife" she claimed to be (407).[64] According to their logic, if she did not accept the patriarchal authority of the state, attend church services, or acknowledge her domestic responsibilities, she must also disregard the sexual mores of English society: "when they saw that they could not persuade her, nor make her yield in anything, they brought ridiculous slanders against her, and told her how the boy had confessed that she had sinned with priests" (427).[65] Clitherow's reputation for chastity depends upon her conformity with the religiopolitical order that she rejects, and her narrative demonstrates how the political resistance of recusant Catholic women was frequently read as evidence for sexual promiscuity, even by fellow Catholics.[66] Because they embraced separatism over church attendance and conformity with the state, recusant women were imagined to be outside the ideological space occupied by the chaste and obedient wife. Thus literary representations of women situated at the margins of society—whether through devotional vows that suggested Catholic monasticism, sexual choices that undermined marital chastity, or, in Hero's case, both—can offer indirect reflections on female recusancy.

Recusant women posed a conceptual difficulty, not just for poets and playwrights of the late sixteenth century but even for their own biographers. Mush, as we have seen, was at pains to depict Clitherow's adherence to domestic hierarchies, despite the fact that she frequently took part in religious activities without her husband's knowledge or consent. As a result, Mush's *Life* does more than "reveal to us the sort of traumatic and tension-filled gender and family politics in and through which religious change was often effected during this period";[67] it also reveals that Clitherow and her fellow recusants did not fit easily into the cultural constructions of either post-Reformation England or post-Tridentine Catholicism: they were neither the contemplative nuns of Catholic ideology, enclosed within the ecclesiastical hierarchy and subject to new restrictions imposed by the Council of Trent, nor the obedient and conformist wives of Protestant marriage manuals.[68] Mush's representation of female recusancy illuminates the limitations of even his own hagiographical understanding of Clitherow's martyrdom, as his narrative resists its narrator's attempt to control interpretation, raising questions for the reader about Clitherow's actions and intentions (how did she send her son to the continent without her husband's knowledge? why does she refuse to go to trial? does she deliberately create the circumstances of her own death?).[69] Historians have studied the religious and political effects of women such as Clitherow, but the cultural implications of their paradoxical status in Protestant England have not yet drawn the attention of critics focused on canonical English literature, perhaps because married recusant women's unsettling disruptions of social categories seem to have forestalled contemporary literary representations of them. But while Margaret Clitherow's life and martyrdom were not performed on the London stage or printed in elegiac verse, plays and poems of the late sixteenth and early seventeenth centuries do register both the indeterminacy and the impact of recusant women.

While textual representations of women such as Margaret Clitherow were largely confined to martyrologies, these narratives—shaped not only by religious and political considerations but also by literary concerns—can facilitate new readings of perplexing female characters whose ethics and actions seem at odds even with the poems and plays in which they feature. Hero, for example, is not simply a divisive figure for literary critics; she is also divided and divisive within *Hero and Leander*, and her position leads Chapman to create a remarkably conservative ending to Marlowe's potentially subversive poem. Hero never quite fits into her society; she stands apart, and Marlowe makes her separation visible through a vow of virginity that signifies her religious devotion and individual autonomy. Though the personal and political dimensions of religious choice figure prominently in *Hero and Leander*, these issues have frequently been overshadowed by the erotic force of Marlowe's verse in the first sestiads and by the abrupt shift in the sexual and lyric sensibility of Chapman's continuation.[70] But Hero's initial desire to be a virgin and her ultimate (and ambiguous) renunciation of that vow are not simply aspects of her sexuality; these choices position her as a religious authority and an autonomous woman who lives in Sestos but does not seem entirely of Sestos.

In social terms, virginity marks Hero much as Catholicism marked recusant women: she is at once incorporated into the practice of daily life in her community and yet she remains imaginatively distinct from the world that surrounds her. This division between Hero and her society intensifies throughout the course of the poem: Marlowe imagines a Hero who lives apart but conforms to social expectations while Chapman allegorizes her silent postcoital rejection of the social order. At the same time, Chapman implicates Hero more completely in the ceremonial forms and institutional structures that the lovers have avoided, turning Marlowe's vacillating and sexually conflicted heroine into a figure of religious hypocrisy and deceit. The two halves of the poem enact the paradoxical status of recusant women in English society, as Marlowe's rumination on female exceptionalism and the pressure to conform to a patriarchal sexual order turns sinister under Chapman's pen, which depicts Hero's religious devotion as a misguided subversion of the state-supported ideology of marriage. *Hero and Leander* is thus a poetic instantiation of the implicit conflict between Mush and Huntingdon regarding the interpretation and importance of recusant women.

When Marlowe introduces Hero, he establishes the magnetic force of her presence in Sestos while at the same time demonstrating that her importance is almost wholly dependent upon her position as an independent and potentially disruptive woman—a position that nonconformist Catholic Englishwomen occupied in the wake of Clitherow's execution, as Parliament became increasingly concerned with the question of how to legislate against married recusant women. The enigmatic and untouchable Hero is an object of desire for the gods (Apollo courts her and Cupid rests in her bosom in the early lines of the poem), and her presence in mortal company highlights her singularity. The artificial flowers adorning her veil cause those around her to "praise the sweet smell as she passed, / When 'twas the odour which her breath forth cast" (1.21–2). Hero's countrymen do not know how to interpret her clothing or her physical presence, and she remains separate from them even in the midst of communal celebrations. At the feast of Adonis, Hero ranks "far above" her peers in beauty, and all eyes are upon her (1.103). Yet even those who "near her stood" do so only to observe: "so ran the people forth to gaze upon her, / And all that viewed her were enamoured on her" (1.112, 117–18). Hero travels "thorough Sestos, from her tower / To Venus' temple" and never fully integrates into the community she passes in transit, perhaps because the very attributes which draw men's eyes to Hero—her physical appearance and her clothing—also point to her position as a devotee of the goddess of love.

In these early descriptions, Marlowe establishes how Hero's devotional stance shapes her personal and public relationships: despite the fact that she is well respected and admired, she is very much alone until Leander sees her performing a sacrifice in the temple. While watching this devout act, Leander is "enamourèd"; like the people of Sestos, he falls in love with Hero when her status as a nun is clear (1.162). But Leander does more than gaze: "he touched her hand," and this physical interaction inspires him "to display / Love's holy fire, with words, with sighs and tears" (1.183, 192–93). Hero's virginity, as one element of her devotional affect, is part of what inspires Leander's desire, and yet he immediately asks her to reject the very things that attracted him to her. "This sacrifice," he argues, "Doth testify that you exceed her far, / To whom you offer, and whose nun you are. / Why should you worship her?" (1.209–13). According to Leander, Hero's religious practice elevates her above the goddess she worships, but it also makes her a bad votaress: "thou in vowing chastity hast sworn / To rob her name and honour, and thereby / Commit'st a sin far worse than perjury" (1.304–6). By this contradictory logic, Hero must relinquish a significant aspect of her religious identity in order to properly express her faith.

When Leander attempts to convince Hero to abandon her vows, he posits an alternative no more in line with Venus's sexuality than Hero's virginity. Instead of suggesting the promiscuity of the gods, Leander offers marriage: "virginity, albeit some highly prize it, / Compared with marriage, had you tried them both, / Differs as much as wine and water doth" (1.262–64). Of course, Leander is willing to say almost anything to forward his seduction, but he remains consistent in opposing "fruitless cold virginity" and "single life" with ceremonialized heterosexual partnership (1.317, 321): he calls upon "never-singling Hymen," praises celebratory "banquets," and finally asks Hero to perform "Venus' sweet rites" without clarifying what he imagines those rites to include (1.258, 301, 320). Leander's ideal of sexuality, which associates the loss of virginity with social rituals, could easily fit within a Protestant ideal of married chastity.[71] Even his confusion over whether "some amorous rites or other were neglected" during the lovers' first sexual encounter can be read within an ideological framework that privileges marriage, though it also alludes to the fact that Hero is eager to protect the last remaining signs associated with her virginity (2.64). Yet she is no longer chaste. In her rose-strewn room, Hero "seeming lavish, saved her maidenhead," but her renewed vows of "spotless chastity" were earlier offered "all in vain" (2.76, 1.368).

From her first interaction with Leander, Hero's virginity has seemed both already lost and not yet relinquished. The ambiguity that dominates the poem's conclusion can thus be traced to the mind and body of Venus's nun: while critics have been eager to pinpoint when, exactly, the lovers fully consummate their relationship, the precise moment at which Hero offers or loses her bodily virginity remains mysterious. Her internal renunciation of chastity, on the contrary, leads to immediate linguistic, physical, and emotional signs. Marlowe identifies her as "Chaste Hero" just as she silently acknowledges Leander's appeal: "'Were I the saint he worships, I would hear him,' / And as she spake those words, came somewhat near him" (1.179). Hero quite literally makes the first move, and Leander responds by touching her hand. "These lovers parlèd by the touch of hands; / True love is mute, and oft amazèd stands. / Thus while dumb signs their yielding hearts entangled, / The air with sparks of living fire was spangled" (1.185–88). This emotional entanglement has more immediate and tangible effects than the lovers' explicitly sexual interactions: before the encounter, Hero is chaste; after, she has "yielded" and vainly attempts to recover her formerly "spotless chastity" (1.330, 1.368). In early modern discourse, as we have seen, virginity and chastity—two terms that Marlowe uses almost interchangeably—had meanings that transcended marital status and the physical condition of the hymen. This is certainly true for Hero, and Marlowe queries the meanings of virginity in both individual and social contexts through his portrayal of her nearly instantaneous loss of conceptual chastity and her far more gradual physical transformation.

The social construction of Hero's virginity as a religious choice that simultaneously creates and justifies her singular autonomy survives even after she has entertained Leander's overtures. For the reader, if not the people of Sestos, chastity and virginity thus seem largely meaningless by the end of Marlowe's poem. Chastity is only identifiable from within—Hero knows when she is no longer chaste and futilely renews her vows to Venus in hopes of regaining her chastity—and yet is defined and interpreted by a community of observers. To be considered chaste, then, Hero may privately break her vow of perpetual virginity, but she must, as Susan Frye has written of Elizabeth, remain publicly "remote, self-sufficient, and desirable."[72] Within ancient Sestos, where she performs her devotional identity, Hero's chastity is a sign of her social positioning rather than her bodily purity. She is, in this sense, somewhat like Elizabeth, and Patrick Cheney has argued that, through Hero, Marlowe assails "the sanctity of the Queen's palisade of chastity" in his critique of "Spenser's Elizabethan cult."[73] Cheney reads Marlowe reading Spenser, and, as a result, he offers a nearly allegorical interpretation of the first sestiads of *Hero and Leander* that does not account for the fact that the meanings of virginity and chastity remain contested through the end of Marlowe's poem.[74] While Cheney recognizes the cultural power of chastity in the late sixteenth century, his focus on "the merits of Spenser and his writing of England, especially with respect to England's queen and her erotic cult of chastity" obscures other political contexts in which the ideological conflicts associated with chastity were relevant.[75] Hero, like the many virgins of *The Faerie Queene*, reveals that chastity could be a flexible tool for literary representation—one that might glance at Elizabeth's conceptual dominance while also invoking the social and religious positioning of women other than the Virgin Queen. Chapman's poem goes further, not by restoring "a Spenserian vision of love and marriage within the epic context of English nationhood"—for, as we have seen, this vision was always deferred in *The Faerie Queene* itself—but by critiquing Hero's religious position and explicitly positioning the lovers outside a Protestant ideological framework.[76]

Chapman allegorizes doctrinal conflict in his continuation of *Hero and Leander*, thereby making the subtext of Marlowe's poem explicit: while Marlowe encoded various interpretations of chastity in Leander's clumsy seduction rhetoric, Chapman ventriloquizes a Protestant position through the goddess Ceremony, who advocates state-sanctioned matrimony. Ceremony interrupts Leander's postcoital reverie when she arrives in his chamber leading Religion, with "Devotion, Order, State, and Reverence" as her shadows (3.120). She "sharply did reprove / Leanders bluntness in his violent love; / Told him how poor was substance without rites" (3.145–47). The "amorous rites" Leander worried over in Hero's bedroom were in fact neglected, and Ceremony envisions a society overrun with "rank corn" and "meats unseasoned" should such "civil forms" be abandoned (3.149–51). Chapman's poem celebrates marriage as a communal activity rather than a private handfast ceremony and positions individual relationships within a network of mutual responsibility.[77] Leander easily decides to marry after his visit from Ceremony, but Hero remains torn between her religious duties and her love for Leander. She decides that she "was singular too much before: / But she would please the world with fair pretext" and "still proceed in works divine" while continuing a sexual relationship with Leander (4.193–94, 204). Hero, in other words, chooses hypocrisy and dissembling: she hides her broken vow from the people of Sestos and continues to perform the religious duties associated with her position as Venus's nun. But her devotion is no longer primarily directed toward Venus; instead, "her religion should be policy, / To follow love with zeal her piety; / Her chamber her cathedral church should be, / And her Leander her chief deity" (4.178–81). Love makes Hero into the idolatrous nun that Leander accused her of being in Marlowe's poem, but he has taken the place of virginity as her "idol," and religion has become her coverture (1.269).[78] Protestants argued that the pretext of religious devotion served a similar function for recusant women such as Clitherow, who faced the accusation that "it is not for religion that thou harbourest priests, but for harlotry" (Mush 414). Under the cover of religion, Hero hides a relationship that threatens the ideological system that Ceremony urges Leander to uphold. Chapman's allegory thus literalizes the religious and political issues to which Marlowe alluded in his more flexible and ambiguous depiction of Hero.

Chapman's Hero is more fully incorporated into her society, and her priest-like office provides her with the authority to openly defy Venus and undermine the religious and social system of which she is a part. She officiates at a marriage ceremony for "her consort vowed / In her maid's state"— Hero's fellow votaress, Mya—that elides distinctions between vowed virginity and married sexuality (5.35). The wedding of Alcmane and Mya allows Hero to "covertly . . . celebrate / With secret joy her own estate" (5.9–10). She continues to perform the role of Venus's nun but uses that position to support an understanding of virginity that positions it along a continuum that eventually results in marriage, just as Spenser did in *The Faerie Queene*. Here, too, the transition from virgin to wife prompts formal disruptions: in the inconclusive ending of Marlowe's poem, in the editorial desire to provide clarity to the sexual encounter, and in Chapman's continuation of a poem that was arguably "designed to be a fragment."[79] And Hero resists a marital telos: she hides her relationship, dooming herself in either a Protestant or a Catholic formulation of marriage, chastity, and sexuality. Despite the fact that Hero's religious devotion seems to have been misdirected—Chapman imagines a Venus who intends to prove that one of her servants can be chaste, regardless of her own sexuality—her virgin vows are still broken without a marriage vow to replace them. Hero, the nun who can travel freely between her tower and the town, becomes a dangerous figure of sexual freedom. She cloaks herself in "religious weeds" and hopes that "when her fault should chance t'abide the light" the people of Sestos will "cover or extenuate it" (4.13, 5.50–51). These transgressions against religion and the state are only superficially solved through the lovers' tragic fate, which Chapman treats as the inevitable coda to their disruption of the social order.

A comparison of the two different versions of *Hero and Leander* printed in 1598 reveals the very ideological tensions that Chapman attempted to resolve. Just as Chapman's Ceremony hopes to impose form and order on Hero and Leander's relationship, so too does the edition that includes Chapman's continuation impose form and order on Marlowe's fragment. Instead of a continuous narrative poem, as it is in Edward Blount's edition, the *Hero and Leander* "begun by *Christopher Marloe*; and *finished by* George Chapman" appears in sestiads headed by brief arguments.[80] This formal change mimics the cantos of *The Faerie Queene*, and suggests that Chapman would like to see narrative closure not only for Marlowe's no-longer-virgin nun but also for the many characters in Spenser's poem whose marriages are promised but never completed. Both Marlowe and Chapman built upon the conflicted representation of chastity and marriage in *The Faerie Queene*, but Chapman worked to contain the troubling implications of Marlowe's incomplete narrative, in which sexuality does not foreclose female autonomy. Instead of pointing toward the virginity of queen or convent, Marlowe's Hero suggests a devotional practice and social position akin to the recusant women who troubled Protestant notions of chaste married femininity in Elizabethan England. The representational multiplicity of her vow of virginity results in a fragmentary poem that resists both the marital and tragic closure that Chapman's continuation demands.

"As Easy Broke as They Make Forms": Mirrors of Virginity

Measure for Measure is not a narrative poem, nor is it unfinished, and yet the formal effects of female virginity—its disruptions and fragmentations, visible in language and narrative—mark this 1604 play as a culmination of the late Elizabethan religious and political discourses I have been tracing in this chapter. Unlike Marlowe and Chapman, Shakespeare explicitly designated his would-be nun a Catholic and associated her with an order that would have been familiar to contemporary audiences.[81] This theatrical representation of potential female monasticism had its analogue in the movement of Catholic women from England to the continent—a migration that increased in the early decades of the seventeenth century, after the first post-Reformation English convent was founded in Brussels in 1598.[82] Thus, though it was staged only six years after the print publication of *Hero and Leander*, Shakespeare's *Measure for Measure* depicts an even more fraught religious and political landscape than that of ancient Sestos: sexuality is corrupted by the bawds and openly condemned by the Viennese state in the person of Angelo, while marital relations lead to personal disappointment, civic unrest, and the threat of death. Religion provides temporary relief for women such as Isabella and Mariana, who attempt to choose lives of quiet devotion away from city life, but their faith is overshadowed by the machinations of the Duke disguised as a friar, whose robes and ultimate unveiling implicate religious life in the problems of the state. Shakespeare expands upon the devotional and social questions that Marlowe posed in *Hero and Leander* and Chapman attempted to resolve in his continuation of the poem, first by transporting Isabella into an explicitly political realm and then by testing the limits of her faith in response to governmental pressure rather than reciprocal sexual attraction.[83] Isabella's speeches—and her famous final silence—invoke contemporary choices made by women joining female communities on the continent, but rather than offering a direct representation of these new English nuns, Shakespeare creates a character who provokes chiastic forms and linguistic paradoxes that register the indeterminate signification of female virginity. Isabella thus allows Shakespeare to consider the issues associated with Catholic women and their devotional practices more broadly: as the problem at the center of *Measure for Measure*, she provides a theatrical means of confronting the increasingly complicated position of recusant women in relationship to both the English state and the Catholic religious hierarchy.

Measure for Measure, a play known for its political and theological stakes, was first performed less than two years after James took the throne, and Debora Shuger has called it "a sustained meditation on its own political moment—the political moment of James's accession, but also, and more significantly, of the Reformation's aftermath."[84] In tracing the effects of the Reformation, scholars such as Julia Reinhard Lupton and Sarah Beckwith have offered compelling readings of the play's engagement with Catholicism, and others such as Alison Findlay, Natasha Korda, and Jessica Slights and Michael Morgan Holmes have focused on Isabella's association with the convent in general and the order of St. Clare in particular.[85] I build on these readings of *Measure for Measure*'s post-Reformation context and its exploration of female monasticism in order to show how Shakespeare's representation of vowed virginity in crisis offers a distinctively literary response to the religious and political resistance of Catholic Englishwomen. Since Shakespeare wrote *Measure for Measure* at the height of parliamentary debates concerning female Catholicism and in the wake of the first English monastic foundations on the continent, it is hardly surprising that his Catholic heroine seems torn between the life of a nun and the death of a martyr.[86] Isabella is a novice who hopes to enter a convent of Poor Clares, a religious order known for its asceticism. In pamphlet literature on monasticism, Protestant writers referred derisively to "the poore bare-footed Clares" and claimed that Jesuits would have nothing to do with these nuns because "they are not rich, and therefore not a fit bit for their palate."[87] But such austerity is not enough for Isabella: she claims that she desires "a more strict restraint / Upon the sisterhood, the votarists of Saint Clare."[88] Her response to Angelo's demand that she relinquish her virginity in exchange for her brother's life emphasizes her willingness to suffer and die rather than forsake her moral and spiritual system: "th' impression of keen whips I'ld wear as rubies," she says, "And strip myself to death, as to a bed / That longing have been sick for, ere I'ld yield / My body up to shame" (2.4.101–4). She thus resembles both the women of the English recusant community like Margaret Clitherow, who "never feared nor once shrunk at any worldly affliction or pain sustained for the Catholic faith and her conscience," and their daughters, who left England in order to fully practice their faith in continental cloisters (Mush 397).[89]

Isabella's wish for "a more strict restraint" produces linguistic effects that reverberate throughout the play; when she expresses desire—for restraint, withdrawal, virginity, martyrdom—her interlocutors frequently turn to chiastic formulations. Immediately after Isabella questions the convent's rule, for example, Francisca responds to Lucio's arrival by articulating the order's restrictions: "When you have vow'd, you must not speak with men / But in the presence of the prioress: / Then if you speak, you must not show your face, / Or if you show your face, you must not speak" (1.4.10–13). These final two lines incite a recursive movement on the part of the reader, a doubling back that contains Isabella's physical body within her choice to speak or be silent. In traversing not speaking/speaking/not speaking, they also point further back, to Claudio's description of his sister's facility "with reason and discourse" and especially her "prone and speechless dialect" (1.2.184, 182). The paradox of Claudio's description—for how can dialect be speechless?—suggests that Isabella, like Elizabeth before her, creates representational difficulties for those who would portray her. Shakespeare draws attention to this parallel not only in naming his nun Isabella (a variant of Elizabeth), but in his structural echoes of the moment when Spenser suggests that Elizabeth's chastity may reveal the inadequacy of art: "If pourtrayd it might be by any liuing art. / But liuing art may not least part expresse" (*The Faerie Queene* 3.proem.1.9–2.1). Here, the chiastic turn crosses stanzas, heightening the reader's experience of an enforced return and reevaluation of Elizabeth's chastity and its availability for representation. Isabella poses a similar problem for characters in *Measure for Measure* and for readers of the play, and provokes responses that take the shape of chiasmus or antimetabole, forms in which a second phrase or clause is the mirror or near mirror image of the first.[90] Recent work on chiasmus in early modern poetry reveals its relationship to religious change,[91] and I argue that Shakespeare's use of chiastic structures contributes to this broader discourse while clarifying the implications of the narrative ruptures provoked by the female virgins of *The Faerie Queene* and *Hero and Leander*.

The interplay of Isabella's bodily integrity, verbal facility, and social circulation creates an interpretive crux for other characters in the play.[92] Since virginity cannot be "with character too gross" writ on her body, as Juliet's pregnancy is on hers, it at once holds no meaning and too many meanings (1.2.154). When Lucio greets her at the convent door, he names her as a virgin before adding a conditional: "Hail, virgin, if you be" (1.4.16). Though he withdraws his "if"—explaining that "those cheek-roses / Proclaim you are no less"—the physical sign of Isabella's body is nonetheless not a reliable marker of either her sexual status or her religious position (1.4.16–17). Instead, Isabella depends upon speech and, as many critics have noted, prompts a series of misunderstandings when she refuses to acknowledge that her words may have multiple meanings. She suggests that she will bribe Angelo (with "true prayers") (2.2.151), agrees to sin with Angelo (by begging Claudio's life), and tells Claudio that he may live (condemning him to die when he accepts the conditions under which he could be saved). Throughout the play, then, Isabella's language, like her body, prompts a recursive interpretive process: in order to understand what she means, we must continually reevaluate what she has said in light of what she is saying.[93] At its most condensed, this appears as a fractured chiasmus: "There is a vice that most I do abhor, / And most desire should meet the blow of justice; / For which I would not plead, but that I must, / For which I must not plead, but that I am / At war 'twixt will and will not" (2.2.29–33). This is not a perfect example, because Isabella is not a perfect rhetorician. The slightly askew formal patterns of her language suggest reason under duress. Here, she creates a parallelism that flirts with chiasmus and anaphora: the repetition of "for which I" at the beginning of two lines and two seemingly parallel clauses ("would not plead"; "must not plead") creates the impression of order, but the chiastic move of ending one line with "I must" only to have it reappear as "I must not" in the first clause of the next line suggests a rupture in parallel logic. The enjambment at the end of this second "for which I" line further disrupts the parallelism: by ending the line but not the sentence on "I am," Shakespeare creates the momentary impression that Isabella herself is the vice for which she would not and must not plead. But the final line reveals that Isabella describes not her ontology but rather her current mental state, "at war 'twixt will and will not," which points us back to what she "abhors" (will not) and "desires" (will) in the first two lines.[94] It is no surprise that Angelo's response is a curt "well, the matter?" given that Isabella circles around the substance of her petition in a rhetorical maneuver that we might, with Claudio, identify as a kind of "speechless dialect."

This is not to suggest that Isabella is unskilled. Rather, her flexible use of rhetorical forms demonstrates the insufficiency of language to represent the conflicts and compromises of her position.[95] When she turns her attention to her interlocutor, her strategy shifts, and chiasmus enables a swift dismantling of Angelo's theory of a justice system based on the equivalence of crime (act) and punishment (law). "If he had been as you, and you as he," Isabella argues, "You would have slipped like him, but he, like you, / Would not have been so stern" (2.2.64–66). The conditional Isabella proposes, in which Claudio (he) is Angelo (you) and Angelo (you) is Claudio (he), forces Angelo to consider another form of equivalence. By asking him to imagine himself as Claudio, Isabella unsettles Angelo's precise sense not only of self but of justice. The second chiastic formulation in these lines—you would slip if you were like him, but if he were like you he would not be stern—suggests that equivalence is not a simple one-to-one relationship; instead, it requires evaluation and modification. Isabella's language reveals an adaptable sense of self and world produced in part *by* her desire for a strict restraint; while what she means (in speaking and in signifying) is not always clear to her interlocutors, her rhetorical patterns establish structures of containment that she would translate from the walls of the cloister to the government of Vienna.

And Isabella's arguments do effect change in Angelo, though not the change she desires. After encountering her, he finds himself trapped in chiastic formulations but unable to grapple with his fractured sense of self. "When

I would pray and think," he complains, "I think and pray / To several subjects" (2.4.1–2). Again, enjambment points us to a self divided: like Isabella, whose "I am" is torn between will and will not, what at first appears to be Angelo's balanced ability to "pray and think" / "think and pray" is in fact torn between "several subjects." Isabella negotiates her chiastic divide as a balancing act: she contains and represents multitudes. On the contrary, Angelo claims that his chiastic balance is fragmented into multiple subjects outside of himself—but in identifying heaven and Isabella, he reveals that in truth he is divided by "the strong and swelling evil / Of my conception" (2.4.6–7).[96] Isabella prompts Angelo's internal fragmentation and, in response, he attempts to pin her down to a single understanding of what it means to be a woman: "Be that you are, / That is a woman; if you be more, you're none" (2.4.134–35).[97] The obvious pun of none/nun suggests that to be a perpetual virgin is actually to be many things at once—and nothing at all. As more than a woman—akin, perhaps, to the Virgin Queen—Isabella simultaneously has no value in a system of social circulation predicated on marriage and sexuality and has a very clearly defined religious and social position. We might thus identify a chiasmus hidden within Angelo's formulation, since to "be that you are" is, for Isabella, to be a nun. Angelo positions "a woman" as both more and less consequential than a vowed virgin: more in the sequential logic, wherein to be chaste and self-sufficient (more than a woman) is actually to be "none"—not a woman or anything at all; less in the chiastic logic, wherein a virgin is more than a sexed body and identifies as a nun. In responding to a woman who means more than he would like, then, Angelo's language exceeds his control, demonstrating in miniature how early modern literature registers the meaningfulness of Catholic women.

Angelo's inability to hold his words to a single meaning of womanhood follows directly from a conversation about female frailty on the one hand and creativity on the other. When Angelo suggests that "we are all frail" and that "women are frail too," Isabella offers a simile that crystallizes the formal effects of Catholic women that I have been tracing in this chapter (2.4.121, 124). They are as frail, she claims, "as the glasses where they view themselves, / Which are as easy broke as they make forms" (2.4.125–26). Women may be easily broken, but they make forms just as easily, in a startling modification of the Aristotelian gendering of form (masculine) and matter (feminine).[98] Isabella's mirrors, like Spenser's mirrors for Elizabeth in *The Faerie Queene*, are multiple and multiplying, but instead of proliferating virgins, Isabella describes both fragment and increase: the analogous relationship of breaking and making creates an image of a shattered mirror, endlessly producing and reflecting forms. As Slights and Holmes argue, in "yok[ing] women with mirrors through their shared ability to create forms," Isabella simultaneously points to women's frailty, sexual fecundity, and "their ability to fashion themselves."[99] I would further point out that the play, especially in Angelo's response, reveals that the forms women make are not only their own or their children's. The capaciousness of Isabella's image leads to the chiastic fragmentation of Angelo's language into the multiple meanings that I analyzed above—it leads to formal effects, in other words, that themselves suggest a broken mirror.

Measure for Measure ends in a flurry of chiasmus, from Isabella's condemnation of Angelo[100] to the Duke's coupling of Mariana and Angelo: "her worth worth yours" (5.1.497). The final scene is particularly revealing of the "chiastic exchange in embodied experience" that James Knapp has identified in *Measure for Measure*, as individuals mirror one another only to demonstrate the necessity of recursive evaluations of the self and others.[101] Mariana, who took Isabella's place in Angelo's bed and is now "neither maid, widow, nor wife," looks suspiciously like a nun when she claims Angelo as her husband (5.1.180).[102] The Duke, upon Mariana's entrance, asks that she "show [her] face, and after speak" but Mariana refuses to reveal herself until Angelo bids her (5.1.168). She thus abides, in part, by the chiastic rules of Isabella's convent, where "if you speak, you must not show your face, / Or if you show your face, you must not speak" (1.4.12–13). Isabella's willingness to sacrifice another's virginity results in two interchangeable and ultimately inscrutable women: at the end of the play, it is not clear whether either of them will be settled as maid, widow, or wife. The question of what Isabella means thus remains open. From Lucio's "Hail, virgin, if you be" to Angelo's demand that she "be that you are / That is a woman; if you be more, you're none," Isabella's religious choice leads to questions about her sexual and social position that manifest in formal mirroring and the play's inconclusive final scene.

Isabella is pulled away from the female community of nuns—and from her own strongly voiced religious system—first by Angelo's attempted seduction and then by the Duke's marriage plot. At the play's end, the audience is left with the image of a Duke disguised as a friar proposing to a silenced woman who wishes to be a nun.[103] These Catholic figures of chastity are transformed into secular, marriageable characters, closely resembling the situation in England at the Reformation, when some former nuns and priests did choose to marry. James Ellison has argued that this "final tableau" is "unmistakable in its Protestant message."[104] But this marital solution is just as incomplete as those of *The Faerie Queene* and *Hero and Leander*: Isabella never responds to the Duke's proposal, which he defers to a "fitter time" (5.1.493).[105] Natasha Korda shows that "the textual fissure produced by this silence has been filled by a cacophony of critical voices," and suggests that there is in fact "ample evidence within both the text and its cultural contexts . . . to support *both* Isabella's acceptance of the Duke's offer of marriage *and* her return to the nunnery."[106] While the fissure that Korda describes is interpretive rather than textual—Isabella's silence leaves the Duke's proposal hanging as an open question to be answered by audience and readers—I would argue that there is a textual fissure in the play's final moments, as well. In the Duke's final chiastic proposal and his inconclusive concluding couplet, Shakespeare formally registers Isabella's silence as an embodiment of Francisca's earlier chiastic formulation of the convent's rules.[107]

For the Duke, chiasmus does not fragment into multiplying mirror images or offer a recursive process of interpretation. Instead, it is a closed circuit that suggests marriage as perfect equivalence: "her worth worth yours," as he says to Angelo (5.1.495). In the final lines of the play, he poses a similar chiasmus as a marriage proposal: "Dear Isabel, / I have a motion much imports your good, / Whereto if you'll a willing ear incline, / What's mine is yours, and what is yours is mine" (5.1.534–37). The Duke thus attempts to close a circuit that Isabella keeps open by maintaining a protective silence. She refuses to be enclosed within his possessive pronoun, and instead protects her own self possession by refusing to speak, as Francisca suggested early in the play: "if you speak, you must not show your face, / Or if you show your face, you must not speak" (1.4.12–13). Isabella's chastity is held within her silence, and the Duke registers her lack of response by concluding the play not on the rhyme of "incline" and "mine" but with a second concluding couplet: "So bring us to our palace, where we'll show / What's yet behind, that['s] meet you all should know" (5.1.538–39). When Isabella does not verbally accede to his attempt to impose a marital telos grounded in masculine possession, the Duke slips from an enclosed chiastic formulation to a communal proposal that suggests moving forward in order to recover and remember what has passed. The final two couplets of the play thus refuse narrative closure and instead signal the necessity of recursive reading.

While the Protestant Reformation shifted the religious and political landscape of sixteenth-century England, the literature of the post-Reformation period reveals the fissures within that transformation. *Measure for Measure* illuminates one such fissure in its representation of Isabella, who embodies multiple aspects of Catholic femininity: her choice of chastity provides her with a tool of political power, a language for resistance, and a religious justification for her final choice of silence. Perhaps, at the end of the play, Isabella will flee to her monastery, as some Catholic women fled proposed marriages in England to enter convents on the continent. Jane Martin, a lay sister in the English convent at Cambrai, for example, might have married "a gentleman of a good estate in England, but shee rather chose to lead an humble life in Religion, than to appear great in the world, therefore refused the offer made her & prevailed with the gentleman who would have married her, to bestow his wealth upon a Seminary of English in Flanders, which he did at his death oblidging the sayd seminary to provide for her & settle her as she should desire."[108] Shakespeare does not allow his audience or his readers to settle on a single interpretation of this character because, at his historical moment, it was impossible to settle on a single interpretation of the Catholic woman. *Measure for Measure* takes a complicated view of female Catholicism, one that is informed by multiple and competing discourses, including not only anti-Catholic propaganda and the Catholic martyr tradition exemplified in Margaret Clitherow but also the writings of sixteenth- and seventeenth-century Englishwomen who desired lives in the convent that remained connected to a world outside their enclosure. As I have argued, authors such as Marlowe, Chapman, and Shakespeare engaged the political dimensions of female chastity in their representations of vowed virgins, thereby creating characters whose dramatic and poetic disruptions mirrored the social and political disruptions of early modern Catholic Englishwomen. *Hero and Leander* and *Measure for Measure* reveal that the conceptual reconfigurations associated with religious reform remained dynamic and competitive even after decades of Protestantism: the Elizabethan ideological system that found its fullest literary expression in Spenser's *The Faerie Queene* was dominant but never unquestioned, whether in the Catholic poetics of Anthony Copley's *A Fig for Fortune*, which depicts a "Virgin in bright majestie" who explicitly does not bear "*Elizas* name," or in the doctrinally ambiguous and now canonical literature of Marlowe and Shakespeare.[109] In the chapters that follow, I will trace the literary effects of Catholic women and their self representations through the first half of the seventeenth century, as books and monasteries gradually displaced courtrooms and prison cells as the primary locations for female religious and political dissent.

CHAPTER 2

To the Nunnery: Enclosure and Polemic in the English Convents in Exile

The female virgins of late Elizabethan literature, whether votaresses of Venus or novices of the Poor Clares, were products of a culture in transition. At the same time that Elizabeth fashioned her virginity into a sign of royal power, Catholic women exposed the fissures in a religious settlement that did not allow for monastic vocations. Some traveled to the continent to join foreign and newly established English cloisters, while others practiced their faith with relative impunity due to the conflicting legal positions of female coverture and married recusancy. These women, who put pressure on ideals of married chastity, influenced both the narrative and form of poems and plays that explored their political and social significance. The presumptive marriages of *The Faerie Queene, Hero and Leander*, and *Measure for Measure* recede before us, as each text suggests a telos thwarted by the demands of character, of book history, and of death—or fulfilled only in protest. Yet even as discourses associated with Catholic femininity helped shape the formal properties of canonical English literature at the turn of the seventeenth century, Catholic women themselves were seldom acknowledged as authors or participants in literary creation.

In the decades that followed, as the establishment of new English convents on the continent gained momentum, plays such as John Webster's *The Duchess of Malfi* and pamphlets like Thomas Robinson's *The Anatomy of the English Nunnery at Lisbon* depicted women as victims of a religious culture that depended on the control of female bodies through enclosure and the corruption of holy books—two of the interlocking manifestations of depravity that undergirded anti-Catholic polemic.[1] While pamphleteers like Robinson addressed the convent directly, in exposés of specific orders or more general critiques of monasticism, the most explicitly anti-Catholic drama of the early seventeenth century responded to the revived interest in monastic life among English Catholics only obliquely. Unlike Shakespeare, who explored the legal pressures on faith and choice through a young woman who wished to be a nun in 1604, later playwrights shied away from direct depictions of the convent or its inhabitants while reviling Catholic devotional materials and the clerical hierarchy.[2] By not including nuns in their condemnations of Catholicism,[3] playwrights such as Webster and Middleton effaced the vibrancy, popularity, and literary activities of the early modern English convents, even as they critiqued the concept of female enclosure through treatments of forced chastity and confinement. Plays like Webster's *The Duchess of Malfi* were deeply invested cultural productions that obscured—and have continued to obscure, in our own critical discourse—early modern English nuns' literary engagements with the religious politics of their native country. Rather than deriding nuns as writers, transcribers, translators, and compilers, English authors instead depicted them as objects to be manipulated by corrupt religious and political authorities. They thus repudiated Catholic women's literary contributions as nothing more than empty echoes, produced at the behest of priests or not at all. Such representations created a double bind, in which neither the presence nor absence of texts produced by Catholic women could successfully demonstrate their unconstrained participation in literary culture.

These competing strands of early seventeenth-century literature—on the one hand, anti-Catholic Jacobean drama and, on the other, the writings of Catholic women—were woven together by the pamphlets that informed both literary representation and polemical discourse associated with religious conflict. This chapter traces these connections in order to demonstrate how physical markers of faith and history—ruins, relics, books, bones—enabled Protestant authors including Webster and Robinson to critique Catholic devotional practices as excessively focused on bodies and materiality, while at the same time practicing their own substitution of presence for absence. In place of real English nuns, living in exile on the continent, Webster staged a poisoned book and the broken walls of an abandoned cloister. In place of political epistles and illuminated manuscript histories crafted by the nuns of Syon Abbey in Lisbon, Robinson described the bones of dead babies, false relics, and interfoliated books. But these same substitutions, when dissected and reconstituted within the convent, could authorize nuns' literary projects rather than effacing them: in a manuscript response to Robinson, the nuns of Syon imagine an allegorical trial in which Truth evaluates *The Anatomy of the English Nunnery at Lisbon* in material terms, first dismissing the pamphlet because it is printed rather than handwritten and then enumerating the many flaws in its materialist logic. By responding to a single pamphlet that shared its anti-Catholic DNA with Italianate revenge tragedies, they offered both a rebuke and an alternative to the English literature that would deny their authorial agency.

For Webster and Robinson, women occupied an untenable and abject position within a Catholic culture that celebrated and exploited the material at the expense of the spiritual, and Webster attempted to deny the contemporary appeal of the cloister through his portraits of the Duchess and Julia in *The Duchess of Malfi*. Both women hold liminal positions at the boundaries between the social categories delineated for women in *Measure for Measure*. The Duchess is widow and wife, compelled to remain single by her brothers, who wish to control her body and property, but secretly married to her steward Antonio. This relationship, largely confined to her bedchamber, enables her to redefine chastity and enclosure in a domestic space. Julia is wife and mistress, seduced by a religious man into a relationship that leads to her death. The Duchess's torture and death, like Julia's death by poisoned book, depend upon the manipulation of material signs that suggest contemporary debates over the theatricality of Catholic worship, the status of the book, and women's role within the church. Nearly a decade later, Thomas Robinson explored a similar set of concerns in *The Anatomy*. Like his fellow pamphleteers, Robinson treated the convent as a thinly disguised prison, where nuns were "mewed up" to face poverty and sexual exploitation at the hands of "Impostors and cheating Copesmates."[4] But Robinson's pamphlet was markedly different from others of the period in its focus on a single convent, Syon Abbey, which had survived the dissolution intact and eventually settled in Lisbon. Robinson's pamphlet builds on the specificity of literary representation in order to portray women who entered continental cloisters as powerless and silly creatures, incapable of resisting priests who wielded authority through sexual dominance and corrupt books.

Robinson's prurient depiction of monastic sexual exploits is grounded in literary culture, from the imagery of anti-Catholic plays to the convent's alleged reading materials and writing practices. Yet even as he made female participation in literary culture nearly unthinkable, his summary of Syon's history and description of monastic life also offered specific details for refutation. As active participants in textual exchange and production, the English nuns of Syon Abbey in Lisbon produced a manuscript response to Robinson that emphatically debunked his claims. Rather than accepting his positioning of them as the passive victims of enclosure, they transformed controversialist language into the basis for self-representation. By situating themselves within a physical space and book culture that featured neither the tragic excesses of Jacobean drama nor the bawdy priests of anti-Catholic polemic, they sidestepped the double bind that would erase or invalidate female monastic writing. Their rhetorical sophistication enables a complex series of reverse substitutions: in the absence of material proof, they provide textual presence through exegesis and thereby build an argument that not only enumerates Robinson's errors but also offers an alternative literary culture for English Catholics.

Books, Bodies, and Ruins:
The Spectral Convent in Jacobean Drama

In *The Duchess of Malfi*, female enclosure and priests' books are twinned manifestations of Catholic perversion: clerical control over women's bodies is mediated by the book and articulated through and against a symbolic cloister. Webster identifies claustration, and especially the practice of unwilling female enclosure, with vividly material forms of Catholic corruption, while displacing female monasticism geographically and temporally. Female religious enclosure is foreign and anachronistic—a ruined cloister in the Italian countryside and on the English stage.[5] As a result, even those readings of the play that are attuned to its engagement with religious controversy have not considered how Webster's treatment of his female characters might evoke contemporary concerns regarding the newly established English continental cloisters.[6] The Duchess and Julia are emphatically *not* nuns: not vowed virgins, not obedient, and not willingly enclosed. Yet Webster's deviations from his source texts suggest his interest in exploring the status of women within Catholic culture: while earlier versions of the Duchess of Malfi's downfall hint at a critique of ecclesiastical hypocrisy in their description of the Cardinal, they do not address issues of enclosure, female autonomy, or material culture.[7] By exploring concepts associated with Catholicism and the cloister through a series of interactions between the Duchess and her male interlocutors and inventing the character of Julia, Webster transforms a well-worn story of the dangers of class mobility into a damning portrait of a religious system that destroys women, degrading any choices they might be capable of making and leading to the death of the soul, the body, or both.

Webster's interest in institutional Catholicism and its relationship to women is especially visible in comparison with the moralizing of authors such as William Painter and Thomas Beard, who condemn the Duchess for her wanton appetites and Antonio for his social climbing. Painter, for example, describes the marriage between Antonio and the Duchess as "a Maske and coverture to hide hir follies & shamelesse lusts."[8] His version of the narrative is explicitly didactic, written in order to warn "good Ladies" against following her example: "these Histories be not written to train and trap you, to pursue the thousand thousand slippery sleightes of Loves gallantise, but rather carefully to warn you to behold the semblable faultes" (185r).[9] Despite a latent sympathy for the Duchess, expressed at the moment of her death in his condemnation of her brothers as "two ministers of iniquitie," the class contamination effected by her secret and lustful marriage is nonetheless the prime object of social critique in Painter's text (192r). "Shall I be of opinion," he asks, "that a housholde servaunt ought to sollicite, nay rather suborne the daughter of his Lord without punishment, or that a vile and abject person dare to mount upon a Princes bed? No no, policie requireth order in all, and eche wight ought to be matched according to their qualitie" (183r).[10] Painter focuses almost exclusively on the interactions between the Duchess and Antonio until their marriage is discovered, when her brothers appear as figures of vengeance whose violent reaction to their sister's marriage is explicable—if not fully acceptable—within the social logic Painter endorses. The brothers are not to be admired, but neither they nor their social and religious positions are at the center of the text. The Cardinal is critiqued for not conforming to "Christian puritie" in the murder of Antonio, but the true fault remains with the victim, who "ought to have contented himself with that degree and honor that hee had acquired by his deedes and glory of his vertues" (194v).[11] In the logic of Painter's text, the brothers reassert social order and correct their sister's sexually motivated transgression by killing her and her husband, though they go too far in killing their children, "who by no meanes could prejudice or anoy the duke of *Malfi* or his title" (192r).[12] Order is restored, even if by excessive means.

Webster borrows Painter's language of folly, lust, and class consciousness, but does not follow his didactic aims. Instead, he places Painter's argument for chastity and social purity in the mouths of the Duchess's brothers, who are identified with images of Catholic corruption from the beginning of the play.[13] Bosola compares Ferdinand and the Cardinal to "plum-trees that grow crooked over standing pools; they are rich, and o'erladen with fruit, but none but crows, pies, and caterpillars feed on them."[14] This sinister metaphor of twisted trees, a fetid pool, ripe fruit, and hungry scavengers could just as easily appear in Protestant propaganda, which identified priests and Jesuits as "Popish Caterpillars," especially in their relationships to women.[15] "It is a pittifull thing," wrote the pamphleteer Lewis Owen, "to see so many proper Gentlewomen, well borne and bred, to be so cheated, and deceived, by these Romish Impostors or Caterpillars."[16] While the brothers are the trees at the heart of this anti-Catholic image of rot, abundance, and decay, they are also caterpillars who attempt to feed upon their sister. In urging her not to remarry, they imply that widowhood offers a renewed opportunity for bodily purity, in contrast to those whose "livers are more spotted / Than Laban's sheep" (1.1.289–90). Contemporary Catholic spiritual guides such as *The Treasure of Vowed Chastity in Secular Persons* associated such widowed purity with virginity and monasticism. This Jesuit text, dedicated to the recusant Anne Vaux, claims that "there be not wanting in these our dayes, amongst secular persons very many, as well Widdowes, as Virgins, who aspyring to perfection, have a desire (as farre as they may conveniently) to sequester themselves from the troubles and incombrances of the world, thereby to imploy their mindes more freely and securly in the service of God."[17] Such women may find that "to live in Monasteryes . . . is not so convenient," but nonetheless wish to emulate the spiritual practices of the cloister, including some form of sequestration.[18]

But the brothers do not use this language of faith and religious devotion, and Webster is careful not to draw his audience's attention to the positive aspects of the convent. Instead, their attempt to prevent the Duchess's remarriage is grounded in ideas about sexuality and decay available in Painter's text, in a broader discourse associated with the trope of the lusty widow,[19] and in the depictions of Jesuits and women in Protestant propaganda.[20] Ferdinand tells Bosola that "she's a young widow / I would not have her marry again," and argues "they are most luxurious / Will wed twice," a position also communicated by Painter (1.1.246–47, 288–89). While Ferdinand refuses to explain his reasons in this scene, he later reveals that he "had a hope, / Had she continued widow, to have gained / An infinite mass of treasure by her death" (4.2.275–77). Ferdinand is unable to separate this desire for the Duchess's estate from his desire for control over her body: he drives himself mad imagining "her in the shameful act of sin / . . . with some strong thighed bargeman" and damns her for sullying "that body of hers, / While that my blood ran pure in't, was more worth / Than that which thou wouldst comfort, called a soul" (2.5.41–42, 4.1.121–23).[21] In his obsessive synthesis of sex, money, and power, Ferdinand is a close relation of the Jesuitical caterpillars portrayed in Protestant propaganda. According to the pamphleteers, women with money were sent to the Jesuits, who "dispossesse them of all worldly cares and vanities, and (like subtill Alchymists) refine them out of their silver and golden drosse, into a more sublime estate and condition, and will cherish and nourish them, even in their owne bosomes: such a burning zeale have they towards them."[22] Like the Jesuits, Ferdinand is motivated by a combination of greed and lust in his imprisonment of the Duchess. Webster thus undercuts Painter's treatment of the Duchess and Antonio's marriage by associating his source material's social and sexual ideology with the play's most villainous characters. His target is not the social disruption effected by the Duchess's marriage but rather a Catholic religious and social system that imposes chastity and enclosure for material rather than spiritual ends.

Rather than treating the Duchess's relationship with Antonio as the product of the uncontrollable sexual appetites that Painter and Ferdinand imagine or as "the entrance into some prison" that the Cardinal threatens (1.1.315–16), Webster suggests that marriage offers the Duchess an opportunity to appropriate and reconfigure the restraints her brothers place upon her.[23] Her courtship of Antonio is marked by her claustrophobic attempts to imagine herself free not simply of their moral code but also of physical enclosures.[24] First, she compares her steward to a too-small house: "this goodly roof of yours is too low built; / I cannot stand upright in't, nor discourse, / Without I raise it higher: raise yourself, / Or if you please, my hand to help you" (1.1.406–9). The Duchess uses a metaphor of building and improvement to signal her intent to raise Antonio's social status. But she also imagines that their marriage will relieve the pressures of enclosure and expand the restricted space that her brothers have left for her, space in which she can neither "stand upright . . . nor discourse." Antonio's response reveals that he sees the danger in pressing the boundaries of enclosure. "Ambition, madam, is a great man's madness, / That is not kept in chains, and close-pent rooms, / But in fair lightsome lodgings, and is girt / With the wild noise of prattling visitants" (1.1.410–13). This is far from a straightforward denial of ambition; instead, Antonio transforms the Duchess's metaphor into a meditation on madness, class, and space. His language foreshadows the play's later scenes, in which a "wild consort / Of madmen" make "noise and folly" both outside and inside the Duchess's chamber, but its immediate effect is an alteration of the Duchess's conception of space and enclosure (4.2.1–2, 5). As Antonio imagines it, the "chains, and close-pent rooms" that restrict the madness of poor men are no more threatening than the "fair lightsome lodgings" that foster the madness of great men. He hints at the possibility of a self-imposed enclosure, in which he "will remain the constant sanctuary / Of [the Duchess's] good name" (1.1.450–51). In an implicit response to Antonio's formulation, the Duchess alters her view of restricted space, disregarding all that lies "without this circumference"—the enclosure created by their embrace (1.1.459).[25] The Duchess and Antonio thus subvert her brothers' efforts to encloister her: they confine their marriage to the bedchamber, making the most of secrecy despite the births of three children.[26]

Numerous critics have noted Webster's attention to interiority, domesticity, and privacy in the relationship between the Duchess and Antonio and some have suggested that their marriage may offer a Protestant alternative to the play's Catholic milieu.[27] But none has explored how the play's treatment of enclosure relates to the religious politics associated with the convent in the first decades of the seventeenth century. In theorizing a form of domestic enclosure, the Duchess and Antonio suggest that companionate marriage is an alternative to the alignment of widowhood and virginity advocated by her brothers for all the wrong reasons and, for many English Catholics, located in continental cloisters. Webster thus attempted to further mar the reputation of monastic life without mentioning it directly or alluding to its contemporary appeal, just as political figures became increasingly concerned about Catholic women migrating to the continent. In a letter of 1612, Sir Thomas Edmondes, the English ambassador to France, notified King James of a plan "to erect in the suburbs of this towne [Paris] a Monasterie of English Nunnes."[28] He had warned his French contact that "the establishment of those Seminaries and Nunneries for English, which gave occasion for the receiving and entertayning of all the discontented persons of our state, were the first, and principall causes of the jealousies bitwixt us and Spaine" (1191).[29] Edmondes linked the foundation of new English convents on the continent to larger questions of international relations: female religious houses "serve for nothing els but to drawe great numbers of others by their example and enticements out of the realme and to make our state the more odious abroad by the shew of great persecutions in England" (1191). He feared France would provide direct and sustained material support to these English Catholics, in the form of newly established religious foundations created for relief of England's religious minority.[30]

As the diplomatic correspondence reveals, female enclosure was understood to be an important political issue in seventeenth-century England. A woman's choice to practice her faith within a continental cloister had implications not only for domestic religious policies but also for relations with foreign powers. Webster's depiction of the Duchess as a woman who rejects forms of enclosure associated with the convent in favor of a secret marriage, and who dies at the behest of religious and political authorities, thus encourages a reading of marriage as a crypto-Protestant alternative to the Catholic state. The Duchess's relationship with Antonio is a strategic political choice as much as it is the loving act of a private individual, and Webster's tragedy is grounded in the futility of her resistance to the "rank pasture" that surrounds her (1.1.297).[31] Her family is ultimately separated by the dual powers of church and state, as embodied in the Cardinal and Ferdinand.[32] Since she defied their demands that she practice nonmarital chastity, they imprison her within her own home, thereby undoing the collective work of redefining that space performed by the Duchess and Antonio during their courtship.

In drawing out the religious implications of the Duchess's torture and death, Webster further associates her with female monasticism and Protestant resistance to it. She reacts to Ferdinand's anger over her secret marriage in explicitly Catholic terms, saying that she will not "be cased up, like a holy relic" (3.2.140). In imagining herself as a possible object of Catholic devotion while confined to a restricted physical space, she raises the specter of the convent, where nuns both preserved saints' relics and could themselves be imagined as holy relics cased up for devotional purposes. In the Protestant imaginary, the cloister was not far removed from the prison: nuns "must remaine locked in, like so many prisoners, all the dayes of their lives, while the Jesuites are sharing their portions."[33] Thus, when the Duchess's estate is "seized into th' protection of the church" by the pope at the Cardinal's "instigation," Webster again alludes to warnings that priests and Jesuits lured women into the convent in order to steal their money as well as their chastity (3.4.32, 35). The Duchess remains resolute in her opposition to these efforts by her brothers and, in comparing herself to a "wretch . . . broke upon the wheel," suggests that she might be interpreted as a Protestant martyr to the Catholic state (4.1.81).[34] The materialist, theatrical, and ceremonial torture she endures is coded as a Catholic attempt to inflict mental anguish on a Protestant sensibility: Ferdinand succeeds in manipulating the Duchess's sensory perception of material signs, especially the wax figures that she is told are the dead bodies of Antonio and their children. Margaret E. Owens argues that these waxworks evoke "devotional traditions involving votive figures" and thus "may be linked to the play's thematic preoccupation with the abuse and perversion of Christian ritual."[35] Even if Webster was not aware of this tradition, these artistic representations of death offer a vivid example of the brothers' materialist aesthetics.[36] Physical objects stand in for and are said to *be* the bodies of the Duchess's loved ones, but the audience soon learns they are false impressions: wax figures posing as flesh.

Webster's condemnation of Catholic doctrine and devotion lies at the heart of the Duchess's torture scene, and yet his heroine cannot be fully reconciled to the reformed faith. She is at once of both religions and of neither: while her secret marriage and her martyrdom are marked by a Protestant sensibility, the Duchess remains steeped in a Roman Catholic world. She accuses Ferdinand of "violat[ing] a sacrament o'th' church" when he calls her children bastards, and Bosola suggests sending "her a penitential garment to put on / Next to her delicate skin, and furnish[ing] her / With beads and prayer-books" (4.1.39, 119–21).[37] After death, her spirit haunts a "piece of a cloister," further aligning the Duchess with England's Roman Catholic past (5.3.4). Instead of tying his eponymous character to a coherent doctrinal sensibility, whether Protestant or Catholic, Webster adopts conflicting rhetoric and images in order to explore how women might negotiate and resist a Catholic social hierarchy and materialist worldview from the inside.[38] The Duchess famously dies in the fourth act, her secret marriage no proof against her brothers' spies and authoritarian control over her body and her estate. But Webster suggests that there might be an alternative for women in his characterization of Julia: what if, instead of attempting to withdraw into a domestic arrangement and live a covertly reformed life, a woman were to participate in the very corruption that so much of the play condemns by attaching herself to a powerful figure in the church?

Julia is not a part of Painter's narrative, but Webster may have discovered the inspiration for her character in Thomas Beard's *The Theatre of Gods Judgements* (1597). After his chapter "Of whoredomes committed under colour of Marriage," which relates the story of the Duchess, Beard focuses on "priests whoredomes" in his chapter "Of unlawfull marriages, and their issues."[39] His elucidation of the paradox of clerical celibacy reads like an apt description of Ferdinand and the Cardinal's initial conversation with their sister: "making marriage one of the sacraments of the Church," Catholics "doe neverthelesse despise it as a vile and prophane thing."[40] Beard goes on to describe bishops who "suffer their priests to keepe harlots" and certain villages "where it was not onely winked at, but also commaunded, that every new priest should have his privat whore for his owne tooth."[41] Julia, the Cardinal's mistress, thus enables Webster to build upon the broader anti-Catholic discourse present in Beard's text, which maintains Painter's interest in class contamination but offers a stronger condemnation of the Cardinal's cruelty. Webster's Cardinal is a signal example of "the corruption of the times"; too corrupt, even, to be pope (1.1.18). "He strews in his way flatterers, panders, intelligencers, atheists, and a thousand such political monsters. He should have been pope; but instead of coming to it by the primitive decency of the church, he did bestow bribes so largely, and so impudently, as if he would have carried it away" (1.1.153–57). Rather than working for the good of religion (specifically coded here in terms of the primitive church), the Cardinal works for his own ends. He makes "religion a stalking horse to intend [his] owne profit."[42] The details of his character—from his secret mistress to his involvement in murderous schemes—reflect the belief that members of the Catholic hierarchy cared only for "great wealth and reputation, to bee counted great States-men, and contrivers of weighty matters; not caring in the meane time, for the securitie of them by whom they worke their villany."[43] The Cardinal works his villainy through many other characters in the play, including his brother and Bosola, but his most telling interactions are with Julia.[44] Their relationship parallels that of the Duchess and her brothers, but enacts more specific concerns involving the confluence of women, priests, property, and the book.

Webster's representation of a churchman who takes a married woman as his mistress is typical of Protestant propaganda, which argued that Jesuits and priests could not be trusted with other men's wives. In their first scene together, Julia outlines the parameters of her affair with the Cardinal. Almost immediately, she reminds him, "you have prevailed with me / Beyond my strongest thoughts" (2.4.6–7). Julia, a married woman who pretends "to visit an old anchorite / Here, for devotion" in order to rendezvous with her lover, is the realization of pamphleteers' fears: a Catholic woman whose "strongest thoughts" are not enough to resist the manipulations of a priest (2.4.4–5). As Edward Hoby explained to the dedicatees of his 1609 *A Letter to Mr. T. H.*—the women he called "Romish Collapsed Ladies"—priests "busilie swarme about your sexe, which, by reason of your lesse abilitie of judgement, is soonest inveigled with their wiles."[45] For Hoby and his contemporaries, religious seduction was closely aligned with sexual seduction, and women who converted to Catholicism were likely to become "collapsed ladies" in more ways than one.[46] John Gee, for example, relates the story of how "a certaine *Catholick collapsed Lady* . . . departed from her Husband (yet living) and went over to *Bruxels*, and was admitted into the order of *Nunnery*."[47] When "there appeared in her some passion incompatible with *Nunship*," this still-married woman "came over into *England* a companion with a *Religious Jesuit*, since of great note, *F. D.* and remaining afterwards an inlarged *Nun* in *London*, was (as it seemeth) more visibly taken with a disease befalling that sexe, called *flatus uterinus*."[48] Gee erases the distinctions between married recusant women and encloistered religious women in his depiction of a married woman who leaves her husband to become an "inlarged *Nun*." Her physical freedom is ultimately indistinguishable from sexual freedom: she is enlarged, or set free, from the convent, only to be quite literally enlarged with pregnancy. So, too, is her collapse to Catholicism nearly indistinguishable from her sexual collapse, as Gee implies that her pregnancy is the fault of a "*Religious Jesuit*."[49] Protestant propagandists thus linked religious conversions to implications of debauched sexuality by tracing both to "the subtiltie of [clergymen's] words."[50]

In *The Duchess of Malfi*, Julia similarly falls victim to the seductive words of a religious man. The Cardinal's courtship is marked by metaphors of wounding and disease borrowed from love poetry: he has "a piteous wound i'th' heart, / And a sick liver" that only Julia can cure (2.4.37–38). But by the play's final act, he has come to see Julia as the disease; she is his "lingering consumption" (5.2.224). To destroy her, he uses poison both figurative and literal. First, he tells her that he ordered the Duchess strangled, "a secret / That, like a ling'ring poison, may chance lie / Spread in thy veins" (5.2.260–62). Immediately thereafter, he demands that she swear upon a book, presumably the Bible, that she will not reveal his secret. "Most religiously" she swears and kisses the book (5.2.272). The two poisons—of the secret and of the book— merge in the Cardinal's explanation for Julia's impending death. By claiming that "thy curiosity / Hath undone thee: thou'rt poisoned with that book," the Cardinal implies that the poisoned book is a manifestation of the poisonous secret Julia was so curious to learn (5.2.273–74). His poisonous words and deeds, from his seduction of a married woman to the murder of his sister, are transformed into the material of a book.[51]

Priests who participated in book culture were a perpetual concern for English Protestants, since the words of Catholic clergymen were always suspect, always potentially poisonous, whether expressed verbally or textually.

Pamphleteers and other Protestant authors accused members of the Catholic clerical hierarchy of corrupting books, whether by physically altering the pages or by hiding the true words in Latin or mistranslations. Robert Burton asked, "what else doe our Papists but by keeping the people in ignorance, vent and broch all their new ceremonies and traditions, when they conceale the Scriptures and read it in Latin, and to some few alone, feeding the people in the meane time with tales out of legends, and such like fabulous narrations? Whom doe they begin with, but collapsed ladies, some few tradesmen, or sooner circumvent?"[52] Webster's Cardinal is only slightly more villainous than the priests who populated the Protestant imaginary: he, too, uses a "fabulous narration" to lure Julia, first to his bed and then to her death. Books as material objects recede in Burton's depiction of a hidden scriptural text supplanted by tales told from legends (saints' lives), in a displacement that seems to reverse the obsessive materiality of Webster's play but actually performs a similar movement from spiritual truth to false shows. Both authors draw attention away from the possibility that women might have unmediated relationships to religious texts—and away from the convent as a possible locale for female autonomy, authorship, and readership—and instead suggest sensational narratives of seduction and collapse accomplished via the very materials of Catholic devotional culture.

Yet, just as Sir Thomas Edmondes's 1612 letter to James reveals growing concerns over Catholic women entering cloisters abroad, so too it suggests a growing awareness of the relationship between the English convents and continental book production. Immediately after describing the plan to build a new "Monasterie of English Nunnes," Edmondes warned James that "besides that the principall of the clergie neere were in hand at the sollicitation of the Nuncio to establishe pensions out of the Churche contributions for six English priests to answer in English all such books as should be sett forth in England against the Romish religion" (118v). As the newly endowed monasteries would draw "discontented persons" away from England, so the pensions would give them the opportunity to print and spread their discontent. Edmondes imagined an exchange of texts and bodies between England and the continent that would "produce all the bad practise that may be against our state" (119r). The king's response to two of Edmondes's letters—which touched on a variety of issues, including a suspected plot to control the Queen of France through a love spell—addressed only the twinned problems of the establishment of English convents and pensions for book-writing priests: "wee have seene your last leters of the fourtenth of this moneth; and in them, all that wee thinck needfull to be aunswered, is the matter about the Nuns and Preists."[53] James discussed the matter with the Ambassador of France, and was told "that for the Preistes to be founded on such a ground, and with such an intention, he thought it unreasonable; for the Nunnes, he held it a matter of lesse accompt" (127r). While the French Ambassador believed that a monastery of English nuns was less threatening than a group of priests paid to write English pamphlets, James disagreed. He countered with "reasons upon both," and instructed Edmondes to "sollicite the dissolution of it" (127r). James may have intended "it" to refer to both matters, but his use of the term "dissolution" necessarily evokes the history of England's monasteries.

For James and his ambassador, the erection of a new female religious house in France was at least as pressing as the parallel growth of the exilic book trade. Yet even in the diplomatic correspondence, nuns remained distinct from book-writing priests. Early modern drama participated in this segregation of Catholic women and religious or controversial books. Plays that explore the cultural transformations attendant upon religious reform seldom suggest that women might be involved in reading, writing, or publishing books; instead, vulnerable and immured female bodies are positioned in relationship to literally and figuratively poisonous books, together demonstrating the irreligious and lethal nature of institutional Catholicism.

In his two female characters, Webster depicts alternate modes of responding to the patriarchal pressures that Protestant pamphleteers associated with the Catholic hierarchy: the Duchess subverts her brothers' restrictions by embracing Antonio's understanding of enclosure, while Julia is complicit in the system of ecclesiastical power, acquiescing to the courtship of the Cardinal and directly benefiting from the fall of the Duchess through the acquisition of Antonio's lands, "ravished from his throat / By the Cardinal's entreaty" (5.1.42–43). Neither woman avoids a tragic death. Ultimately, their differing attempts to negotiate sexual alliances and to control property are frustrated by the whims of Ferdinand and the Cardinal.[54] Webster's representation of women struggling within and against the demands of a Catholic hierarchy reveals what English Protestants saw as the untenable nature of *any* woman's position in a Catholic political and religious framework.[55] The tragedy of *The Duchess of Malfi* is thus, in part, Webster's reflection on the tragedy of female monasticism, though it includes no nuns.

Webster's play does include a former convent, seemingly haunted by the Duchess's ghost. Among "the ruins of an ancient abbey" is a "piece of a cloister . . . / Gives the best echo that you ever heard" (5.3.2–5). This echo sounds suspiciously like the Duchess—" 'Tis very like my wife's voice," says Antonio—and voices an interest in protecting her husband (5.3.26). The echo tells Antonio of his wife's death and, at that moment, he sees an image of "a face folded in sorrow" (5.3.45). The Duchess, it seems, may be both heard and seen in the remains of a monastery. This scene thus reads like the fulfillment of Cariola's description of the Duchess as "like some reverend monument / Whose ruins are even pitied" (4.2.33–34).[56] The Duchess *becomes* the ruined cloister, simultaneously a monument to her own "reverend history" and a striking illustration of the corruption of the church (5.3.11). As Antonio, who "love[s] these ancient ruins" puts it, "Churches and cities, which have diseases like to men, / Must have like death that we have" (5.3.9, 18–19). The disease of the church in *The Duchess of Malfi* is embodied in the Cardinal and Ferdinand and manifested though the Duchess's torture and martyrdom.

Webster imagines the death of the Duchess as akin, in some way, to the death of Catholicism in England: both are laid to rest amid the ruined abbeys. But the Duchess's death also signals what English Protestants saw as the continued corruption of post-Reformation Catholicism, particularly in its relationship to women and female monasticism. Even after the convents were dissolved in England, transformed into "a wall, / Piece of a cloister" that could no longer enclose, women continued to travel to monasteries on the continent. There, they were vulnerable to what Protestant propagandists depicted as the daily tragedies of enclosure: loss of property, altered texts, domineering priests. Webster stages a more extreme version of these tragedies—the Cardinal poisons his book with more than words, and the Duchess dies for resisting the demands of celibate enclosure—and his dramatic representations helped to shape the language and the tone of pamphlet literature that imagined Catholic clergymen manipulating the enclosed women in their charge.

Bad Books: Literary Allusion and
Textual Substitution in the Convent

In rigorously denying that women could be active religious agents or participants in Catholic book culture, Webster simultaneously diffused and obscured what James and Edmondes saw as an imminent threat: that English women might wish to become nuns, align themselves with foreign countries, and have some association with continental book production. Protestant pamphleteers, who offered similar visions of sexual degradation and financial motivation in their depictions of the dangers of female religious enclosure, also worked to discredit continental Catholicism and deny that women might find anything positive in monastic life. But they could not follow Webster in ignoring contemporary English convents, which grew increasingly popular in the recusant and exilic Catholic communities during the first decades of the seventeenth century.[57] Instead, polemical authors extended the materialist focus of anti-Catholic drama by offering details of place and person, books and bodies. As the only pamphlet centered on a single convent, Thomas Robinson's *The Anatomy of the English Nunnery at Lisbon* is particularly notable for its narrative of Syon Abbey's history before and after the dissolution, its attention to monastic reading materials, and its catalogue of specific nuns. First published in 1622 and reprinted throughout the seventeenth century, *The Anatomy* was one of the best known anti-Catholic pamphlets in early modern England, and it remains a popular touchstone for both historians and literary critics. Like Webster's play, Robinson's exposé of Syon provides insight into the ways that post-Reformation English nuns were ignored or diminished by contemporary authors and thus erased from literary history. Robinson's rhetorical and representational strategies efface female contributions to monastic book culture even as he professes sympathy for individual nuns, who function as tragic signs of a depraved society. In their vulnerability, they elicit pity rather than scorn, enabling an authorial stance of generous condescension for women trapped in a religious culture not of their own making, thereby dismissing the possibility that actual women in Italy, Spain, or the Low Countries might contradict such representations.

Contemporary readers of *The Anatomy* included the playwright Thomas Middleton, who incorporated Robinson's depiction of Jesuits trafficking in seduced young women into the pawn's plot of *A Game at Chess*, as well as Robinson's fellow pamphleteers, many of whom referenced his book as an authoritative source on the inner workings of an English convent displaced to continental Europe.[58] Today, *The Anatomy* is most frequently cited in one of two ways: first, as a representative example of Protestant propaganda—almost any scholar writing on Syon Abbey in the seventeenth century now seems compelled to invoke Robinson in order to deny the historical merits of his claims—and second, as the source of a glancing critique of one of Shakespeare's narrative poems.[59] For Robinson was not content simply to rehash the conventions of monastic satire or the sensational materialism of anti-Catholic drama and polemic; instead, he incorporated both classical and contemporary literary allusions to contextualize his project and illuminate the convent's book culture, including the claim that the convent's confessor, Father Seth Foster, read *Venus and Adonis*, the *Jests* of George Peele, and other similarly "scurrilous" material to the nuns.[60]

Though it is famous as a reference to Shakespeare, this description of the priest's reading material captures the thrust of Robinson's repeated accusations against Father Foster as a seducer of England's Catholic daughters. In Robinson's depiction, Foster manipulates the women in his charge by means of his control over the convent's book culture, exposing them to corrupting (and corrupted) texts in order to "more freely enjoy the scope of his lascivious and sacrilegious desire" (14). This portrait of "silly seduced women" at the mercy of a religious hierarchy that denies them access to the Word is, as we have seen, only one example of many in post-Reformation English literature (14). The perception of female monasticism that these representations helped to foster has proven tenacious in the centuries since, and even the most reluctant citations of Robinson suggest that modern scholars feel unable to ignore his book's description of the convent in Lisbon, unreliable and hyperbolic though it may be. This continued dependence on *The Anatomy* reveals that historians and literary critics are in a position similar to that of Robinson's earliest readers: in the absence of first-hand evidence, we rely on representation to lessen geographical and historical distance.

The first edition of Robinson's pamphlet further reveals that literature and representation are at the heart of his polemical project. The epigraph on the title page, replaced in all four subsequent printings with a woodcut and explanatory poem, reads "Virg. Lib.I. Æneid. – – *Cæcumq' domus scelus omne retexit*."[61] This line, translated "uncovering all the dark crime of the house," appears in Venus's narrative of Dido's past: her marriage to Sychaeus, to whom "her father had given her, / A virgin still"; his death "sacrilegiously" committed "before the altars" by her brother Pygmalion; Pygmalion's "cozening" and "deluding the sick woman with false hope"; and the dream in which Sychaeus reveals the nature of his death to his grieving wife:

> But the true form of her unburied husband
> Came in a dream: lifting his pallid face
> Before her strangely, he made visible
> The cruel altars and his body pierced,
> Uncovering all the dark crime of the house.

He urged her then to make haste and take flight,
Leaving her fatherland.[62]

Dido stands in for the reader of Robinson's pamphlet, accepting a revelation of wickedness performed at the altar of God. But she also evokes the nuns whose ruin he purports to reveal, both in the transformation Venus describes—she is a figure of chastity and exile whose life has been destroyed by a wicked man—and through her position in the early modern imaginary as an enigmatic figure of female constancy *and* sexual frailty. The seventeenth century inherited two competing narratives surrounding Dido, both of which include the story outlined above. In the non-Virgilian histories, Dido, the founder of Carthage, kills herself rather than remarry after her husband's death. In Virgil's account, Aeneas arrives while the walls of Carthage are being built, Dido is seduced by him and his story of Troy, and she kills herself after Aeneas abandons her in favor of his own imperial journey.[63] Robinson's title page suggests the nuns at this convent in Lisbon are Dido's daughters through an allusion that treats the founder of Carthage as the pitiful victim of male transgression.[64] I would nonetheless argue that such an allusion cannot completely elide the Dido who awakes from this dream vision— "captaining the venture" to Carthage "was a woman" who became a powerful agent of imperial conquest—and that this is one possible explanation for the disappearance of the epigraph in future printings of *The Anatomy*.[65]

The Virgil epigraph, allusive and elusive, frames a text that purports to offer a "plain" discourse of Robinson's "*owne experience*" as eyewitness ("oculatus testis") to the convent's hypocrisy and sin (A3r, A4v). His account is a striking blend of the quotidian (the nuns' travels on the continent, the songs they sing, the food available in the convent) and the grotesque (violated confessional rooms, nuns with the clap, dead babies in the walls), constructed around the nuns' supposed violation of their vows of poverty, chastity, and obedience. Robinson claims that he collected this information after being "inticed to abide with [Father Foster] in the house," where he was employed "dayly in copying out certaine Treatises of Obedience, which hee had composed for the Nunnes" (1). He points to this scribal position as the source for his detailed information about the convent's history and its inhabitants: "I continued in writing over divers bookes for them, and amongst the rest, the Register of their House, whereby I came to some understanding of their estate, beginning and successe untill this present, which for the satisfaction of the Reader, I thought good to set downe as briefely as I could" (2). Robinson's self-representation as a writer bookends *The Anatomy*, which concludes with his ultimate removal from the convent, precipitated by Foster's discovery of "a blotted Copy of [Robinson's] Articles" enumerating his principal allegations against confessor and convent—a rough draft, it seems, for the pamphlet itself (29).

Robinson's development as a writer is closely related to the books he encounters in the convent, and he crafts his authorial persona as an active and engaged reader whose familiarity with book culture allows him to interrogate priestly authority. As copyist and compiler of Foster's authorial works, he claims to inscribe the misdeeds that Foster incarnates through the physical corruption of textual materials. Robinson's detailed description of the process of book production at the convent is worth quoting at length:

> having made these books of Obedience, he caused mee to write
> them out faire, omitting in many places a Leafe, and in some two
> or three together, which contained any false doctrine and unallow-
> able perswasions to draw them to obedience in unlawfull things;
> and being finished in this sort, he bringeth them to Father *Newman*
> to be signed with his approbation and testimonie, that there was
> nothing in them repugnant to the Catholique faith; which beeing
> done, hee then interserteth and soweth in the aforesaid omitted
> Leaves, and so delivereth them to his daughters to be practised,
> who take the approbation at the end of the booke for a sufficient
> warrantie of all the doctrine therein contained. And this is a
> principall furtherance to his sacrilegious lusts: for I am verily
> perswaded that not one amongst them will (for feare of being
> disobedient) refuse to come to his bed whensoever he commands
> them. (18–19)

In this anomalously sympathetic account, neither the doctrines of obedience, the Catholic hierarchy that approves them, nor the nuns with "feare of being disobedient" are fundamentally in error. Instead, Robinson treats Foster as the source for a "false doctrine" of obedience that is able to flourish because the priest alone controls Syon's book production. Just as Webster embodied a lethal religious culture in his portrait of the Cardinal and his poisonous book, Robinson reifies Catholic villainy in a specific individual's textual practice in order to suggest that enclosed women are never safe from clerical manipulations. The corruption of the book, accomplished through the insertion of leaves and sowing of false doctrine, leads directly to the corruption of the nuns' bodies: deviant textuality anticipates and prefigures deviant sexuality.

Robinson's legacy thus lies not only in his fascination with nuns' sexuality but also in his more mundane description of nuns' passive relationships with their books. Women are the victims of the monastic book culture Robinson describes—a culture marked by illicit reading materials, access to "idle Pamphlets printed in *England*" (which Robinson claims make their way to the convent by means of "Father *Newman* an *English* Priest, who hath an office in the Inquisition house to peruse all English books that are brought into *Lisbon*"), and books materially altered to include false doctrine (17). Male superiors limit female access to the textual community of which they are a part, allowing the nuns only circumscribed forms of engagement with the written word. They are not allowed to write uncensored letters to their families in England; instead, Foster "will make them to Article one against the other in writing" (14). Robinson summarizes one such document, the content of which matches its function as a tool for the disruption of female community: "It was my chance one day to finde a paper of these Articles in a walke in the Friers Garden, which had unawares fallen from him; being drawne by one Sister *Anne*, alias *Josepha Bingham*, against Sister *Suzan Bacon*: Wherein the said Sister *Susan* stood accused, for blaming her ghostly Father, and the Abbesse and Prioresse of partialitie to some of their children more then to others" (14). The very thing Sister Susan verbally complains about—a social system marked by favoritism and division—is reinscribed through Sister Anne's written document, which suggests her own favored position in the eyes of the convent's hierarchy. Female monastic writing is here just another sign of Foster's dominance, and the absence of truly female-authored texts in the convent serves as Robinson's justification for his own textual intervention: he writes *for* the nuns, "in whose behalf I am bound to intreat their friends to enter into a further search of their miserable estate and condition . . . themselves not being able to send any word thereof, because all their Letters must bee given to him to be sent into *England*; which if they contain any thing contrary to his mind, shal never be sent; for hee will peruse them all" (30). Robinson presents himself as the benign protector of seduced women and an alternative to Foster's corrupt textual patriarchy. His printed book will serve as the material proxy for the nuns' letters, unwritten, unsent, and unread.

The content of Robinson's pamphlet serves as a gloss on its epigraph, erasing female agency not only from contemporary monastic practice and book culture but also from the history of literary constructions of national identity. Like Dido, imagined by Virgil as a brief diversion from someone else's imperial destiny, nuns are relegated to the margins of English history. The subjects of Robinson's pamphlet—the Bridgettine nuns of Lisbon, formerly of Syon Abbey in England—could trace the history of their foundation to Henry V. Theirs was the only English convent that survived the dissolution: a group of the Syon nuns fled to the continent under Henry VIII, returned briefly at the invitation of Mary, and eventually settled in Lisbon in 1594 after years of wandering through the Low Countries and France.[66] Their order thus served as a material link to England's Catholic past.[67] Robinson established this context in the opening pages of *The Anatomy*: "the Nuns thereof doe challenge (and indeed truely) a succession from the Abbey of Sion in England, now belonging unto the earle of Northumberland, which house, together with another Monasterie of Carthusian Monkes, called Shyne, beeing both scituated upon the Thames, were erected and built by King Henry the 5. at his returne from his famous Conquest in France" (2). Robinson simultaneously acknowledges and dismisses the nuns' link to England: what was once Syon Abbey is now Northumberland's house. Other pamphleteers followed suit, making the transition from the "late dissolved Abbey of Sion" to the earl of Northumberland's "very faire house" a synecdoche for the Reformation as a whole.[68] Nuns, in these formulations, belong only in England's past; they are a brief diversion from the nation's Protestant destiny.

Like Webster, Robinson deploys a number of interrelated strategies in his attempt to condemn the contemporary practice of female monasticism. While *The Duchess of Malfi*'s juxtaposition of domestic secrecy and doctrinally inflected imprisonment as competing modes of enclosure offers an oblique commentary on the newly established English convents on the continent, the documentary nature and popularity of *The Anatomy* reveal that seventeenth-century Protestants were interested in learning more about the Catholic Englishwomen who entered cloisters abroad. Robinson cultivated this interest by listing "The Nunnes of this House" on his final pages—a striking catalogue of the women who populated the convent, which Robinson offers his readers in case "any of them amongst these insuing names finde either a Sister or Kinswoman, or Friend, let him sigh to thinke on their misery, and use his best indeavours to free them" (30–31). But these gestures at full revelation are another form of displacement, as Robinson's factual information turns his readers' attention away from his many unverifiable claims.

Both Webster and Robinson thus substitute vivid details for what they do not wish to acknowledge: the immense appeal of female religious enclosure in Webster's case, and nuns' involvement in monastic book culture in Robinson's. Together, anti-Catholic drama and polemic reveal that precisely what seventeenth-century authors wish to hide is what we should work to uncover.

Collective Truth: Female Authority and Manuscript Polemic

As I have demonstrated, *The Anatomy of the English Nunnery at Lisbon* depicts a monastic book culture controlled by a single masculine authority, and it suggests that the alternative lies not in the nuns' own writing—for who could imagine that nuns wrote?—but in the substitution of Protestant pamphleteer for Catholic cleric. Robinson thus erased the long history of the convent's collective interventions in both print and manuscript, including a 1594 printed Spanish history attributed to "las Monjas de Sion" and an early 1620s illuminated manuscript signed by "Sister Barbara, Abbess, and other English Sisters of the Order of Saint Bridget."[69] In what remains of this chapter, I trace selected examples of Syon's participation in post-Reformation manuscript and print publication, culminating in a collective manuscript response to Robinson. Within seven months of *The Anatomy*'s appearance in the Stationer's Register in May of 1622, members of the convent received, read, and wrote a rebuttal to it.[70] The relatively short interval between the print publication of Robinson's pamphlet and its arrival at the convent suggests that the Syon community did have ready access to "idle Pamphlets printed in *England*" as Robinson claimed, but other elements of the manuscript force its reader to question not only the pamphlet's content but also its undergirding assumptions about individual authorship and monastic authority. In what follows, I will analyze how this unsigned text manipulates authorial voice and the flexibility of anonymity, establishes generic classifications, and adopts literary figures and forms in order to construct a communal textual identity, thereby revealing the significance of literary acuity in the vibrant and politically engaged writing of early modern nuns.

The manuscripts and printed books written by and about the Syon nuns after the Reformation reveal the convent's contemporary engagements with England's religious politics. When, for example, the dangers of life on the continent led one group of young nuns to journey back into England during the 1570s, a number of manuscripts recorded their efforts to secure patronage for the convent.[71] Elizabeth Sander wrote of the substance of their time in England in letters to Sir Francis Englefield, a Catholic exile on the continent and patron of Syon.[72] Her descriptions of the difficulties endured by English Catholics—including an account of her repeated imprisonments—were ultimately translated into Spanish and printed in Robert Persons's 1590 *Relacion de Algunos Martyrios* and Diego de Yepes's 1599 *Historia Particular de la Persecucion de Inglaterra*.[73] Sander's letters became, in these printed editions, material evidence in a lengthy case against English Protestants. Their Spanish print publication suggests that Persons, Yepes, and Joseph Creswell—the compilers of these volumes—were hoping to encourage popular support for the English exiles who had begun erecting monasteries, schools, and convents in Spain. Both books also included brief histories of Syon and city-by-city descriptions of the nuns' exile.[74] A more detailed history of the order was printed in 1594, on the occasion of their arrival in Lisbon: Persons wrote the preface for the *Relacion que embiaron las Religiosas del Monesterio de Sion de Inglaterra*, but the history itself was signed by "las Monjas de Sion."[75] The nuns of Syon, in other words, were the named authors of texts printed in support of their order's continued survival. Life in a post-Reformation English convent in Spanish territory did not preclude female participation in book culture or political discourse centered on questions of national and religious identity.[76] Instead, it provided a motive for such engagement.

In exile on the continent, the nuns maintained Syon's pre-Reformation textual practice—including a reading library of print and manuscript books that facilitated strategic print publication—in support of the composition of explicitly political texts in both print and manuscript.[77] In the early 1620s, they created an illuminated manuscript as a gift for King Philip III of Spain, which was simultaneously a more direct intervention into Spanish/English relations than the nuns had previously attempted and an explicit bid for economic support.[78] Written in Spanish and accompanied by miniatures illustrating the nuns' history, the text of the manuscript includes a petition to the Infanta Maria of Spain, an account of the foundation of Syon Abbey, and a detailed description of the Bridgettines' exile from England.[79] At the height of speculation over the Spanish Match,[80] the nuns of Syon attempted to support and participate in the marriage negotiations, in the hopes that the Infanta Maria would become "Her Royal Highness the Princess of Wales," as she was hailed in the petition.[81] The nuns thus confirmed the worst fears of Protestant propagandists, who warned that the Spanish Match would lead not only to the restoration of Catholicism but also to Spanish rule over

England. The manuscript expresses the hope that "this marriage of Your Highness [has] opened the door for our holy Catholic faith to enter England."[82] This very scenario—the Infanta Maria as a catalyst for the restoration of Catholicism in England—was cause for concern in Thomas Scott's *Vox Populi*, a pamphlet written against the prospective marriage. Scott imagined that English Catholics "hoped hereby at least for a moderation of fynes and lawes, perhaps a tolleration, and perhaps a total restauration of their religion in England . . . . So that by this marriage it might be so wrought, that the state should rather be robd and weakened."[83] Collectively, Protestant pamphleteers worked to undermine the Catholic supporters of the Spanish Match, and Robinson's attack on Syon in 1622 was likely part of this larger political project.[84]

Robinson's epigraph suggests a direct literary connection to the nuns' illuminated manuscript. Where the first edition of his pamphlet was framed by a quotation from the *Aeneid* identifying the nuns with Dido, the manuscript's account of the convent's exile compares the Syon community to Aeneas, Virgil's wandering—and nation-building—hero: "this convent can say, like the famous Trojan pilgrim, *Quae regio in terris nostri non plena laboris?*"[85] This interjection appears after an extended comparison of the order with its founder, Saint Bridget, that interweaves biblical analogy and exegesis. The convent in exile is like Bridget, who is like Abraham. It is like Aeneas. It is like Tobias and Joseph. This shift between religious and classical allusion begins to suggest what I will be arguing about the convent's manuscript response to Robinson: the nuns' participation in manuscript and print culture is marked by literary skill as well as religious and political goals.

Syon's history of authorship and publication reveals that rather than a "plain" discourse of Robinson's *"owne experience," The Anatomy* is a text with specific motivations, including the erasure of any form of political efficacy or literary engagement on the part of the convent's female inhabitants (A3r, A4v). The manuscript response dissects *The Anatomy*, laying bare its rhetorical strategies and reconstituting its component parts into a defense of the convent. While they could not invite concerned readers of Robinson's pamphlet to enter their enclosure in Lisbon, their narrative strategies disable the representational power of *The Anatomy* while at the same time offering an alternative reading of the convent's post-Reformation religious and political history. The manuscript response is thus far more than an archival curiosity demonstrating that nuns could write for themselves; instead, it offers a powerful critique of how and why female monastics were silenced in Protestant propaganda and effaced from literary history. By recognizing how literary forms, genres, and hermeneutics shape this remarkable text, we can begin to acknowledge the myriad strategies that early modern nuns used not only to intervene in contemporary religious politics but also to prevent the erasure of female intellectual engagement from the historical record.

In opposition to Robinson's insistent eyewitness "I," the voice of the convent's response is variable and flexible. The first line of the manuscript declares that "about the first of December 1622, Syon had a full notice and syghte of a most slaunderous printed lybell, sett forth by one Thomas Rbinson against them."[86] Even after the destruction of their abbey in England, "Syon" remained the collective appellation for the monastic community based in Lisbon, but this introductory description does not seem to be written in Syon's collective voice: the community is comprised of "them" rather than us. This first paragraph suggests an anonymous and omniscient narrator and it does so in order to emphasize the impartiality of the response:

first of all, because the goodnes or the badnes of the author, is not impertinent, that the reader credite or discredite his worke, therfore they are first of all to speak of the author himselfe, and then of his booke or lybell, and not as he doth of them, making himselfe both the accusor and witnes, but as those who proceed judicially, bringing in his owne evydence, and hand wrightinge, which he cannot deny, against him, as in the dclaration heere following, it shall by and by apeare. (42v)

"They"—the plural Syon—"will speak" in the "dclaration heere following," and the authorial voice of the second section of the manuscript—which shifts into the first person plural, with repeated references to "us" and "we"—does seem to represent the collective voice of the community. This framing device offers a seemingly detached description of the ensuing narrative as a kind of trial, in which the convent will provide material evidence to contradict Robinson's tautological use of his self-proclaimed eyewitness status as the proof of his claims. The author or authors of this manuscript use multiple forms of anonymity strategically in what amounts to an implicit challenge to Robinson's insistent naming of both himself and the men and women associated with the convent at Lisbon.[87] As Marcy North has argued, "Catholic authors manipulated anonymity's ambiguities to make it a more effective protective device and to further their own side's religious and political platforms. They show how anonymity allowed for the creation of complex authorial identities that often proved more important and more useful than names."[88] Anonymity in this manuscript is not an absence to be filled in with a name but rather a complex strategy that itself serves as a partial response to the claims of Robinson's pamphlet.

From the outset, then, the very voice in which the manuscript is written suggests the necessity of qualifying a central stylistic claim of the introduction: that "it was then no tyme to prolong the answere of it, with longe discourses & exquisite termes, and phrases" (42v). To suggest that "exquisite termes, and phrases"—the adornments of rhetoric and literature—were neglected in the community's haste is itself a rhetorical maneuver, of course, and it precedes a figurative and allusive characterization of Robinson in the second section of the manuscript, entitled "A declaration of such deeds and actions, as Thomas Robinson set forth of himselfe, and left in his owne hand wryghtinge" (43r). The collective voice describes how "the father Confessor" gave Robinson "certaine bookes of meditation, and of such lyke devotion . . . to be written or coppyed forthe," but this partial validation of Robinson's claim to have been Foster's copyist in the convent (they later deny that he ever saw or copied the register) serves primarily as the foundation for a description of Robinson's authorial practice that weds the materials of book production to biblical allusion (43r). Upon gaining access to the convent's scribal materials, Robinson "takinge hould uppon, and covering himselfe with a sheepskine . . . craftely framed a certaine narration, in Inglishe ryme, of his former sinnes" (43r). This is a sophisticated elaboration upon Matthew 7:15—"Take ye great heede of false Prophets, which come to you in the clothing of sheepe, but inwardly are ravening wolves"—a passage that had evolved into a popular and adaptable topos for both Catholic and Protestant authors by the seventeenth century.[89] Robinson is the wolf, crept into the sheepfold of the monastery, but his sheepskin is not simply figurative: it is the material on which he writes his narration, the parchment leaf that he simultaneously takes "hould uppon" and "cover[s] himselfe with" in order to "insynuate himselfe, in this humble ^manner,^ and penitentiall shape or figure" (44r). The authors of the manuscript response thus turn Robinson's description of monastic book culture against him: the false pages he writes in the convent are not bound into a book of obedience but crafted into his own narrative history.

The material specificity of this figurative classification of Robinson forms the basis for an extended analysis of the autobiographical manuscript he left at the convent, which the authors of the manuscript response cite by leaf, side, and margin: "in the first leafe whearof," "even theare in the margine, he confesseth that," "in the seaventh leafe and second syde he sayeth" (43r–v). Literary technique shifts into what Jesse Lander describes as one of the formal markers of early modern polemic: "elaborate protocols of quotation and citation, of both authorities and opponents, are developed in the maelstrom of polemic. Here, the 'fixity' of the printed book matters, as polemicists accompany their copious quotations with exact page citations, which allow the reader to check for accuracy."[90] Of course, neither the response nor the manuscript it cites is fixed in print. Instead, the authors redeploy this polemical technique as a fictive device in support of their attempt "to give satisfaction, to their ^fore^ sayed frinds or catholikes, who happely have seene or heard" of Robinson's pamphlet—which, they later note, "nameth neyther place nor chapter" in describing the supposedly manipulated books of obedience (42v, 50v). Their intended audience cannot check Robinson's autobiographical manuscript for accuracy—it is a unique document, enclosed in a convent in Lisbon—but the detailed page-by-page reading experience produced in the manuscript response creates the fiction of evidentiary proof that the nuns suggest is missing in Robinson's treatment of their book culture. Rather than claiming the status of eyewitness on behalf of the community or any individual in it, the manuscript authors instead treat books as witnesses and thereby directly counter Robinson's claim that nuns cannot interpret or engage textual evidence. In their descriptive summary of "his owne evydence, and hand wrightinge, which he cannot deny," the physical marks of Robinson's hand are as essential as the material pages upon which he wrote, and the authors repeatedly invoke "his owne booke and hand wrightinge" and "his owne carrackter and hand wrightinge" as evidence against him (42v, 44v, 45v). Since the facts cannot be verified by outside readers—a copy of Robinson's manuscript would, of necessity, erase his hand in it, rendering its physical relationship to him invisible—the authors instead adopt one of the generic markers of polemic as a tool for transforming representation into the illusion of reality.

The authors of the manuscript response, in other words, are both skilled literary craftspeople *and* skilled literary critics, deploying figurative language and polemical reading practices to characterize Robinson's authorial position and analyze his manuscript. Syon's participation in a specifically literary project of analysis and authorship is especially visible in the authors' formal and generic classifications of Robinson's writing, including their description of his manuscript as "a certaine narration, in Inglishe ryme" (43r). Instead of copying the convent's "bookes of meditation, and of such lyke devotion," he writes this "Inglishe ryme" delineating his premonastic life and travels, including participation in English piracy expeditions—a displacement of devotional literature by poetry; religious texts by profane (43r).

The authors' characterization of Robinson's printed pamphlet builds upon this critique of the manuscript poem: they claim that Robinson printed *The Anatomy* on his return to England because "he knewe it to be necessary for him to frame an apt ^or dexterous^ tale, and give some plausible account, as well of his sea jornye amongst pyrotts, as of his land Jornys amongst Catholikes" (45r). Indeed, their most effective opening salvo is not an attack on Robinson's character as a pirate—it is this classification of his pamphlet as a "tale." As they point out,

> if you reade but the story of pope Joane, and howe . . . she laboured
> of chylde birthe: and of the fishe ^pond^ of saint Gregory full of
> drowned childrens heads, to the number of sixe thouzand, and a
> thousand such lyke, you shall easely perceave, that it is neither
> greate or newe matter, that our persecutors easely permitt men of
> their owne secte, to publishe infamous lyes against us: who seeke
> not liberty as they doe, but have holly rules, and most worthy
> superiors. (45v)

The collective voice here identifies itself with the nuns—the "us" who "have holly rules, and most worthy superiors"—and proceeds to note the similarities between Robinson's work and pamphlets such as *The Friers Chronicle* or *The anatomie of the Romane clergie*, propaganda that looked to the medieval past for oft-recycled stories of papist bogeymen (and women).[91] For the nuns, Robinson is the mirror image of Burton's papists in his use of fantastic tales to deceive and exploit. Robinson is unable to move beyond discredited notions of the Catholic hierarchy and its religious women: his printed claims about their involvement in the Lopez plot and the Gunpowder Plot are simply extensions of earlier lies about Catholic saints and bear no relationship to the actual circumstances of life on the continent for English women religious. Robinson's *The Anatomy of the English Nunnery at Lisbon* is, in other words, merely a sensationalist fantasy that adapts conventional antimonastic satire in order to condemn post-Reformation English Catholicism.

Even as the authors dismiss Robinson's accusations by lumping his writing into a series of questionable generic categories, they articulate their response in literary terms in order to craft a competing representation of post-Reformation English Catholicism in exile. At the end of the second part of the manuscript, the collective voice announces that the narrative perspective will shift yet again in its third and final section: "nowe it followeth, to speake of his other booke, or rather lybell an^d^ badd speeches of others, the which being nothing else, but a conflicte of falshood against the truth: the modest reader must give truthe leave, to call falshood a lye, and the falsifyer a lyer; which if she should not, she should not be her selfe, nor speake the truth" (45v). To put it more succinctly: the bulk of the manuscript response, which addresses the substance of *The Anatomy* in a point-by-point rebuttal, is written in the voice of the allegorical figure of "truth." This first person singular (and feminine) narrator defends the nuns in a textual trial that elaborates upon the literary skills the authors have already demonstrated and adds further "exquisite termes, and phrases" that demonstrate Syon's rhetorical and literary sophistication (42v). Truth speaks on behalf of Syon as a singular entity, while treating the nuns whose individual good names Robinson lists in the final pages of *The Anatomy*—from Abbess Barbara Wiseman to Maudlyn Shelly, Katherine Dendy and Elizabeth Cole "of the Kitchin" (Robinson 31–32)—as if they were possessed of a collective yet singular "good name" ("Papers" 54v). The manuscript's form and rhetorical strategies thus directly contradict what the nuns identify as one of Robinson's claims about Foster: that he "setteth one againste another, leaste that they should joyne all in one, and so altogether complaine of him" (50r). Rather than complaining of Foster, the nuns "joyne all in one" to complain of Robinson.

In contrast to their collective self-representation, the authors identify Robinson with "the poysonable, and conninge craft of a Crocadell: who after he hath most wickedly, and in the hyest degree slaundred them, and done the worst he cane to kill thear good name, then to lamente & weepe over them, seeminge to give them a remedy, therby to credite hi^s^ lyes, and overthrowe patient Syon" (54v). The metaphorical image of Robinson is not incidental here: at the same time that the authors craft a plural identity for the convent's inhabitants out of the contradictory tension of voice and grammatical person exhibited here and throughout the manuscript, they deconstruct Robinson's authorial identity. For how can you believe someone's claim to be an eyewitness when in fact he is never what he seems? The show of "devotion or contrition" is everywhere "thrust into his narration, wherby of an angell of satan, he labours to transfigure himselfe into angell of lyghte" (44v). Robinson is a wolf in sheep's clothing, a pirate in penitential garb, a man in show but a crocodile in sentiment, and this series of identifications transfigures his self-representation in *The Anatomy*.

Individual identity is unstable and partial in the manuscript response, and the unnamed authors dismiss the lure of individualism in favor of a collective identity associated with Syon. The monastic whole that emerges out of the three narrative voices that shift and sometimes meld offers the convent's implicit rebuttal to Robinson's titular claim that he has "truly anatomized this handmayd of the Whore of Babylon; laying open her principall veines and sinewes" (A4r). Robinson textually penetrates and disassembles the walls of Syon's enclosure, but the manuscript is at once a material sign that the community inside is intact and a textual exploration of how walls might be reconstructed through words. For when the authors reach Robinson's claim that Father Foster would "daily without any companion goe into the Nunnes Cloister" (27), their response suggests a complex process of literary substitution, in which formal qualities of the text replicate the physicality of the convent's walls. They explain that Foster could not enter the enclosure, "for to goe into the Nuns, first theare is a speake house, with a grate for the nuns to speake with the seculars, and those of the house ^& this speke house^ hath a locke and key, and within this is the inclosure doore, which the nuns lockes on ^within^ their syde" (54r). The manuscript's description of the nuns' enclosure is nearly as impossible to penetrate as the enclosure itself: layers of sequential clauses and grammatical confusion, along with words and phrases inserted into the text, double for the walls, doors, and locks which separate the nuns from their confessor and from Robinson's accusations against them.[92]

A similar process of textual substitution appears in the authors' deconstruction of Robinson's version of Reformation history: where he creates a parallel between the (supposedly fake) saints' relics held in monasteries and the bones of innocents that he claims to have found in a wall of the convent, the nuns extend his analogy in order to provide both a counter narrative of history and a carefully reasoned rebuttal of his more scandalous implication. They begin by contradicting his claim that the bones of Thomas of Canterbury were burned by Protestants at the Reformation. "For in the pryme or begininge of heresye, thear was a multitude of true and zealus catholikes and religious, who neither abandoned their fayth nor yet theire relickes, but kepte them with great reverence" (48r). In their account, the Reformation is not an immediate transition into Protestantism: instead, many people in England retained their faith and protected the material aspects of it.[93] But they do not fully contradict Robinson's depiction of the dissolution; they admit that "kinge Henry to have the ritche shryne, burnt so much of this saints body, as he found their: but as for the other parts or bones, of that so beloved and miraculus martir of their owne country, which the sayed Catholikes had in their custody, they weare safe enough layed up from the persecutors discovering" (48r). In this articulation of history, England is the Catholics' "owne country" and King Henry is the "persecutor" who desecrates religion for material gain. Despite the fact that he is England's king, Henry plays the role of barbarian invader.[94] The reality of the Reformation and the destruction associated with it cannot be denied, but the nuns point out that not all has been lost: Henry is only able to burn that which has not already been saved.

From their discussion of saints' relics, the nuns turn to Robinson's accusation that they have given birth to bastard children and buried the remains in the convent wall. Robinson is so enamored of this idea that he includes it twice, explaining the second time that he "did chance to make a hole in a hollow place in a wall . . . out of which hole I pulled sundry bones of some dead children" (28). The nuns again note Robinson's tendency to echo the claims of other Protestant propaganda, since "this is a common calumation, which all heretickes have ever accustomed to put uppon monesterys, and Religious women inclosed" (49r). But they also carefully analyze the specifics of Robinson's argument: they point out that "theare is hardly a more publicke place in any community of women, wherunto workemen and others, must necessarily have recourse: And therfore it cannot be that such a place should be chosen by plottinge and polliticke father Foster, as he cauleth him; to committ such secresy of so much importance and consequence unto." Why, they ask, would they choose to bury the bones in the wall, when they could put them "in some secret corner, that by the moysture they myght rotten be the sooner, and lye the saffer" (49r)? They convert Robinson's sensationalist and tragic vision of murdered children into matter for practical exegesis: why, indeed, would they bury their bastard children in such an obvious place? Their analysis of the particular details of Robinson's accusation also provides the basis for a broader examination of the pamphlet's internal incoherence. "If," they explain, "their had bine any such thinge, yet he would make all thinck that none of them had the understandinge, briefly to be bourne them, and disperse their ashes in the ayer, as those of Robinsons sect did, with the bones of sainte Thomas, to have no more memory of them"

(49r). They thus extend Robinson's analogy between the bones of saints and the bones of innocents in order to undermine his allegation: the nuns would have to be fools not to follow Protestants in burning that which contradicts their religious ideology. But they also make a more subtle point here: that Protestant attempts to erase memory are necessarily contingent. Burning the bones of Thomas of Canterbury does not have the desired effect; the saint is still remembered. In the nuns' version of the story, memory remains possible because some of the relics were preserved. The material body acts as a witness and a memorial, but so too does their manuscript and, ironically, Robinson's pamphlet. The "true and zealus catholikes" will remember Thomas of Canterbury, with or without his relics, as will the Protestants who attempt to destroy his legend (48r).

In Syon's manuscript response to Robinson, literary technique is essential to the construction of a text that serves as both appeal and evidence. The manuscript's second section, in which the first person plural voice speaks explicitly as the nuns, demonstrates that Robinson's depiction of a corrupt monastic book culture controlled by a domineering priest is necessarily false. Rather than allowing themselves to be portrayed as "silly seduced women," the nuns participated in shaping the manuscript that would serve as their self-representation (Robinson 14). The interconnected representational strategies of Webster's play, Robinson's pamphlet, and the manuscript response produced at the convent reveal how dramatic props and settings—wax figures, a poisoned book, ruined walls—relate to the substitutive logic of Protestant polemic, in which livid details stand in for what is hidden behind convent walls. In order to see what anti-Catholic drama and pamphlet literature make invisible, we must read monastic texts not only with an eye for historical fact and material witnesses but also with an ear for literary tropes and techniques. This practice enables a more flexible understanding of the rhetorical construction of communal textual identities and offers a corrective to the idea that Catholic women—and nuns in particular—were victims of, rather than participants in and shapers of, early modern book culture.

CHAPTER 3

A Game of Her Own:
The Reformation of Obedience

Material remnants of England's religious change—defaced statues, ruined cloisters, burnt bones—remained part of its geographical and textual landscape, from country houses that were once convents to polemical invocations of saints' relics. For the nuns of Syon, the dissolution of the monasteries served as a touchstone in their order's exilic history, enabling them to assert the continuity of English monasticism over a century of doctrinal upheaval and to suggest the cohesion of their community in Lisbon. The new English convents established on the continent had no such history on which to draw, but orders such as the English Benedictine nuns in Cambrai, founded in 1623, nonetheless emphasized individual members' familial ties to a pre-Reformation Catholic community and worked to recover an English mystical tradition grounded in medieval texts.[1] Far from simply provoking nostalgia or remorse on the part of sympathetic readers, these connections were part of a larger project of recollection and reinvention: female monastics adapted not only the ancestral and textual bodies of medieval Catholicism but also the ideological conflicts associated with the Henrician Reformation to their lives in exile, writing devotional texts that offer surprising insights into the religious politics of early seventeenth-century literature.[2] This chapter will explore how debates over temporal and spiritual authority provoked by Henry VIII's break with Rome reverberated a century later in the writings of a Calvinist playwright and an exiled English nun. *The Spiritual Exercises* of Dame Gertrude More, great-great-granddaughter of Sir Thomas More, offers a striking depiction of how the vow of obedience was interrogated within a monastic community and thus helps to explain why Thomas Middleton situated his treatment of female obedience in the conceptual (if not the physical) space of the convent in *A Game at Chess*.

Obedience—the question of whom to obey, when, and how much—was central to both Catholic and Protestant representations of spiritual crisis and progress in the sixteenth and seventeenth centuries. This led to sometimes troubling contradictions: as one of the monastic vows, obedience to the Catholic clerical hierarchy was frequently condemned in Protestant propaganda as blind or unthinking, yet Catholics were required to affirm their political obedience to the state by attending church services, regardless of rational objections to this form of religious compulsion. The potential follies of monastic obedience had been subject to satire even before the Reformation, but Henry's rejection of the papal hierarchy and subsequent seizure of both church property and religious authority initiated a crisis of faith grounded in the nature of obedience. Middleton drew on this history in his exploration of the implications of obedience and its opposite within religious orders and political systems in *A Game at Chess*, but his treatment of recent events has frequently overshadowed this aspect of the play. Historians and literary critics have focused almost exclusively on *A Game at Chess*'s political allegory, which depicts Prince Charles and the Duke of Buckingham on their infamous trip to Spain to secure Charles's marriage to the Infanta Maria in 1623. Middleton transplanted the language and imagery of contemporary Protestant propaganda onto the English stage less than a year after their return, leading to an unprecedented nine consecutive performances in August 1624, before the play was closed by order of the Privy Council.[3] As a result, political context overshadows political content, leading scholars to peer into the parliamentary factions and coterie circles that might have supported a theatrical depiction of the state intrigue surrounding the Spanish Match rather than exploring how Middleton's engagement with religious and political controversy goes beyond pamphlet literature, most notably in the pawns' plot, a struggle over faith, sexuality, and obedience that is dominated by the experiences of two women and generates much of the play's narrative momentum.[4] Gertrude More's writings on obedience enable a new perspective on Middleton's political allegory, revealing his participation in an aspect of religious conflict less immediately relevant than the Spanish Match but far more significant to the long history of sixteenth- and seventeenth-century religious politics: namely, the increasingly complex discourse on obedience, which focused on the distinction—or lack thereof—between earthly and divine authority for individuals writing from a variety of different confessional perspectives. English nuns, especially those who wrote and translated monastic rules and devotional texts, engaged the question of obedience in both life and literature: their entrance into Catholic religious orders vividly illustrated their refusal to conform to the Jacobean state, and their manuscript and printed books grappled with the potential conflict between obedience to a temporal hierarchy and devotion to God.

More represented herself as a contemplative scholar whose most immediate spiritual relationship was with God, but her writings nonetheless addressed local conflicts over the proper form of prayer and spiritual direction for female monastics. In the wake of controversy over the teachings of Cambrai's spiritual director, Augustine Baker, and his removal from the convent by members of the English Benedictine Congregation, More wrote an extensive defense of Baker's work that condemned blind obedience as readily as her Protestant countrymen did.[5] For her, "blind faith" was not the "meere blind zeale and devotion" that Protestant pamphleteers condemned for leading women "to bee Nunnes."[6] Instead, More redefined religious obedience in terms of her independent contemplative practice and her reasoned interpretation of both scripture and the Benedictine rule.[7] At the same time, both More and the later editors of her *Spiritual Exercises* suggested that her defense of Baker and her written confessions marked her not only as Sir Thomas More's descendant but also as his intellectual successor in resisting unlawful authority, a line of descent traced in texts—from the *The Workes of Sir Thomas More Knyght* printed in 1557 to *The Life and Death of Sir Thomas Moore* written by Gertrude's father, Cresacre More, and printed in 1631—as readily as in blood. Gertrude More's devotional writings treat obedience and authority as contingent categories, dependent not only upon community hierarchies but also upon the individual's experience of the divine, and thus echo concerns regarding the royal supremacy that arose during the Henrician Reformation, offer a striking complement to the 1628 parliamentary debates over the Petition of Right, and anticipate the central questions of the English Civil War. *The Spiritual Exercises* helps to illuminate how literary treatments of female obedience such as the pawns' plot in *A Game at Chess* both participated in and helped provide a language for early modern understandings of the individual's place within a hierarchical community, thereby making Middleton's play meaningful beyond its allegorical moment.

The imaginative force of post-Reformation English nuns and their participation in the discourse on obedience inflects Middleton's play, rendering his allegorical depiction of the failed Spanish Match secondary to a pawns' plot in which narrative disrupts figuration. Middleton pointed directly to the English cloisters in Spain and the Low Countries by borrowing from Thomas Robinson's *The Anatomy of the English Nunnery at Lisbon*, which was printed just two years before *A Game at Chess* was staged. Following Robinson, the pawns' narrative of doctrinal and personal conflict queries the limits of female monastic obedience, which is mediated by devotional texts and corrupt priests. In scenes featuring the White Queen's Pawn and the Black Queen's Pawn, Middleton confronts religious obedience by examining how two women maneuver within and against the authoritarian hierarchy of the Black House. In so doing, Middleton's play transcends the particular circumstances of the 1620s: he builds upon the scaffolding provided by a recent political event but offers a more thorough rendering of how religious and political conflict emerges from within institutional hierarchies when the play turns away from Charles, Buckingham, and the Spanish court. Like *The Spiritual Exercises*, written less than a decade later, *A Game at Chess* looks backward and forward simultaneously, in a perspectival gaze that remembers the Reformation and anticipates the Civil War. While the political allegory focuses on conflict between opposed groups—Catholic and Protestant, Spanish and English, Black House and White—the play as a whole treats that externalized struggle as a symptom of the internecine conflict generated by the interplay of authority and obedience within a seemingly unified religious and political order. Pairing *The Spiritual Exercises* with *A Game at Chess* thus reveals what literary history has overlooked in the post-Reformation period: that debates over the place of obedience in English political and religious life, which would culminate in the Civil War, developed in tandem with—rather than in opposition to—a concurrent debate in the Catholic Church regarding the place and authority of female monastics.

"A Turning of Religious Obedience"

In the early seventeenth century, Catholic women who left their homes in England to enter convents in France and the Low Countries were often forced to confront a difficult question: to whom does an English nun owe her obedience? To God? To pope? To priest? To abbess? To king? As exiles from their country and often from their families, these women entered an ecclesiastical hierarchy that was at once foreign and familiar. The English Reformation had unsettled the relationship between spiritual and temporal authority, casting obedience to the monarch—expressed through oaths and signified by regular attendance at church services—as the primary duty of an English subject.[8] At the same time, the spread of Protestantism led to the disruption of traditional religious hierarchies; in this new religion, priests, popes, and saints were no longer necessary intermediaries between an individual and God. By entering religious orders, young women presumably rejected these alterations, pledging themselves "to obeye there lawfull superiors in all offices and exercises, be they never so base or meane," according to the Cambrai *Constitutions*.[9] But obedience was rarely so simple, and the *Constitutions* also offer advice for nuns who encounter conflicting demands from their superiors. This was not just a hypothetical: at Cambrai, differing advice regarding spiritual practice led to accusations of disobedience on the part of individual nuns and, eventually, investigations into the reading materials held by the community. Thus, while the Cambrai nuns identified obedience as "the essence of Religion," they simultaneously explored its relational significance in their interactions with religious authorities.[10] In what follows, I trace the interrelated practices of prayer and manuscript production at Cambrai in order to demonstrate how Gertrude More's scrutiny of religious obedience has relevance beyond her cloister.

The devotional texts produced at Cambrai reveal that monastic obedience was never a matter of naïve submissiveness or an unconflicted and automatic product of nuns' vows: a nun's personality and spiritual tendencies, her position in the convent, and the convent's devotional character contributed to the development of individual obedience, and, in a monastic environment, the development of individual obedience necessarily affected the larger community. In the first half of the seventeenth century, the relative demands of temporal and spiritual authorities at Cambrai had far-reaching implications in the wake of a local controversy over monastic devotional practice. The order was established in 1623, and Father Augustine Baker served as its formative spiritual director from 1624 until 1633. Baker was a proponent of contemplative prayer for enclosed nuns—an affective rather than intellectual experience that bypassed Jesuit exercises of meditation on an image or idea. The dominant strain of post-Reformation monastic instruction, however, was based on the Ignatian model of discursive prayer. Baker attempted to mediate between medieval mysticism, especially as it was practiced in England, and post-Tridentine continental spirituality, but his direction of the Cambrai nuns—and especially their elaboration upon his spiritual instructions—ultimately led Father Francis Hull, the convent's chaplain, to accuse Baker of promoting an antiauthoritarian mode of prayer and the nuns of practicing it.[11] Hull took his concerns to the General Chapter of the English Benedictine Congregation in 1633 and, while Baker's teachings were approved, both men were forced to leave the convent in the aftermath of the controversy.

The nuns of Cambrai nonetheless adhered to the principles Baker outlined in numerous manuscripts on contemplative prayer, and they produced impassioned defenses of the convent and its devotional life that circulated in both manuscript and print. The books written in the years following Baker's departure cover a wide variety of religious issues, but they invariably engage questions of authority and obedience, as the nuns struggled to come to terms with charges that Baker had encouraged disobedience to clerical authorities. These texts, along with the many manuscript and printed books written at other convents in the seventeenth century, reveal that the books of obedience that Thomas Robinson identified in *The Anatomy* as the products and tools of religious men—books that nuns may read but not write—were, in fact, frequently translated, transcribed, or compiled by nuns. Elizabeth Evelinge, an English Poor Clare, translated the *Rule* of St. Clare for print publication in 1622, along with two other translations in 1622 and 1635.[12] Alexia Gray's 1632 edition of *The Rule of the Most Blissed Father Saint Benedict* was not only a translation but also an adaptation, which used feminine pronouns to signal Gray's intended audience.[13] And the recent publication of *The English Convents in Exile*, a six-volume edition of original documents written by and for nuns, reveals that these print publications only scratch the surface of female monastic book culture in the seventeenth century.[14]

Among the manuscripts written at Cambrai and at the order's daughter house in Paris were a number of "Collections." These books were made of fragments and extracts: writings assembled from multiple authors, sometimes transcribed by more than one scribe, pieced together and bound in the remnants of older volumes.[15] But unlike the fragmentary books described in Robinson's pamphlet—instructional volumes manipulated by a priest to hold leaves of false doctrine, with the intention of luring young nuns into a corrupt form of obedience—the Cambrai and Paris collections were often produced by the nuns themselves. The sisters controlled the content, the form, and often the argument of these books, which range from heterogeneous compilations on diverse topics to carefully edited volumes on a specific theme. In one example of the former, the scribe of Dame Margaret Gascoigne's manuscript *Devotions* describes the composition of such collections: "two bookes she wrote beside, being chieflie, if not alltogether collections out of other Authors, for her owne use which I thinke maie be of verie good use for some others allso; and some of those collections I shall perhaps transcribe and adde heerto; and for such of them as have no Author specified above them, I know not how farre they maie not be esteemed to be of her owne originall penning."[16] Collections, in other words, hold the potential for two forms of authorship: of the volume as a whole, which may include various authors, and of individual selections within that volume. Gascoigne's scribe attributes value to both forms of authorship. The possibility of "original penning" is worthy of particular mention, but the volumes compiled by Gascoigne "maie be of verie good use for some others" even if they are "alltogether collections out of other Authors."[17]

The process of creating collections at Cambrai evolved out of the particular form of religious devotion recommended by Baker: he believed "that Contemplation or (which is all one) Spirituall praier, and the perfection of it, is the ende of our Rule and profession, who are of St Benets order."[18] In order to achieve true contemplation, Baker encouraged the sisters to read. "Good bookes," he explained, "are a necessarie food for your soules; for by them you are (as by the voice of God) incited to devotion, and nourished in it, and greatlie holpen and directed in your spirituall course."[19] To facilitate the nuns' prayer, Baker wrote and compiled a number of books during his time at Cambrai—books which served both as spiritual instructions and as models for the nuns' own collections. Baker peppered his writings with quotations and paraphrastic instructions from a wide range of theologians, contemplatives, and mystics, including Francis de Sales, Walter Hilton, Alvarez de Paz, and Hildegard of Bingen, but he also acknowledged that books alone, even when read devoutly, would not invariably lead to true contemplation.[20]

In *The Life and Death of Dame Gertrude More*, Baker outlined the conditions by which reading spiritual books could lead to contemplative prayer and, thereby, to the writing of devotional texts. Before Baker joined the convent, More "sought for all the meanes, which naturall reason did suggest unto her for her helpe. She redde over all the bookes, that were in the howse, or she could gette from abroade for her purpose, printed and Manuscript, and redde them seriously: and store of bookes there were in the howse" (*Life* 22). But reading as a function of "naturall reason" does not help her. Instead, she must learn to read affectively, with a focus not on the words of the text but on her interior state; Baker calls this form of worship "the exercise of Amorous affections" (36). In order to reach contemplation, More "selected out of St. Augustins Confessions and Meditations and out of the workes of other such like affective Praier-men, great store of amorous actuations of soule, which wonderfully fitted her foresaid Propension. And thereby she camme (commonly) to have a verie efficacious Praier, and that of much Recollection and internall sight of herself" (36). This practice of selective reading ultimately leads to authorship and scribal reproduction:

> using at the first onlie out of necessitie such ejaculations, as she
> gotte out of bookes, she camme in a short time to use other
> meerelie of her owne framing, as suggested to her by her owne
> nature or spirit, or by the divin spirit, which often times she used
> to sette downe in writing for her helpe in times of more ariditie.
> And those so expressed in writing, some others in the howse
> comming to see them, liked so well of them, that they used to
> copie them out. By this meanes in time there was in the howse
> great store of those Amorous affections of her collection or fram-
> ing, that were written or scattered heere and there in divers and
> sundrie bookes and papers. (44–45)

The process Baker describes is cyclical and, at the community level, self-sustaining: an individual nun chooses passages from spiritual authors to aid in her prayer; reading these passages enables her to practice a more affective form of prayer, through which she finds inspiration to write her own aids to prayer; other nuns collect her writings in order to aid in their own prayer, and the cycle begins anew.[21] Thus, Dames Gertrude More, Margaret Gascoigne, and Barbara Constable, along with their often anonymous religious sisters, created a dynamic book culture that originated in their life of prayer.[22]

Even when writing devotional texts, the nuns kept a wary eye and pen fixed on what Abbess Catherine Gascoigne called the "obligations and exter-nall obediences" demanded of them as Catholics and contemplatives, En-glishwomen and exiles.[23] Gertrude More's *The Spiritual Exercises* is one such text: a compilation of her manuscript materials that includes devotional con-fessions, mystical poetry, and a polemical defense of Baker's instructions.[24] More's book was printed more than two decades after Baker's departure and her death in 1633, when the English Benedictine Congregation attempted to censor Cambrai's autograph Baker materials in the 1650s.[25] From its first pages, *The Spiritual Exercises* is marked as a book compiled and printed at a particular time and place, with a purpose that extends beyond the straight-forward representation of More's devotional practice. Francis Gascoigne, a priest and the brother of Abbess Catherine Gascoigne, was responsible for the printed edition of More's work, which had circulated in manuscript at both Cambrai and Paris.[26] His dedication to Gertrude's sister Bridget More, the prioress at Paris, simultaneously invokes and deflects a potential controversy surrounding the print publication of More's confessions: he considers the possibility that the book may "chance to fal into the hands of any such as may reject, or cry it down: (as some few did the *Ideots Devotions* of the same *Spirit* lately set forth)" but then claims that "the whole Book hath nothing in it almost but Scripture."[27] Gascoigne makes this seemingly disingenuous claim—if the book is composed of almost nothing "but Scripture," why would anyone want to "cry it down"?—in order to signal how More's inter-vention into a matter of local religious controversy is grounded in the careful explication of scriptural passages, while leaving ambiguous whether those "some few" were members of the English Benedictine Congregation who ob-jected to Baker's influence on the Cambrai and Paris nuns.

What Arthur Marotti has called the "double context" for *The Spiritual Exercises'* print publication—the "renewed attack" on Baker's teaching and "the instructive use . . . of the personal devotional writing of nuns"—results in a book that looks outside the convent walls as readily as it delves into the struggles of an individual soul.[28] More's apology for Baker is printed before her spiritual confessions, and entitled "This Devout Souls Advertisement to the Reader. With an Apology for herself, and her spiritual Guide, and Direc-tor the V.F. Augustin Baker. Wherein is excellently described a true interne, contemplative Spiritual Life, and the maner how to live happily in it, with right, and true Obedience to God an man" (More A7). The theory of obedi-ence outlined in the "Advertisement" frames and contextualizes the spiritual confessions advertised on the book's title page, transforming More's account of contemplative prayer into a polemical tract that intervenes in contemporary debates regarding spiritual direction, religious faith, and political allegiance.

The local conflicts at Cambrai offer the occasion for More's engage-ment with the vow and practice of religious obedience: in describing the controversy over Baker's instructions, More suggests that even religious au-thorities may err when it comes to matters of the individual's spiritual life, though she is careful to avoid mentioning Hull by name. Instead, he is "the Confessor whose place deserveth an extraordinary respect" but whose in-structions are nonetheless nearly worthless (A28). According to More, "of

al in this howse I could never see, but one who could discourse, and distin-
guish his points in, and of Obedience, and draw out of them a setled quiet,
and satisfactory course, but that when he is gone they be as far to seeke as
they were before in the understanding of it" (A28). Hull's spiritual direction leaves the nuns adrift, and his teachings on obedience are particularly
at fault because they depend on his presence and authority. In contrast,
Baker leads the nuns to God: "this therefor was that which made me so affect F. Bakers instructions at first when he delivered them: because I saw
they were grounded upon *God*, (not upon him) *who* could never fail what-
soever became of him" (A28). Rather than relying upon an earthly confessor
or intercessor, Baker's teachings authorize the nuns to look directly to God
for prayer, consolation, and instruction. No wonder, then, that both Hull
and the English Benedictine Congregation were concerned that this practice of contemplative prayer might authorize various forms of disobedience,
from a refusal to alter one's spiritual course despite a superior's concerns
to the critical engagement with ecclesiastical politics evident in the "Advertisement."

More does little to alleviate concerns regarding monastic disobedience,
instead offering clear descriptions of how a nun might silently withstand the
potentially fallible instructions of her religious superiors. "*God*," she explains,
"wil prosper us by those exercises that *he* thinketh good, and not by those of
our own inventions" (A93). Thus, rather than "applying blindly the practice
of Saints to our imperfect case," an individual must "simply regard *God* in
the best maner she can" (A93). For More, difficulties arise when the spiritual
path of the individual is disrupted by a religious superior who believes most
strongly in his own inventions: "And this not prospering any other way or by
any other means then *God* pleaseth, may be very wel applyed in some sort to
the case where the director out of his own head, and out of his own customs
would have the soul pray in that maner he hath good by: And if *God* lead her
by another way then he hath gone, she is wrong howsoever it be indeed"
(A94). The spiritual director's "own customs" are no more trustworthy than
an individual's "own inventions," despite the fact that such customs might be
grounded in the traditions of the church. In the hypothetical case More describes, when the confessor "misliked her course and would not tel her why
nor wherefor," the nun "stood upon her gard, and held her peace, having before endeavoured by al informations she could, and as wel as she could to
expres her-self, that she might do things with his good leave, and liking. I say
she held her peace, and was confident that her cours was never the wors for

his fearing, and meant not by the *grace of God* to alter it" (A95). More treats this case as an exemplar, declaring "for my part I say, I shal follow her example the best I can" (A95). The unnamed contemplative could be any nun, at any convent, urged to abandon her spiritual course in favor of the guidelines endorsed by her superior. In such a case, More asks "what would you advise the poor soul to do?" (A96). Her answer—"what I do, and upon what reasons I do it"—shifts the focus of her "Advertisement" from an abstract discussion of a supposedly hypothetical scenario into a set of guidelines for passive monastic disobedience justified by the scriptural interpretations she weaves throughout the text (A96).

The central questions of More's "Advertisement" revolve around obedience: who defines it? How? And to whom does a contemplative owe her obedience? As the above example of a nun at odds with her superior demonstrates, these are not abstract questions for More, who explicitly positions her concerns in the context of her monastic life and religious vows. She fears "a turning of religious Obedience," and exclaims "O my *God* was this *thy* meaning when we vowed our selves to *thee!*" (A57). But she also looks beyond the convent by framing her own response to this question in scriptural terms: "*Thou bidst us give to Cæsar what is Cæsars, and to Thee what is Thine*" (A58). More thus simultaneously defines monastic obedience as an expression of the soul's devotion to God while emphasizing the importance of distinguishing among various forms of obedience, including that owed to a temporal or political authority as opposed to a spiritual or divine authority. She is most immediately interested in rebutting critics of Baker's teachings, many of whom argued that he encouraged the nuns to disregard religious superiors in their search for God, but her biblical exegesis has broader implications for a post-Reformation England still struggling to define the appropriate relationship between religious worship and allegiance to the monarch.

Christ's admonition to "'render therfore the things that are Cæsars to Cæsar: and the things that are Gods, to God'" brackets More's discussion of the difference between "true Obedience" and "pretended Obedience" in the "Advertisement" (A102).[29] From her opening description of how her spiritual course is "taxed now by the same words in a manner which were alleaged against our blessed Saviour. *We have found this man subverting the people, and forbidding to give tribute to Cæsar*" to the first and final lines of her final paragraph—to "*Give to Cæsar that is Cæsars, and that to God, that is Gods*" and "*to give that to God that is Gods, and that to Cæsar that is Cæsars*"—More makes good on Gascoigne's prefatory claim that her "Book hath nothing in it almost but Scripture" (A9, A111–12). But rather than offering a collection of biblical quotations and reflections, More dilates upon two passages that describe the same moment in Christ's teachings and conclude with identical aphoristic statements.[30] This exegetical focus undergirds her definition of true obedience, which More argues must enable certain forms of (what looks like) disobedience. "The effect of *Obedience* if it be true Obedience," she explains,

> is very profitable to a soul, and never prejudicial: *but it is when we give that to Cæsar, that is Gods,* that it succeeds il with us by obeying: for by this pretended Obedience we darken, and obscure our soul contrary to *Gods* meaning, and intention. And it is always seen that when a soul suffereth her self to be put out of her way by a director, or Superior, that when she thinks she hath done al she can, as to the doing their wil, yet she is further from it then she was before, and both the Superior, and she mis of their desire. . . . she being now so obscured that she knows not *what to give God, and what Cæsar.* (A102)

In order to explain the crucial distinction between superficial obedience to superiors and true obedience to God, More inverts the biblical passage from which she quotes. The Pharisees, in an attempt to "entrappe him in his talke," ask Christ whether it is "lawful to give tribute to Cæsar."[31] In response, Christ tells them to give the coin of tribute and taxation, a temporal signifier, to Caesar and to offer God the devotion that is due unto him. More adheres to the meaning of the scriptures, but instead of focusing on the Pharisees' question—which is intended to trap Christ into offering that which is Caesar's to God—More argues against giving that which is God's to Caesar.

The Rheims translation of the New Testament models this shift in emphasis in its annotation of Matthew 22:21: "Temporal duties and payments exacted by worldly Princes must be payed, so that God be not defrauded of his more soveraine dutie. And therfore Princes have to take heede, how they exact: and others, how they geve to Cæsar, that is, to their Prince, the things that are dewe to God, that is, to his Ecclesiastical ministers."[32] While the first clause suggests that duties to princes "must be payed," the annotators subsequently make clear that these worldly tributes should not interfere with the "more soveraine" position of God. The conclusion—that princes and their subjects "take heede" of what they demand and what they give—reads like a warning or a threat, and a marginal note makes the implications for England clear: "Neither must temporal Princes exact, nor their Subjects give unto them, Ecclesiastical jurisdiction."[33] In other words, the Rheims translators implicitly condemn the royal supremacy, which gave Henry VIII jurisdiction over the English church. More builds upon this earlier commentary on what is owed to God rather than to Caesar in order to more broadly reject the claims of earthly authorities. Where the Rheims annotation aligns God with his "Ecclesiastical ministers," suggesting that the things owed to God may be offered to his substitutes on earth, she uses Matthew 22:21 to relegate even religious superiors to the role of Caesar. More's interpretation of the Bible thus lessens the importance of members of the ecclesiastical hierarchy in favor of emphasizing the relationship between the individual and God, and does so within a textual tradition that ties questions of authority and obedience to the Henrician Reformation.

More's arguments in defense of a nun's ability to pursue the devotional practice best suited to her individual temperament reconfigure the sixteenth-century controversy over royal supremacy in which Sir Thomas More figured prominently. The prefatory material of *The Spiritual Exercises* prepares the reader for this connection by positioning Gertrude as Thomas's spiritual heir.[34] The first two facing pages of the book feature a poem that invokes Sir Thomas More and an engraving of Gertrude More in her habit. Embedded within the poem, which calls upon "Renowned, *More* whose bloody Fate / England neer yet could expiate," is a fourteen-line poem by Gertrude More.[35] The relationship between More and her ancestor is reaffirmed within the body of the "Advertisement," when she invokes him ("as sir *Thomas More* saith") to explicate her own intention to serve God alone: "if there were no world but this and that my soul were to dy with my body yet I would choos to serve, and please *him alone*, and none but *him*" (A86). Gertrude, like Thomas, will not allow her devotion to God to be corrupted by earthly authorities. As Nancy Bradley Warren has argued, Gertrude More is introduced in the context of Sir Thomas More's martyrdom in order to create a physical link between England's pre-Reformation Catholics and seventeenth-century English nuns in a "textual experience of martyrdom, suggesting that the body of Gertrude More's text suffers in common with her, the monastic community, Baker, her martyred ancestor Thomas More, and, ultimately, Christ."[36] I would add that this relationship, articulated through bodies and suffering in the prefatory poem, moves beyond a corporeal lineage in the text of the "Advertisement" and the "Confessiones Amantis" to focus on questions of faith, doctrine, and political resistance—an intellectual heritage as much as an embodied connection.

Gertrude More's confessional writings build simultaneously on the consanguineous tie to Sir Thomas More established in the prefatory poem and the God/Caesar frame that grounds her defense of Baker, the convent, and her own devotional practice in the "Advertisement." References to the relative claims of God and Caesar serve as scriptural tags throughout her writings, marking moments when questions of obedience come to the fore and suggesting her position as the intellectual heir of both Sir Thomas More and his daughter, Margaret More Roper. In the "Confessiones Amantis," the repetition of this biblical allusion reveals that More's devotional practice is inseparable from her defense of that practice. Like the "Advertisement," the confessions communicate a firm sense of the limits of authority and obedience, but they are less explicitly tied to the events at Cambrai. Instead, they offer a suggestive echo of the political and religious events that shook England a century earlier, when Sir Thomas More was engaged with a similar set of questions. When Gertrude More critiques overbearing superiors on God's behalf, especially those who "stand upon points usurping that to themselves which *thou* hast reserved to *thy self*," the threat of usurpation changes the tenor of the God/Caesar dyad (B210–11). If, "out of blindnes we give Cæsar that which was *Gods*," we simultaneously allow those Caesarean superiors to supersede God's divine authority (B210). More casts religious superiors not only as temporal—and potentially tyrannical—rulers but also as unwitting heretics. They are silently transformed into approximations of kings whose "subjects . . . wil not wel know what to do" (B211). More's language echoes the conflict that led to Sir Thomas More's execution and martyrdom, when the 1534 Act of Supremacy established King Henry VIII as the head of the English church, thus blurring the boundaries between spiritual and temporal authority in English religious life. Gertrude More attempts to redraw these boundaries by establishing God as "the only true teacher of *Humility*, true obedience and perfect *Pryer*," thereby expanding upon her ancestor's objections to the Act of Supremacy and implicitly rejecting the arguments of Henrician religious and political theorists who would offer "true obedience" to the king (B211).

In letters to his daughter, Margaret More Roper, Sir Thomas More related how the royal supremacy came to be framed as a matter of temporal obedience rather than spiritual conscience:

but than (said my lorde [of Canterbury]) you knowe for a certenty
and a thynge without dout, that you be bounden to obey your
soverain lorde your king. And therefore are ye bounden to leave of
the dout of your unsure consciens in refusing the othe, and take
the sure waye in obeiyng of your prince, & swere it. Now al was it
so, that in mine own mind me thought my self not concluded, yet
this argument semed me sodenly so suttle, and namely with such
authorite comming out of so noble a prelates mouth.[37]

Because "the king linked the issue of ecclesiastical authority with the issue of
worldly obedience, decoupling it from its theological roots," obedience was
defined in terms of political conformity to the royal will.[38] More, though,
rejected this definition, and recognized that obedience could all too easily
suppress an individual's conscience, especially when spiritual men wield
temporal authority or vice versa—as when a member of the ecclesiastical
hierarchy offers an argument for the royal supremacy. In such instances, the
individual must remember that he or she is not "bounden to obey" at the
expense of his or her duty to God. More was imprisoned for refusing to affirm the Act of Supremacy in 1534 and executed in 1535; the print publication
of his letters in the 1557 *The Workes of Sir Thomas More Knyght* provided Marian subjects and later English Catholics—including the nuns of Cambrai,
who held a copy in their library—with a detailed defense of the "unsure consciens" of this Catholic martyr.[39] His printed works also served as a rejoinder to
the work of Henrician propagandists such as Stephen Gardiner, a conformist
whose 1535 *De Vera Obedientia* was grounded in "the sure waye in obeiyng"
that More rejected.[40] Gardiner argued that "as many as are the kinges subi-
ectes (which is the congregacion / that we call the churche) are all bounden
throughlye to obeye. For the kinge is commaunded / to governe the people."[41]
On the eve of the English Reformation, both Protestant reformers and Catholic supporters of the royal supremacy "had come to envisage the king's
authority as minister of God as extending now beyond the temporal to en-
compass the spiritual."[42] A century later, Cresacre More, Gertrude More's
father and Cambrai's patron, chronicled his ancestor's steadfast resistance to
this position—what Gertrude More might have called a "turning of religious
obedience" (A57)—in *The Life and Death of Sir Thomas Moore*.[43] This biography, written in the years before Gertrude More's death, outlines a theory of
obedience for the "good subject" of a Christian realm: it is "the dutie of a

good subject, except he be such a subject, as will be an evill Christian; rather to obey God then man, to have more care of offending his Conscience, then of anie other matter in the world."[44] For both More and his great-great-granddaughter, God alone deserves true and boundless obedience.

The textual genealogy outlined here—from the works of Sir Thomas More printed in 1557 to the works of Gertrude More printed in 1658, by way of the Rheims translation of the New Testament (1582) and Cresacre More's biography of Thomas More (1631)—demonstrates the political and historical significance of Gertrude More's scrutiny of her own spiritual practice and her convent's structure of governance. *The Spiritual Exercises* elaborates upon Sir Thomas More's principle of conscientious disobedience: Gertrude More explicitly rejects the notion that a subject may be "bound to obey" a superior at her soul's expense and critiques men who "would be so absolute that there is no power left in the soul thus under such to have relation, or confidence in *God*" (A101, A56).[45] Writing against authoritarian religious superiors and delineating her own devotional practice allows Gertrude More to offer a general condemnation of any "absolute government" that would subvert or supplant God's authority, be it the government of Francis Hull, Henry VIII, or Charles I (A56). In the early 1630s, such a position resonated not only with events decades in the past or future, but also with the 1628 parliamentary debates that resulted in the Petition of Right, which established limits on royal power and emphasized both the primacy of the law and the rights of the subject.[46] While More does not invoke the petition, her emphasis on the spiritual rights of the individual suggests the relevance of her exploration of obedience and authority to a broader—and centuries long—English political discourse.[47]

More draws attention to the political analogues for her argument in what initially seems like a call for absolute obedience: she suggests that "if *God* require that seculars should obey the Prince, and the Laws of the Realm, so far as it may be done without offence to his own Laws," then so too must "Religious persons" obey their superiors (A20). Like her countrymen in Parliament, she distinguishes between "the Prince" and "the Laws of the Realm," but she does so in order to evade both forms of authority, along with that of religious superiors. For, as we have seen, she maintains a crucial caveat throughout the "Advertisement" and "Confessiones Amantis": all forms of obedience must follow "*God Almighties* good *wil*," enabling the individual to "regard *God* in all and walke solicitously with *him*" (A21). This focus on the intimate and physically proximate relationship between the individual and

God draws upon the work of another significant ancestor: Sir Thomas More's daughter, Margaret More Roper. In her 1524 translation of Erasmus's *Precatio dominica*, or *A Devout Treatise upon the Pater Noster*, Roper wrote, "let every man here in erthe / with good mynde and gladde chere obey thy wyll and godly preceptes."[48] As Jaime Goodrich has argued, Roper's text is a work with political implications related to the understanding of Reformation-era obedience.[49] Roper's translation not only "refut[es] the argument that Catholics practice mindless conformity to papal authority," but also suggests that the intimate relationship between individual and divinity explored by More has roots in "Erasmus's contention that Catholics can plumb God's mind," which "gives humankind a larger agency for salvation within the divine framework than is possible within Protestantism and so confutes Protestant emphasis on faith alone."[50] In suggestive echoes of *A Devout Treatise* that link the intrafaith struggles of the early sixteenth century to divisions among Catholic religious orders in the seventeenth, More reveals that her book is as deeply rooted in the political circumstances and theological questions of Henrician religious conflict as it is in the spiritual circumstances of life as an exiled English nun.

The religious and political divides occasioned by the Reformation—not only between Catholics and Protestants but also within the various religious orders of the Catholic Church—are the fault lines running beneath More's explication of the Cambrai controversy over spiritual direction and contemplative prayer. "When shal it be said," More asks, "that the multitude of beleivers are of one hart and soul? When shal al be united in the bonds of true *peace*?" (B211). More hopes that the Protestant Reformation and its effects may be reversed, but in order to imagine "the primitive Church" renewed, she presents her reader with a conditional: "if Saint Benets his, S. Francis his, S. Ignatius his, *&c.* children were perfectly, as this life wil permit, united together, and with one hart, and consent seek and labour to advance *thy* honour and praise, as our founders do in Heaven, which if we did then would the *Spirit* of the primitive Church flourish, and *thy* torn and mangled members be healed and perfectly set againe together" (B249–50). This image from the "Confessiones Amantis" is almost identical to a passage in the "Advertisement," suggesting its central importance to both More's political intervention and her devotional practice (A66–67). Her prophetic voice imagining a church in pieces brought together again echoes Roper's translation of Erasmus, which suggests that the religious community will not achieve the "full perfection of felicite" until "all the membres and partes of thy sonne be gathered together / and that the hole body of thy sonne / safe and sounde be joyned to his heed / Wherby neyther Christe shall lacke any of his partes and membres / nor good mennes soules theyr bodyes."[51] More transforms Erasmus's image of the divine body reconstituted into a vision of the future reunification of the Christian world predicated on the unification of the Catholic contemplative and apostolic orders. "Then sinners, and hereticks would easily be converted by them to thee. . . . Then they by prayer conversing in a familiar, and tender maner with *thee* would speak so that none would be able to resist thee in them" (B250). Adapting the Protestant rhetoric of a primitive church to apply to pre-Reformation Catholic religious orders, More critiques seventeenth-century monastic dissension as an extension of the doctrinal divisions initiated in the early sixteenth century, both of which prevent Christian believers from being "perfectly set againe together" (B250).

While More's "torn and mangled members" could refer to any number of conflicts within the seventeenth-century English Catholic community, which was by no means a homogeneous or easily defined group, her naming of specific religious orders suggests that she was less interested in issues related to recusancy, church papistry, or missionary activities in England than in continental English monasticism.[52] Obedience had become a particularly fraught issue for the newly founded cloisters in the wake of a series of controversies over Jesuit instruction for enclosed nuns: the Poor Clares at Gravelines, for example, were divided on whether to accept Jesuit or Franciscan directors—a spiritual dispute that eventually led to a physical split, when a group of nuns left Gravelines to establish a new convent in Aire in 1629.[53] The English Benedictine foundation at Brussels endured similar divisions for decades, and more than one group of nuns attempted to leave the convent to establish cloisters under Jesuit instruction, including the successful foundation of a convent in Ghent in 1624.[54] Jaime Goodrich has argued that "it does not seem coincidental that the Ghent Benedictines printed the Rule and Statutes in 1632, a year in which a second group of pro-Jesuit nuns left the Brussels Benedictines to found their own house even as yet another English Benedictine house, in Cambrai, faced accusations of unorthodox spiritual practices," and she identifies this publication as an intervention into "an ongoing competition between English Benedictine convents over spiritual primacy."[55] More offers a similar intervention by specifically invoking St. Benedict, St. Francis, and St. Ignatius in her anatomization of the church, arguing against Ignatian spiritual direction within the context of a broader claim about how competition among Benedictines, Franciscans, and Jesuits could be held responsible not only for the splintering of English monastic communities but also for the disunity and controversy afflicting early modern Christianity as a whole. She rejected Jesuit instruction as a nun at Cambrai and in the "Advertisement," reminding readers that "Saint Ignatius . . . absolutly forbad them the care, and government of Religious women" (A64), and pointing out "the reason as I conceive which maketh the Nunns of Contemplative orders prosper so il under their hands: Becaus they put them into Exercises of discourse" (A63). More's arguments against authoritarian superiors and Jesuit instruction not only intervene in debates over spiritual direction within the Catholic Church but also run contrary to Protestant depictions of nuns as unwitting pawns of Jesuits who hold "an usurping authoritie over them."[56] For More, those "Superiors and Priests [who] stand upon points, usurping that to themselves which *thou* hast reserved to *thy self*" are versions of Henry VIII, who usurped control of the church and his subjects' consciences from God's representative on earth (B210–11). At the same time, More broadens the scope of arguments concerning monasticism and obedience to include any superiors or priests—not just Jesuits—who would usurp God's authority. As such, *The Spiritual Exercises* reveals both the heterogeneity of early modern English Catholicism and the limits of masculine authority in the convent.

Reading *The Spiritual Exercises* in full—from its prefatory material linking Gertrude More to Sir Thomas More's martyrdom to its printed confessions, which build upon the defense of contemplative prayer included in the "Advertisement"—necessitates a rethinking of Protestant narratives of authority and obedience within the Catholic Church. More represents herself as a contemplative scholar whose most immediate spiritual relationship is with God, drawing upon her family's religious history to suggest the political implications of personal faith and individual devotional practice. She explains that "only living in Religion and pleasing our Superiors wil not advance us in the way of perfection, nor practising a blind Obedience which hath in it neither reason nor discretion" (79–80). "Reason" and "discretion" are essential for More: it is impossible to mistake her for the parodic models of female monasticism created by authors from Spenser to Middleton. By redefining religious obedience in terms of independent contemplative practice and reasoned interpretation of both scripture and post-Reformation political discourse, *The Spiritual Exercises* forces readers to reconsider these literary representations of nuns in relationship to More's articulation of the broader implications of female monastic obedience to questions of religious change and conflict.

The Religious Politics of Disobedience

Texts written in the decades before either the writing or publication of More's *The Spiritual Exercises* register the significance of nuns to questions of obedience, as we have already seen in pamphlet literature and in a play like *Measure for Measure*, which queries the limits of political authority in relationship to woman who wishes to enter a cloister. More's writings, with their close attention to the internal divisions that might plague a religious community and their emphasis on the priority of the individual's experience of God, can shed new light on the subtleties of these early seventeenth-century literary representations of religious and political conflict, highlighting even the complexities of a political allegory whose interpretive clarity has long hinged on its relevance to a specific political event. Thomas Middleton's *A Game at Chess* encourages spectators and readers to treat its characters-cum-chess-pieces as elements of a puzzle to be decoded: written in response to the political and religious crisis of the Spanish Match—the proposed marriage of Prince Charles to the Infanta Maria—the play depicts contemporary Englishmen and Spaniards as readily identifiable Kings, Dukes, and Knights on opposed sides of a chessboard.[57] Yet Middleton's pawns resist allegorical identifications, forcing the reader to step outside the play's game in order to confront its full implications. In the Induction, a liminal space between allegorical chess match and early modern audience, Ignatius Loyola calls special attention to the Black Bishop's Pawn and Black Queen's Pawn, his "son and daughter."[58] He suggests that the pawns' presence may disrupt the chessboard's rules and hierarchies: if they are truly his disciples, they will play against their own house in order to "rule . . . not observe rule" (71). Thus even before the first act, Middleton reveals that the "great game" at the center of his play may give way to the subversive energies at its periphery, where characters like the Black Queen's Pawn plot against their fellow pieces and prevent cohesive allegorical readings (78).

The pawns confirm that *A Game at Chess* is less indebted to a particular patron or immediate circumstances than it is to a set of religious and political concerns generated by the English Reformation. Allegory is not the point but the occasion, enabling Middleton to project outward from a single historical moment to a broader rendering of gender and obedience in post-Reformation religious politics. This extra-allegorical reading is only fully legible by attending to devotional texts like More's *The Spiritual Exercises*, which delineates the parameters of female obedience and reveals the relevance of monastic obedience to political life both inside and outside the cloister. By recognizing that Middleton addresses a similar set of issues in his play, we can see how Catholic women render his political allegory secondary, as the Black Queen's Pawn, identified as a "Jesuitess," forestalls clear analogical readings and instead necessitates close and careful attention to narrative details and their implications (2.1.187). In what follows, I will review how contemporary audiences and readers interpreted the pawn's plot in order to contextualize my reading of how Middleton's exploration of female obedience unsettles the search for a singular and stable structure of meaning behind an allegorical veil—and thus reveals how literary criticism has unintentionally replicated the early modern erasure of Catholic women.

Scholars of *A Game at Chess* have followed its earliest spectators in attending to the identifiable political allegory[59]—in which the devious Black Knight, representing the Conde de Gondomar, schemes against the Fat Bishop (De Dominis, the archbishop of Spalato) and the White Knight and Duke (Charles and Buckingham)—while neglecting the literary and political implications of the pawns' plot.[60] Seventeenth-century plot summaries typically ignore or elide the pawns: in a letter of 6 August 1624, John Woolley describes how "Gundomars diuilish plotts and deuices are displaid, and many other things to long to resight, the Conclusion expresseth his H: returne and a Mastery ouer the k. of sp: who being ouer come is putt into a great sack with D: Maria, Count of Oliuares, Gunde-|mar, and the B. of Spalato."[61] Woolley is willing to enumerate the fate of the play's obvious political figures, but the pawns' plot is hidden among the "things to long to resight" for him and many of his contemporaries.[62]

Of the dozens of contemporary notices of *A Game at Chess*, only one mentions the pawns specifically. Thomas Salisbury's manuscript poem on the play, written in December of 1624, describes the White Queen's Pawn as "a Lady! hard besett / to become Nunne: but came off cleerely yet," the Black Queen's Pawn as a "seculare Jesuitesse," and the Black Bishop's Pawn as "a Shy Jesuite."[63] Like other commentators—both early modern and modern—Salisbury is most interested in who or what the chess pieces represent, but he is unable to fully account for the White Queen's Pawn, identifying her simply as "a Lady" and instead focusing on what she *almost* becomes: a nun. This is surprising, given recent critics' attempts to identify the White Queen's Pawn with the English church. T. H. Howard-Hill, editor of the Revels edition of *A Game at Chess*, argues that "the Pawn's plot, in which the Black Bishop's Pawn and Black Queen's Pawn—both Jesuits—attack a figure representing the pristine virtues of Anglicanism, is primarily a moral allegory. It has even less political significance than the comparable allegory of *The Faerie Queene*, Book I because no contemporary reporter even noticed the main plot of the play."[64] Of course, a contemporary reporter did notice the pawns' plot, but Salisbury's interpretation does not align with Howard-Hill's. Rather than seeing the attempted seduction of the White Queen's Pawn as a moral allegory, Salisbury views it literally: in his description, Anglicanism is not "hard besett" by the corrupting forces of Jesuitical Catholicism; instead, a "Lady" nearly becomes a "Nunne."

For Salisbury, the pawns' plot is a struggle over individual faith, in which the failed attempt to convert the White Queen's Pawn comprises the bulk of the action. This aspect of the pawn's plot initiates the main action of the play, as the Black Queen's Pawn sees the White Queen's Pawn and exclaims, "I ne'er see that face but my pity rises" (1.1.1). She proceeds to describe her fears for this "daughter of heresy," doomed to be "lost eternally" (1.1.5, 4). By manipulating the language of virtue and salvation, the Black Queen's Pawn is able to make "a little passage" in the work of conversion before she leaves the White Queen's Pawn with the Black Bishop's Pawn (1.1.69). But becoming a nun, in the Protestant imaginary, was not a simple matter of conversion, and anti-Catholic pamphlet literature nearly always portrayed religious seduction as a prelude to sexual or economic seduction. The Black Queen's Pawn implicitly makes this connection when she describes the Black Bishop's Pawn with "all his young tractable sweet obedient daughters / E'en in his bosom, in his own dear bosom" (1.1.39–40).[65] While Salisbury was right that the White Queen's Pawn is "hard besett / to become Nunne," her entrance into a Catholic religious order is not exactly the point—it is a means to various ends. Her conversion will allow the Black King to "make some attempt upon the White Queen's person"; it will facilitate the Black Bishop's Pawn's attempt to transform religious obedience into sexual obedience; and it will help the Black Queen's Pawn to entrap the Black Bishop's Pawn (2.1.23–24).

Obedience is introduced to the reader of *A Game at Chess* as that which prevents a woman from engaging with the world of court politics and makes her vulnerable to religious and sexual ruin. In the play's first act, the Black

Queen's Pawn explains the Jesuits' involvement in matters of state to the White Queen's Pawn, whose innocence seems to prevent her from fully understanding the implications of the political intrigue practiced by these supposedly religious men. The vowed Jesuits are

> maintained in many courts and palaces,
> And are induced by noble personages
> Into great princes' services . . .
> All serving in notes of intelligence,
> As parish clerks their mortuary bills,
> To the Father General; so are designs
> Oft times prevented, and important secrets
> Of states discovered, yet no author found
> But those suspected oft that are most sound. (1.1.53–62)

After giving the game away, the Black Queen's Pawn belatedly declares that "this mystery is too deep yet for your entrance" (1.1.63). She then claims to be "checked by obedience," and hands the White Queen's Pawn over to the Black Bishop's Pawn to facilitate her conversion (1.1.65–66).[66] This is a sleight of hand on the part of both the Black Queen's Pawn and her author: she is not actually checked (or bound) by obedience, and this is the first of many moments when the reader is encouraged to question the force of obedience in the play's depiction of religious politics.

While the Black Bishop's Pawn thinks that becoming a nun will make the White Queen's Pawn "supple" under his authority, her interpretation of obedience does not meet his expectations of sexual submission (1.1.69). When she expresses her intention to "become / Obedience's humblest daughter," she explains that her desire is to "serve virtue / The right way" (1.1.90–94). To remedy this setback in his seduction, the Black Bishop's Pawn decides that the White Queen's Pawn "must be informed to know / A daughter's duty" by reading a "small tract of obedience" (1.1.186–90). Punning on the language of pregnancy—"you will conceive by that my power, your duty," the Black Bishop's Pawn says (1.1.193)—Middleton implicitly follows Thomas Robinson's formulation of deviant textuality as the prelude to deviant sexuality.[67] In Middleton's play, however, the book is not determinative, and the White Queen's Pawn is a careful and critical reader. When she returns to the stage, with the "book in her hand," she is already questioning its contents (2.1). As she reads, she realizes that "here again it is the daughter's duty / To obey her

confessor's command in all things / Without exception or expostulation"
(2.1.1–3). This immediately seems strange: " 'Tis the most general rule that
e'er I read of," she exclaims (2.1.4). She attempts to justify the book's instructions, convincing herself that "boundless virtue" deserves "uncircumscribed"
authority, but even her justification requires some form of the "expostulation" that the book itself forbids (2.1.5–8). This process of active reading is
remarkably similar to the devotional practice associated with the manuscript
culture at Cambrai, and the White Queen's Pawn anticipates the very objections to temporal authority that Gertrude More articulated from within a
religious order.

As a result, the "small tract of obedience" does not function as the Black
Bishop's Pawn had hoped it would: rather than impeding the White Queen's
Pawn's critical faculties and curtailing her virtuous intentions, the book inspires her. The Black Bishop's Pawn realizes his mistake when he sees her
reading. "She's passed the general rule, the large extent / Of our prescriptions
for obedience," he observes, "And yet with what alacrity of soul / Her eye
moves on the letters" (2.1.28–31). The conjunction "and yet" is crucial: *despite*
the Black Bishop's Pawn's most devious intentions, the book has produced
"alacrity of soul" instead of abject obedience. Even when the White Queen's
Pawn begs him to "lay your commands as thick and fast upon me / As you
can speak 'em" and describes "boundless obedience" as "the humblest yet the
mightiest of all duties," the Black Bishop's Pawn is aware that she has
"frighted the full meaning from itself" (2.1.34–42). The book and its definition of obedience depend upon her interpretation. When the Black Bishop's
Pawn reveals himself, asking for a kiss as evidence of her obedience, the
White Queen's Pawn immediately reframes her first reaction to the book.
Whereas she first posited that "the power / Of the dispenser" should be "as
uncircumscribed" as "boundless virtue" (2.1.5–8), she now acknowledges that
the inverse is true, as well: "fond men command, and wantons best obey"
(2.1.64). The nature of obedience, in other words, is dependent upon the nature of authority—and should a religious superior subvert the will of God,
his commands must be dismissed. While the Black Bishop's Pawn thinks
that the White Queen's Pawn has misinterpreted the text—"fright[ing] the
full meaning from itself"—she in fact fully understands the authoritarian
point but rejects the claim that authority must go unquestioned.

Authority in general seems suspect in *A Game at Chess*, and at least one
critic has suggested that the play is a "work opposed" to obedience.[68] But
disobedience is equally problematic for Middleton, who depicts the disruptive

effect of spies and turncoats—extreme examples of disobedient subjects—in the White House. Middleton is less interested in opposing obedience (or disobedience) than he is in imagining various situations that put obedience under pressure. How, he asks, is obedience enforced? Can material objects influence an individual's relationship to authority? What are the motivations for disobedience? How does a disobedient subject affect his or her superiors? Does obedience within a religious hierarchy function in the same way as obedience within a political hierarchy? To answer these questions, Middleton tests a number of scenarios, beginning with the White Queen's Pawn's close encounter with corrupt religious authority.

In the third act, Middleton shifts his focus from the manipulation of obedience by an authority figure to the subversion of authority within a religious order. The Black Queen's Pawn is at the heart of Middleton's speculative examination of possible responses to monastic authoritarianism. While she initially facilitates the Black Bishop's Pawn's religious and sexual seduction of the White Queen's Pawn, the Black Queen's Pawn's actions soon belie her claims for obedience within a religious hierarchy. Indeed, after preventing the rape of the White Queen's Pawn, she explains in an aside that all she does is "for my own turn, which end is all I work for" (2.1.156). In the Black House, where Catholic religious powers are so closely aligned with Spanish political powers that it is sometimes difficult to differentiate the two, the Black Queen's Pawn does not work to forward either of these interests; instead, she demonstrates how an autonomous—and disobedient—religious woman might change the game.

Throughout *A Game at Chess*, the Black Queen's Pawn negotiates the terms of obedience, rhetorically deploying the concept when necessary and undermining it with equal facility. She is not one of the Black Bishop's Pawn's "young tractable sweet obedient daughters" (1.1.39); instead, she is Middleton's representative Jesuit. The Black Queen's Pawn adheres to the principles outlined by Ignatius Loyola, founder of the Jesuits, in the play's induction: she "play[s] against" the Black Bishop's Pawn, but her motivations—self rule? personal revenge?—are not entirely clear (Ind. 69). Critics have consistently misread her character: one accuses her of betraying the White Queen's Pawn "to the lust of the Jesuit Black Bishop's Pawn, whose whim she indulges out of a secret desire to enjoy him herself," while another succinctly claims that she "enjoys pimping."[69] In fact, Middleton's Jesuitess is most interested in seeking revenge against the Black Bishop's Pawn and satisfying her "blood's game" (4.1.148). Editors have identified the "blood's game" as "lust," since the

Black Queen's Pawn ultimately stages a bed trick: she fools the Black Bishop's Pawn into sleeping with her by switching places with the White Queen's Pawn.[70] But her own explanation for her actions belies the limited scope of this gloss: she later claims to be exacting revenge for a relative—or, we might say, her "blood"—who was tricked into sleeping with the Black Bishop's Pawn as a young nun.[71]

When the Black Queen's Pawn denounces the Black Bishop's Pawn, she asks, "whose niece was she you poisoned with child, twice, / Then gave her out possessed with a foul spirit / When 'twas indeed your bastard?" (5.2.104–6). These lines have become something of a crux in readings of the play, as critics elide the niece and instead claim that the Black Queen's Pawn was "poisoned with child." Gary Taylor argues that "the play's other major woman, the Black Queen's Pawn, has already been successfully seduced by the Black Bishop's Pawn, five years before, when she was 'probationer at Brussels'; he has since 'poisoned [her] with child twice,' though he then refuses to acknowledge his 'bastard' offspring."[72] Caroline Bicks—in an insightful reading of female performance and theatricality that brings welcome attention to the relevance of the Black Queen's Pawn's self-identification as a "secular Jesuitess" to Mary Ward's order of unenclosed nuns (1.1.41)—also reads the Black Queen's Pawn as the victim of the Black Bishop's Pawn's seduction. Bicks explains that the Black and White Queens' Pawns "have played the same role opposite the Jesuit—that the Jesuitess herself was seduced by the Black Bishop's Pawn 'when I was a probationer at Brussels' . . . . As with the dumb show, this conflation of the women is literally staged."[73] Bicks offers a careful and convincing reading, but it is worth noting that the Black Queen's Pawn never actually says that she was seduced by the Black Bishop's Pawn. Instead, she asks him, "do you plant your scorn against me? / Why, when I was probationer at Brussels / That engine was not seen; then adoration / Filled up the place and wonder was in fashion" (5.1.90–93). These lines do offer interpretive possibilities, and it seems plausible, even likely, that the Black Queen's Pawn had some previous sexual relationship with the Black Bishop's Pawn, though Middleton does not directly reveal as much. Critics nonetheless transform implication and possibility into fact: the Black Queen's Pawn "has already been successfully seduced" or "was seduced by the Black Bishop's Pawn."[74] Such readings implicitly treat the White Queen's Pawn and Black Queen's Pawn as twinned allegorical renderings of the possible outcomes of religious seduction and conversion. They thus reduce the Black Queen's Pawn to a woman wronged and debased, seeking a pathetic revenge that replicates her original seduction, rather than holding to an allegorical understanding of the soul converted away from God or acknowledging the literal narrative that she offers.

Critics who conflate the Black Queen's Pawn with either her niece or the nearly seduced White Queen's Pawn also erase the other women represented in the climactic scene of the pawns' plot. When the Black Queen's Pawn denounces the Black Bishop's Pawn, she accuses him of being "chief agent for the transportation / Of ladies' daughters. . . . / Some of their portions I could name; who pursed 'em too. / They were soon dispossessed of worldly cares / That came into your fingers" (5.2.97–101).[75] The Black Queen's Pawn speaks for all of the "ladies' daughters" who have been financially and sexually seduced by the Black Bishop's Pawn. Her rejection of clerical hierarchy, demonstrated in her subversion of the seduction effort that the Black Bishop's Pawn claims is part of the "main work" of the Black House (1.1.290), is undertaken on behalf of a community of women. Though the Black Queen's Pawn initially represents herself as a fully independent actor, working for her "own turn," she is in fact motivated by alliances and familial ties (2.1.156).

Rather than straightforward political allegory, the collective female experience of monasticism drives the pawns' plot in *A Game at Chess*. From the Black Queen's Pawn's initial description of the Black Bishop's Pawn's "sweet obedient daughters" to her ultimate identification of those daughters with their recusant mothers, Catholic women are among the most resonant and yet the most invisible figures in Middleton's political and religious game (1.1.39). Where are the nuns? Where, for that matter, is the Infanta Maria? In this play about the Spanish Match, the woman to whom Charles was ostensibly matching himself disappears, along with the women for whom the Black Queen's Pawn speaks but who remain nameless.[76] They are crucial nonetheless: "dispossessed" nuns provide the impetus for the Black Queen's Pawn's actions, and the Infanta Maria is the unacknowledged reason for the White Knight's trip to the Black House (5.2.100). Middleton may find Catholic women nearly unrepresentable, but he cannot ignore them. This is not to say that Middleton has a positive view of female Catholicism; like Webster, he imagines women betrayed and destroyed by corrupt clerics. And yet Middleton seems aware of the fact that Catholic women, and nuns in particular, could affect the world outside the convent. The Black Queen's Pawn's plot against the Black Bishop's Pawn mirrors and anticipates the Black Knight's plot against the Fat Bishop: both the Black Knight and the Black Queen's Pawn manipulate the rules of the game in their pursuit of revenge. The Black Knight schemes to convert the Fat Bishop back to the Black House in order to ensnare him, and the Black Queen's Pawn brings the Black Bishop's Pawn "strangely in again" so that she may personally betray him (3.1.207). Both plots are successful at the expense of the larger game, and the capture of the Black Queen's Pawn at her moment of triumph prefigures the final fall of the Black House: she and the Black Bishop's Pawn are taken immediately after she reveals herself, in a version of the "checkmate by / Discovery" that ends the play when the Black Knight admits to "dissemblance" (5.3.159–61).

The Black Queen's Pawn can be folded into the larger political and religious allegory of *A Game at Chess* as one of the Spanish Catholics who is damned by the failed plot to entrap Charles in marriage and thereby return England to the Catholic Church. In this reading, she is not a specific Catholic woman like Mary Ward but the representative Catholic Englishwoman, alienated from proper allegiance (expressed in her sympathy for the White Queen's Pawn) by the corrupting forces of the Catholic religious hierarchy. But treating her only as an allegorical figure elides how she functions narratively. As a character within the play, the Black Queen's Pawn drives its most compelling plot, initiating and then undermining the Black Bishop's Pawn's seduction of the White Queen's Pawn in a trajectory that is utterly disconnected from the political goals of the Black House. She thus enables us to read allegory otherwise, and reveals that *A Game at Chess* is more than just a play about the Spanish Match and its political significance in the 1620s. The Black Queen's Pawn's self-discovery demonstrates the relevance of female monasticism in the world at large: she describes a convent that obeys the religious hierarchy and yet also produces internal agents of subversion. As a Catholic woman whose actions are informed by both her Ignatian principles and her experience of a female community, the Black Queen's Pawn creates a space for monastic disobedience. Although she has been reduced to a pimp, a whore, and a monstrous "cockatrice *in voto*," she is far more complicated and ambiguous than either the play's other characters or modern critics care to acknowledge (5.2.112).[77] For Middleton, however, she is also an impossible fiction. When she condemns the Black Bishop's Pawn as the "chief agent for the transportation / Of ladies' daughters" and claims that "they were soon dispossessed of worldly cares / That came into your fingers," Middleton borrows her words from Thomas Robinson's *The Anatomy of the English Nunnery at Lisbon* (5.2.97–101).[78] The Black Queen's Pawn may resemble Mary Ward, but she sounds like a Protestant pamphleteer. For Middleton, the disobedient nun is ultimately as unrepresentable as her religious sisters: unless she ventriloquizes Protestants, she is unable to speak.

What, then, can *A Game at Chess* reveal about the influence of Catholic Englishwomen on literary representations of religious conflict and monastic obedience in the seventeenth century? Middleton was certainly not reading Gertrude More, who wrote in the years following the staging and publication of his play, nor was More responding to his depiction of an autonomous religious woman. Yet their respective meditations on the relationship between obedient (or disobedient) subjects and temporal authority figures suggest that both authors were attempting to grapple with a similar set of social concerns. Their convergence might be partially explained by one of the more startling contemporary accounts of *A Game at Chess*, which documents the play's audience: it included "all sorts of people old and younge, rich and poore, masters and seruants, papists and puritans, wise men et[c] churchmen and statesmen . . . and a world besides."[79] This audience of opposite extremes does not seem unlikely—presumably old and young, rich and poor, and masters and servants attended any number of plays, and there is nothing to suggest that these groups would find anything particularly offensive in *A Game at Chess*—until the reader encounters the "papists." What might Catholics have found interesting about a play in which the material of Protestant pamphlets was transformed into dramatic action? Why would they have wanted to see a representation of themselves, or their coreligionists on the continent, plotting against the English throne? Don Carlos Coloma, the Spanish ambassador, suggested one possible explanation in a letter that included some details "a few Catholics have told me who went secretly to see the play."[80] Catholics, in other words, may have attended this play not for allegory but for information: to discover the substance of current anti-Catholic sentiment, to witness the Protestant reaction (according to Coloma's sources, "people come out of the theatre so inflamed against Spain that . . . my person would not be safe in the streets") and perhaps, like their Protestant countrymen, to learn about the geographically distant Spanish and Jesuit participants in international religious politics.[81]

English Catholics relied on letters, manuscripts, and printed books as sources of information on continental religious life, but these material witnesses to the practice of Catholicism in the English cloisters, colleges, and monasteries in French and Spanish territories were subject to loss, damage, and confiscation. Pursuivants captured many packets bound for England, and surviving letters attest to how frequently such documents went astray.[82]

Information from the continent could also cause concern, whether it arrived in the form of Protestant pamphlets that purported to expose the dangers of the convent or in the manuscripts written by nuns and their priests that revealed the internal divisions at some continental cloisters.[83] Claire Walker has argued convincingly that such information may have influenced decisions concerning professions and led recusants to avoid sending their daughters to scandal-ridden convents.[84] Catholics in England were eager to learn about the conditions they might face when practicing their religion in seemingly more hospitable environments. A play like *A Game at Chess*, which avoided the outrageous claims of Catholic blood-lust featured in revenge tragedies in favor of a condemnation of Spanish political machinations, could have appealed to "papists" who desired some insight into continental monastic practices.

Despite Middleton's reliance on Protestant propaganda and his subsequent categorization of nuns as seduced or depraved by their experience of the convent, *A Game at Chess* is nonetheless an attempt to evaluate power struggles within the Catholic hierarchy and to examine their effects on the individuals subject to that hierarchy.[85] Middleton's depiction of the Black Queen's Pawn is, in part, the stuff of paranoid Protestant fantasies: an amalgamation of the fears concerning Catholic women who might enjoy too much freedom and the desire to peer beyond the convent walls and view the illicit activities that may occur, unseen, within the enclosure. But as I have argued, the Black Queen's Pawn also raises the possibility that nuns might resist corrupt authority figures and thereby have some influence on religious politics. The idea that nuns could have their own agendas, distinct from the institutional imperatives of the Catholic Church or the personal schemes of duplicitous priests, is largely absent from Protestant propaganda. Middleton thus provided English Catholics with a glimpse into the Catholic world on the continent—partial, polemical, and prejudiced though that glimpse was. The Black Queen's Pawn simultaneously represented and distorted the antiauthoritarian elements that would later appear in *The Spiritual Exercises* of Gertrude More, and her participation in the internal strife afflicting the Black House suggests that the divisions within and among monastic communities on the continent were widely known in England by the early 1620s, when the convent at Cambrai was founded.[86]

The nuns of Cambrai rejected Protestant representations of submissive or seduced monastic women in their manuscripts and printed books. As female contemplatives who articulated their relationships to religious superiors and to God through the language of obedience, they shared far more with the White Queen's Pawn than with the Black. More read and wrote with "alacrity of soul," transforming her convent's local controversy into the basis for a complex reading of obedience and religious conflict in the world outside the cloister (2.1.30). Like the White Queen's Pawn, she rejected the notion of "boundless obedience" to corrupt authorities and instead offered the substance of her vows to God (2.1.38). In *A Game at Chess*, the convent and its values are dismissed as the tools of hypocrites and frauds, yet the White Queen's Pawn makes a surprising announcement in the play's final scenes: she vows to "never know man farther than by name" (5.2.118). Middleton's representation of an idealized—if easily converted—religious woman is steeped in Catholicism, from the White Queen's Pawn's early enthusiasm for conventual life and monastic obedience to her ultimate renunciation of marriage through a vow of virginity. She undergoes a transformation from idealized Protestant to Catholic convert to a hybrid fusion of the two: a Protestant nun. In her, perhaps, the "papists" at the theater saw a female contemplative whose religious devotion resembled that of the women who left their native country in order to practice their faith. In the 1620s, values originally associated with the convent—virginal chastity and true religious obedience, in particular— remained relevant to any depiction of a religious woman, whether Protestant or Catholic. So, too, by the 1650s, obedience had become a vexed category not only for Puritans in England but also for Catholic monastics living far from the ravages of the Civil War: "the most stronge & bright armour of obedience" was at once a promise and a burden, an offering to God and a rhetorical shield against the depredations of earthly authority.[87]

CHAPTER 4

Cloisters and Country Houses:
Women's Literary Communities

Thomas Middleton's final image of vowed female virginity in *A Game at Chess* poses a sympathetic counterpoint to the aggressive anti-Catholicism of theatrical representation in the 1620s. Yet, like Webster's portrait of the Duchess, Middleton's play joins contemporary pamphlet literature in portraying enclosed women as the victims of a corrupt religious system, and the White Queen's Pawn's solitary epilogue makes visible her distance from the female community of the convent. As the previous chapters have demonstrated, manuscripts and printed books produced at the English convents in exile countered these pejorative representations, but imaginative literature of the first half of the seventeenth century registered monastic interventions only obliquely and ambivalently. Instead of dismissing Catholic book culture outright, authors such as Webster and Middleton reduced the textual communities of Syon and Cambrai from flourishing libraries to isolated and poisonous books, while erasing or denigrating the potential for women's communal life. A central argument of this book has been that the former representational project continues to influence critical discourse on Catholic women and the book.[1] This final chapter will show how the latter contributes to the erasure of alternate narratives of English literary history, which become legible when we shift our focus away from the traces of Catholic women in canonical literature and toward the traces of canonical literature in communities associated with the convent. Catholic women's literary networks reveal a flexible and fluid early modern canon and can help us to better identify the interventions that helped to solidify the canon as we know it, erasing Catholic women's contributions and their significance as literary agents.

Authors in the second half of the seventeenth century began to depict a broad range of fictive and potential female communities that echoed or adapted elements of monasticism. From Katherine Philips's poetic valorizations of female friendship to Mary Astell's proposed religious retirement for the propagation of faith and good works, a great deal of post-Civil War literature explored the possibility that female communities might enable poetic production and intellectual development. The Laudian community at Little Gidding, founded by the Ferrar family in 1625 and organized according to a "quasi-monastic rule" developed by Nicholas Ferrar, offers one point of reference for these representations.[2] Female members of the community produced a remarkable collection of manuscripts, including Story Books addressing history and theology, Biblical Harmonies composed of cut and pasted printed texts, and a presentation copy of George Herbert's poetry. Yet contemporary commentators focused not on the community's literary significance but on its affinities with the convent: Nicholas Ferrar's nieces, Mary and Anna Collett, were virgins and "so resolved to continue" according to a 1641 pamphlet that condemned them for religious devotion practiced "just like as the English *Nunnes* at Saint *Omers* and other Popish places."[3] Hardly surprising, then, that authorship of the Little Gidding materials was long associated with Nicholas Ferrar, whether by wholesale misattribution or by means of the critical tendency to trivialize material practices such as cutting "as a kind of nonwriting."[4] Recent critics such as Adam Smyth and Debora Shuger have corrected this oversight, but it remains telling that even a spurious connection to the English convents in exile helped to obscure the collaborative literary productions of the women at Little Gidding, despite their importance to poets such as Herbert and Crashaw. Seventeenth-century perceptions of popery created the grounds for a literary history in which women like Mary and Anna were made invisible while Nicholas was recognized for the entire community's literary practice—a situation akin to the actual convents, where men like Augustine Baker at Cambrai or Seth Foster at Syon were accused by contemporaries of controlling women's participation in book culture and have since been credited with monastic manuscripts of uncertain authorship.

By repositioning women at the center of the communities to which they were so essential, literary history becomes more capacious, in terms of who participates and what that participation entails. In the mid-seventeenth century, networks of recusant readers and writers mixed strictly religious poetry and prose with a broad range of written materials, from pastoral poetry to love letters. At the center of one such network was a young woman named

Constance Aston Fowler, who compiled a manuscript book of poetry that drew on multiple and sometimes conflicting literary traditions, and did not adhere to a specifically Catholic or even religious selection process.[5] Fowler's miscellany is one of many literary texts associated with members of the Aston and Thimelby families in the seventeenth century, and a handful of historians and literary critics have noted that textual exchange was a community-building activity for this geographically dispersed group of Catholic men and women, whose writing practice spanned the 1630s through the 1680s.[6] Their manuscripts reveal the generic and formal complexity of a recusant literary culture centered on women: we can hear the influence of poet and martyr Robert Southwell[7]—in a Passion poem written from a woman's perspective in Fowler's miscellany and in the way Winefrid Thimelby adopts the tropes of sonnet sequences in letters urging faith, prayer, and support for her convent in exile—and find explicit references to John Donne, a more ambiguous poetic predecessor for committed recusants. Through the quotation, revision, and adaptation of their poetic predecessors and contemporaries, the women of the Aston-Thimelby circle demonstrate their profound engagement with literary history and their own relevance to seventeenth-century poetics.

Because members of the Aston-Thimelby family exchanged letters and poetry over a period of more than fifty years and alluded to poems written decades earlier, I take a miscellaneous chronological approach in this chapter, exploring a range of textual materials published and circulated from the 1590s until the 1680s. Many of these texts are crucially informed by travel to the continent: whether that of a letter writer, its recipient, the distance between the two, or a period of exile enabling firsthand experience of the English convents. I explore, for example, the surprising resonances between Margaret Cavendish's *The Convent of Pleasure*, which incorporates both the pejorative and the celebratory strains of literature focused on female community, and the literary practice of the Aston-Thimelby family. Cavendish may have been inspired by her interactions with English Carmelite nuns in Antwerp, where she lived during the 1650s, and *The Convent of Pleasure* reveals that it was possible to imagine and represent Catholic women's communal literary production in early modern England, albeit in limited ways. Cavendish's play thus offers an important corrective to poems such as Andrew Marvell's *Upon Appleton House*. The response to both Little Gidding and Astell's *A Serious Proposal* demonstrates how deeply ingrained anti-Catholic prejudice had become in English culture, and Marvell's condemnation of the words of "subtle nuns" in the midst of an imaginative history of the dissolution of the monasteries underscores the central role of canonical literary representation in denying the multifaceted significance of Catholic women's communities and literature.[8] By turning to *Upon Appleton House* and *The Convent of Pleasure* after analyzing the poems and letters of the Aston-Thimelby circle, I show how we might reorient our perspective on long-canonical writers like Marvell and newly canonical female authors like Cavendish when we recognize both Catholic women as active participants in early modern literary culture and the seventeenth-century interest in female community as a significant chapter in literary history.

The variety of literary forms and genres adopted by members of the Aston-Thimelby circle demonstrate that communal literary practice anticipates and even surpasses the sympathetic literary representation of female community in plays like *The Convent of Pleasure*. While Cavendish ultimately abandons her experiments with genre and form in favor of a traditional comedy plot—one in which Lady Happy relinquishes an exclusively female space of literary production in favor of marriage—women like Fowler and Thimelby demonstrated an ongoing commitment to literary production and conversation as the basis for community cohesion. Their textual network flourished throughout the seventeenth century, and it included women whose writings reveal multiple perspectives on faith, marriage, and monasticism. By examining their poems and letters as part of an ongoing conversation about the place of poetry in the formation of post-Reformation communities of various kinds, this chapter will demonstrate the significance of Catholic women's collective literary practices to the reception and representations of canonical English literature in the seventeenth century, when Southwell's devotional poetry had been embraced by English Protestants, Donne's heterogeneous verses inspired recusant imitation and response, and Marvell acknowledged the convent as a space of literary production while denying the continued influence of female communities associated with Catholicism.[9]

Poetic Faith: Robert Southwell's Devotional Petrarchism

In the epistle from "The Authour to his lovinge Cosen" prefacing *Saint Peters Complaint* and the Waldegrave manuscript of his poems, Robert Southwell cautioned that poets who "abus[e] their talent" by "making the follies and fayninges of love, the customary subject of their base endevours" have degraded their very office.[10] Following poetic theorists of the 1580s such as

George Puttenham and Sir Philip Sidney, Southwell pointed to the "many parts of Scripture in verse," which "warranteth the Arte to bee good." Yet the poetry that followed this letter went beyond scriptural paraphrase and the tradition of psalm translation most prevalent in England in the late sixteenth century. As Alison Shell has demonstrated, "Southwell's poems met a need for imaginatively engaging religious verse, different from mainstream English religious poetry of the 1590s."[11] Despite the close association between his faith and his poetry—the first printed editions of *Saint Peter's Complaint* appeared in 1595, the year of his martyrdom—Southwell nonetheless initiated a theory and practice of devotional verse that paved the way for poets from Herbert to Milton. Literary critics of the past two decades have done much to restore his place in the history of seventeenth-century verse, suggesting that Protestant poetics and religious lyrics were in fact indebted to Catholic aesthetics.[12] But less attention has been paid to how Southwell's call for a devotional poetics purified of "idle fansies" influenced his female coreligionists in the decades following his death, as England's Catholics attempted to find a language that adequately expressed the ambiguities and contradictions of their post-Reformation faith. In the reading of "Marie Magdalen's Blush" that follows, I trace how Southwell incorporated the tropes of love poetry into his religious poems. By first repudiating and then refashioning Petrarchism, the dominant discourse of love in Elizabethan England, Southwell provided his later readers with an ambiguous poetic inheritance that would come to influence not only canonical English lyric but also the prose explorations of faith, love, and identity written by Catholic women in the mid-seventeenth century.

Southwell called for and modeled a reinvigorated religious poetics that transformed the language of contemporary love poetry into the material for sacred verse. In "Marie Magdalen's Blush," the first poem following "Saint Peter's Complaint" in the 1595 volume, Southwell recuperates the tropes of Petrarchan lyric: instead of the beloved's "cheeks adorned with a sweet fire" imagined by the Petrarchan speaker of *canzone* 127,[13] Mary Magdalene herself describes "the signes of shame that staine my blushing face" in the poem's opening line.[14] These blushes are not available for interpretive—and arguably false or self-serving—readings by a lover; instead, they are anchored to a specific emotion: "The signes of shame that staine my blushing face, / Rise from the feeling of my raving fits" (1–2). These first two lines form an insistent declarative sentence, suggesting that signs are clear and direct representations of felt experience. The female speaker of Southwell's poem thus instantiates the rejection of "the follies and fayninges of love" in the prefatory letter, demonstrating how "a Poet, a Lover, and a Liar" might no longer be "reckoned but three wordes of one signification" by tying physical signs to emotional substance.[15]

Yet Southwell was no stranger to the crisis in representation that defined his period, during which Protestant and Catholic disputation frequently centered on the relationship between sign and meaning. Reformist writings questioned the possibility that things—images, relics, even books—could point to truth,[16] while at the same time emphasizing the Eucharist's status as a sign rather than the miraculous transformation of bread to body. Southwell's description of the Magdalene's blush thus signifies on at least two levels, by repudiating Petrarchan tropes and invoking Reformation religious controversy.[17] In bringing together these two discourses, Southwell critiques not only Petrarchism but also Protestantism, in its alignment of the superficial, the material, and the false: signs here do point to truth, even in a fallen world and a fallen body. But following this declarative, the poem shifts into a more complex rendering of the relationship between signs and substance in another adaptation of Petrarchan love lyric:

> All ghostly dynts that grace at me did dart
> Like stubborne rocke I forced to recoyle;
> To other flights an ayme I made my hart,
> whose wounds then welcome, now have wrought my foyle.
> Woe worth the bow, woe worth the Archers might,
> That drave such arrowes to the marke so right. (13–18)

The weapons that grace wields in its attack are indeed "ghostly": they inflict "dynts" or blows but at first take on no distinctive shape or substance. Yet the grammar of the poem encourages its readers to *think* they can identify these weapons. Grace "dart[s]" its blows at the Magdalene, suggesting that its weapon is thrown: a spear or—more likely following the plural "dynts"— arrows. The enjambment between lines thirteen and fourteen makes such a reading more complicated, as it initially seems that "like stubborne rocke" could modify "dart" or "dynts," offering readers a material anchor that dissolves almost immediately under the weight of its own incomprehensibility: how can something be thrown like stubborn rock? How can blows be like stubborn rock? Instead, "like stubborne rocke" describes the speaker herself, who rejects the efforts of grace in favor of "other flights." As Mary

Magdalene compares the two sets of weapons, her language grows increasingly specific: from "dynts" to "flights" aimed at a heart, and the ultimate revelation of a "bow," an "Archers might," and his "arrowes." In the third stanza, then, Southwell's Mary Magdalene seems to reoccupy the Petrarchan worldview rejected in the poem's opening lines, as she imaginatively returns to the origins of her shame by invoking the objects and metaphors of Petrarchan lyric.

Rather than replacing Cupid's arrows with God's, as he replaced the crimson cheeks of the beloved with the shame-stained face of the repentant sinner, Southwell maintains the Petrarchan tradition but places it on an eschatological continuum in which the actions, themes, and tropes of love lyric lead not to unrequited love or consummated marriage but to guilt, repentance, and eventually grace.[18] The unnamed archer's arrows are essential to this process, as the initial fixity of their meaning becomes elusive:

> To pull them out, to leave them in, is death:
> One, to this world: one, to the world to come:
> Wounds may I weare, and draw a doubtfull breath:
> But then my wounds will worke a dreadfull dome.
> And for a world, whose pleasures passe away,
> I lose a world, whose joyes are past decay. (19–24)

Arrows mean death, but what does death mean? Meaning splits and doubles back on itself: the arrows mean death whether they are pulled out or left in, but death can apply to either the body (this world) or the soul (the world to come). Life, in the form of "doubtfull breath," is possible with sin, but such life will result in "a dreadfull dome." These lines reveal that Southwell's poetic practice does not depend on a simplistic repudiation of Petrarchan "follies and fayninges" but rather offers a model for how religious lyric and religious life might be reinvigorated through an exploration of the language and submerged meanings available in love poetry.

Southwell offered an earlier rationale for his recuperation of the late sixteenth century's most pervasive and popular discourse of love in *Marie Magdalens Funeral Teares*. This 1591 prose meditation on Mary's passion includes a dedicatory epistle "To the worshipfull and vertuous Gentlewoman, Mistres D. A." in which Southwell anticipates not only the theory but also the practice of *Saint Peters Complaint*, as he queries the multiple significations of passion and love:

> For as passion, and especially this of love, is in these daies the
> chiefe commaunder of moste mens actions, & the Idol to which
> both tongues and pennes doe sacrifice their ill bestowed labours:
> so is there nothing nowe more needefull to bee intreated then how
> to direct these humors unto their due courses, and to draw this
> floud of affections into the righte chanel. Passions I allow, and loves
> I approve, onely I would wishe that men would alter their object
> and better their intent.[19]

In treating love as an "Idol" to which men "sacrifice their ill bestowed labours," Southwell transforms iconoclastic Protestant critiques of Catholic worship into an attack on secular speech and writing, but he refuses to destroy a symbol that signifies on multiple levels. Love, in Southwell's formulation, may be redirected from false worship, and it is this redirection that forms the basis of his poetics: secular verse is adopted, adapted, and redeployed in the service of religious devotion practiced or desired by women. While Shell has suggested that Southwell demonstrates "an overt wariness about the place of woman in verse" based on his infrequent invocation of a feminine heavenly muse, he nonetheless explores his own poetic theory through female subjects and in response to a woman's "vertuous request" in the case of this dedicatory epistle.[20]

Gary Kuchar has identified the "D.A." to whom Southwell dedicates *Marie Magdalens Funeral Teares* as Dorothy Arundel, recusant daughter of one of the most visible Catholic families in Elizabethan England and an early member of the Benedictine convent in Brussels, where she professed in 1600.[21] Arundel was also an author in her own right, though the manuscript of her *Life of Father Cornelius the Martyr* is no longer extant. In what follows, I will suggest that the model that Southwell offers to fellow poets is also taken up by women like Arundel: female recusants and nuns whose writings on faith and family engaged the discourses of romantic love and, in so doing, adapted Southwell's poetic theory for seventeenth-century literary and religious practice. Exiled English nuns such as the "pore sinner Sister Magdalen Sheldon" who inscribed the 1602 edition of *Marie Magdalens Funerall Teares* given to her by "her Deare Aunt Mrs Jane Wake" were reading Southwell well into the seventeenth century: Sheldon was born Bridgett Sheldon in 1640 and professed at the Dominican convent in Brussels in 1665.[22] The inscription in her book offers material evidence of the literary ties that linked women who entered convents on the continent with their coreligionists in England. In the letters of the Aston-Thimelby circle, such ties are expressed figuratively: while they did not follow Southwell in disparaging secular verse, references to poetry and metaphorical explorations of love and faith in the letters nonetheless reveal that writers such as Constance Aston Fowler, Katherine Thimelby Aston, and Winefrid Thimelby were engaged in a project that expanded Southwell's exploration of the available and appropriate languages for earthly attachments and religious devotion.

Hearts Divided: Southwellian Metaphor and Epistolary Devotion

Southwell's poetic theory infused the language of Catholic women as they attempted to negotiate secular and religious devotion in the development of a community grounded in textual exchange and shared faith. Just as "Marie Magdalen's Blush" illuminates the complexities of Southwell's rejection of poetry's "idle fansies" in its exploration of the tension between earthly and divine love, the letters of the Aston-Thimelby family—whose correspondents included siblings Constance and Herbert, Herbert's eventual wife Katherine and her sister Winefrid[23]—attempt to negotiate these tensions through formal play, but play performed by and with women as interlocutors rather than poetic symbols. It is no surprise that the contradictions central to Southwellian poetics were still vital to Catholic networks of readers and writers nearly a half century later, but by tracking what could be a simplified Petrarchan conceit of physical hearts as signs of emotional attachment through a series of transformations in single images and across multiple letters, I will demonstrate how Catholic women were central to this engagement with a recusant literary inheritance that included not only martyrdom and persecution but also assimilation into the dominant religious culture.[24] I begin with the letters that Constance wrote to her brother and Katherine before and during their courtship, most of which were exchanged while Herbert accompanied their father, Stuart diplomat and Catholic convert Walter Aston, on his second embassy to Spain between 1635 and 1638. Against this backdrop of international politics, Constance focused on the details of intimate relationships, and yet I will demonstrate that her metaphorical explorations of familial and romantic love offer an extended meditation on the place of early modern poetics in post-Reformation recusant devotional practice.

In the letters of the Aston-Thimelby families, the personal, poetic, and devotional merge in the development and solidification of social networks and collective Catholic identity. Yet scholars have tended to read Constance Aston Fowler's letters as almost entirely personal, concerned as they are with her brother Herbert Aston's courtship of Katherine Thimelby and Constance's own interactions with a handful of family members and friends, rather than as part of a larger seventeenth-century literary tradition. As Julie Sanders puts it, such materials "may seem opaque to readers outside the charmed circle."[25] In order to explicate them and justify their status as texts worthy of literary analysis, more than one critic has noted that the letters bear some generic similarity to later epistolary novels.[26] But it is a mistake to privilege the plot or narrative of these letters over the figures, allusions, and grammatical play embedded within them. Rather than restricting Constance's letters to a historical teleology that justifies their literary significance because they anticipate later innovations in prose fiction, I propose a reading attuned to the contemporary discourses in which a young Catholic woman might have wanted to intervene.[27] These letters, which narrate and negotiate a marital relationship between two individuals, simultaneously explore the available language for other forms of attachment and love. The opacity of Constance's letters is thus not simply a product of their historical association with a "charmed circle" of readers, writers, and intimates; instead, it is a product of their multivalent participation in a discourse of love, devotion, and poetic invention that can be traced through the metaphor of hearts.

Poetry has been recognized as a defining mode of community engagement for members of this literary coterie, but it has most frequently been explored in material terms. Multiple scholars have discussed the writing, exchange, and collection of poems as textual objects—activities variously practiced by Constance, Herbert, their sister Gertrude Aston Thimelby, Katherine, and Katherine's brother Edward Thimelby (among others).[28] But few have analyzed how figurative language and poetic theory infused nearly every aspect of the community's writing practice, often appearing alongside references to poems as material objects.[29] In a letter written by Constance before she discovered Herbert's particular attachment to Katherine, for example, Constance discusses "three copyes of verses" that Herbert promised but did not deliver in exchange "for sending your box to Mr. Henry Thimelby."[30] This failed gift exchange is part of a precise accounting of things that have gone astray in the journey between England and Spain, where Herbert was stationed with their father, including "a letter with six several maners of ribin with it of the newes fassions" and "tw par of gloves and another letter" (22v). Poems, as they are described here, function primarily as objects to be created, exchanged, and collected. As textual artifacts, they form the basis for a scribal community in which, as Helen Hackett has argued, Constance "had a central role . . . as an individual known for her taste and aesthetic judgment and who promoted and circulated the poetry of others." Hackett borrows the term "voucher" from Paul Trolander and Zeynep Tenger to describe Constance's position in the family network, which captures her primary role in the creation of the poetic miscellany and her representation of specific poems within her letters.[31] But these are not the only ways that poetry figures in Constance's correspondence. Earlier in the same letter, Constance initiates an elaborate explication of two heart-based riddles offered by her brother. First: if his letters were as heavy as his heart, they would cost nothing to convey, and second: if a letter could fly to his sister as quickly as his heart, it would never reach her. These lines "seeme paradoxes" to Constance "at first reeding over" but she is possessed "with this strong conceate that it was the highest exspression of constant love as could be writ" (21r). Constance invokes contemporary poetics in the language she uses to describe her process of analysis, and the paradoxes she unpacks should certainly bring to mind Donne's similarly riddling descriptions of love in poems such as "Negative Love" and "The Paradox" (the latter of which was untitled in the 1633 *Poems*). But Constance is not simply a reader of her brother's wordplay. Even in her description of her "strong conceate"—a phrase that encompasses both the thought that Constance has about Herbert's figurative descriptions of his letters *and* the figure that Constance herself creates in response—Constance begins to craft her own witty linguistic play, punning on her first name in proclaiming that Herbert's riddles must express "constant love."

Explication bleeds into invention, as Constance ceases to consider the heart's weight or its speed and instead treats it—like a letter or a poem—as an object. It is a "rellike" that breaks the rules of the gift economy in which these family members participated: "I must needes rest, nae I fear dye indet," Constance complains, "for ther is nor can bee no mirrit in mee that can deserve the least of so Rich a treasure, and therfore very unable I am to make any recompence to you for bestouing of it" (21r–v). She returns to this idea of "recompence" before imagining herself as possessor and protector of her brother's heart, capable of controlling the terms of its eventual "resinement" to a beloved (21v). Here we see that Hackett's description of Constance as a voucher for poetry is anticipated by Constance herself, in this figure of her holding "the ofes of so high a tressurer," capable of presenting her brother's heart to another (21v). Constance concludes her response to Herbert's paradoxical renderings of his heavy and stationary heart with her own elaborate image of his prospective beloved's heart: "she will bee treable harted, for first her own hart must needes bee unighted to yours or elce it werr not worthy of it, and then mine which has bin the keeper of yours I feare will not bee perswaded to part from it, but when it tis to resine up yours to her, it will intowme it selfe in it, so that she will bee able to furnish one that has lost ore given awae ther hart" (21v). In this accretive image, hearts are added onto hearts and the metaphor must bear the weight not only of Constance's affection for her brother but also of the broader community that has a claim on all these hearts. Modifying a common trope of love poetry, Constance describes the heart of the beloved uniting with Herbert's in order to be "worthy" of his. But this follows a long meditation on worth, in which Constance anticipates resigning her place when Herbert finds "a choyce farr more worthy of" his heart (21v). The beloved's worthiness may exist prior to Herbert's heart joining with hers—Constance will "present a hart more worth then all hartes to one onely worthy of it"—or it may result *from* the unification: Constance is "confident she will be that has it, ore elce that will make her so" (21v). This is not, in other words, a simple unification of two equally matched hearts; instead, Constance suggests a possible elevation of the female beloved's heart through her love for Herbert. Constance then must find a place for her own heart, which was a "keeper" of his and thus will not want to separate from it. But rather than imagine a failure of either the gift economy or herself as its treasurer, Constance transforms her heart from a possessor incapable of resigning Herbert's heart to a heart entombed within his. Even before she introduces a possible fourth factor—the "one that has lost ore given awae ther hart"—Constance guides her reader through a dizzying series of reversals, in which power and agency shift from Constance to the triple-hearted beloved to Herbert, back to Constance, then Herbert, and finally to the beloved who will be able "to furnish" another with the surplus of hearts joined to hers.

Jenijoy La Belle, an early and sensitive reader of the letters, suggests that this passage "shows how at times the emotion becomes an artifice, a literary creation, centering around the paradoxes, conceits, and puns in which the affection is couched."[32] While I agree with her claim that "in these letters we see how literature and life come together as the conventions of the rhetoric become one with the conventions of the heart," this idea leads La Belle to an opposition between literature and history, as she argues that the lack of quotidian detail in Constance's letters makes it "seem that Constance did not live in history, but in language: she created a little self-contained world made cunningly of love and rhetoric."[33] But is Constance's world really so self-contained? Or does her poetic exegesis and invention within the letters function like the material exchange and collection of poetry that she negotiates through and outside them—as a community-building practice? Here I would like to return to Constance's final addition to the image of the triple heart, when she imagines that the beloved "will bee able to furnish one that has lost ore given awae ther hart, and yet make ther selfe lettle the poorer" (21v). Who is this "one"? Is Constance referring again to herself, in the loss of her heart to Herbert and then his beloved? Is the beloved supplying a place for Constance's heart, and enriching it despite the loss of Herbert's heart? Or is Constance, as I suggested earlier, introducing the possibility of a separate individual whose lost heart can be replaced with the excess available to the beloved? Constance's linguistic play enables all these options: as she shifts her pronouns from "I," "she," "mine," "yours," and "her" to the more ambiguous "one" and "ther," the closed circuit of the triple heart opens onto the possibility of broader exchange. Constance's figurative treatment of affection, in other words, moves progressively from Herbert's single heart to the dual love of brother and sister to the triple-hearted beloved and finally to the invocation of a possible outsider entering into this intimate world.

Immediately after this gesture toward an inclusive and expansive network of hearts, Constance punningly examines her own conceit: "I can not chuse but smile to thinke what a harty letter you will thinke this when you reed it, for I have taken such a subject for my invenion to worke on that I can not for my life unfasen my selfe from it" (21v). And yet she does unfasten from the heart conceit, turning from a self-reflexive consideration of her audience and her authorship to a narrative of recent events, including a visit from the king during which their elder brother acquitted himself well; the stay of Thomas Weston, son of the lord high treasurer, at the family seat at Tixall; a family gathering with music provided by the earl of Essex; and the prospect of Richard Fanshaw arriving with letters from Spain. This account of "all the newes that is here" includes communal speech ("my brother Aston they say has behaved himselfe very well") and action (dancing) in its description of the relationships among individuals of varying degrees of social distance from the family (22r). Hackett has delineated the extent to which family connections were also social and political connections for the Aston-Thimelby circle, and I would add that the discursive movement of Constance's letter—from poetic invention to social interaction and finally to a detailed account of the poems she would like to receive from Herbert—suggests that her language is not only fully imbricated in history but also constitutive of a community grounded in the literary practice of women. We cannot separate the extensive list of social ties, courtly favors, and communal speech or the material exchange of poetry from the poetic conceit of hearts linked to one another in multiple and shifting ways, with new additions altering and expanding the initially settled familial relationship of brother and sister.

Nor can we separate the social and familial from the devotional. Southwell's poetic theory infused the language of later female Catholic writers as they attempted to negotiate secular and religious devotion in the development of a community grounded in textual exchange and shared faith. La Belle notes that Constance uses a vocabulary that "hints at religious love through words like *relic* and through the complex image of the three hearts being one," but she does not address the significance of such choices or analyze how devotional language inflects the increasingly complex interactions created through and reflected in the letters.[34] Whether or not such language alludes directly to the secular or devotional poetry of someone like Southwell or Donne—and the quotations of Donne in the letters that I examine in the next section suggest that it might—its allusive qualities illuminate the relationship between discourses of religious love and erotic or familial love that Southwell so influentially explored. How does one situate love for a brother, an intimate friend, or a beloved in relationship to love for God, the practice of an outlawed religion, and the diversity of devotional choices within a community of coreligionists?

While Constance rarely addresses such questions directly, she does return to familiar images throughout her letters that suggest the development of her thinking on these issues. When, for example, Constance meets and befriends Katherine Thimelby, who will eventually become her brother's wife, she revises her earlier image of the rich treasure of Herbert's heart and his prospective triple-hearted beloved. Constance uses the language of wealth, value, and possession that she originally applied to Herbert to describe what he would gain through their match: "you wer sure to possess the never decaying tresure, which she her self might bringe you, and my dearest brother lett me tell you I thinke you would find your selfe no looser by what I wish, if you wer so blest as to possess it, for certainly she is soe rich in her selfe, that none can be poore that has the possession of so unvallevable a jewell."[35] Immediately following this description of Katherine's worth, Constance offers a new—and crucially modified—image of an inclusive heart:

> you tw are deare partners in my hart and it tis soe holly devided
> betwixt you, that I have much a doe to gett leave of it to place any
> other friend of mine there, of then in pitty of this hart . . . doe
> what you can to compasse that happynes for your selfe which I soe
> thirst after, that my dearest friend and you being unighted in ᵒⁿᵉ your
> harts may likewise be come one, and soe I may keepe them with
> more ease in my brest then now I can, they being devided. (28r)

In the playful image of the earlier letter, Constance suggested that a heart that admits others might continue to expand, but here she sets limits: her heart can hold no more than two others, and their lack of unification prevents her from extending her affection elsewhere. In this accretion of metaphors that transform and expand, Constance's letters function like a sonnet sequence: reading a letter or poem without reference to other units in the sequence creates a false limit on the multiplicity of meanings available within that single letter and across the accumulated correspondence. It is not necessary, in other words, to read these letters as a nascent epistolary novel in order to understand them as a whole worthy of literary analysis—they are neither a novel nor a sonnet sequence, but they form a generically flexible text capacious enough to include poetic tropes and narrative sequences.

Constance's letters not only address her own relationship with Herbert and the prospective match between Herbert and Katherine; they also emphasize the friendship that has formed between the two women. Through her writings on this friendship, Constance begins to consider the dangers of earthly affection. Her initial desire for unification, explored in the second image of hearts, develops into later reflections on unworthiness and human frailty like those that haunt Southwellian poetic expressions of love for God. Even as she acknowledges her feelings for Katherine, Constance attempts to remind herself and Herbert that human love cannot (and must not) compare to divine love: "doe you not now beleeve I have reson to love her equell with my soule . . . oh that I were worthy what a unspeakable comfort shuld I injoy all my life if I had her but this world would be too great a Heaven for me and I shuld take so much delight in it, that I feare I shuld have much adoe to perswad my selfe from being sorrow to leave it if I leaft her in it."[36] In these lines, Katherine transforms from a treasure or jewel worthy of Herbert's possession into the equal of Constance's soul. She is capable of producing heaven on earth—and nearly transforms into a heaven herself. Constance thus reverses the trajectory of a poem like "Marie Magdalen's Blush" by elevating rather than repenting earthly love, but pulls back from and acknowledges that reversal as part of a conditional clause: "if" Constance "had her" then the world would become too great a heaven—a possibility that inspires "feare" and remains unfulfilled. Constance models a language of courtship for her brother, but with an important difference: as the beloved friend, Katherine may be incorporated into the devotional life of her admirer without precipitating a sinful act.[37] Constance brings herself and her reader to the edge of a sacrilegious displacement of heaven and the soul with the beloved, but her adaptation of the love lyric transforms friendship into the basis for a reflection upon appropriate forms of desire and love. Constance's metaphorical explorations of love invoke Southwellian debates over the value of Petrarchism and its dangers, as she progresses from a celebration of intimate love in religious terms to an acknowledgment of the potential dangers of infusing devotional language and imagery into human relationships. But where Southwell imagined the fallen and repentant Magdalene enabling a recuperation of poetry as devotional verse, Constance imagines female friendship mediating between male/female desire and solidifying a community articulated through both poetic and devotional discourse. Her letters thus enable a new perspective on early modern poetry, shifting attention away from the reception of Southwellian poetics and toward the women who refigured his verse in the creation of their own literary materials and communities.

Remembering Donne: Catholic Appropriations of Protestant Poetics

A communal language allowed the Aston-Thimelby circle to maintain its familial ties and devotional identity despite the fact that its members lived "in so different states and though asonder," as Katherine Thimelby wrote of herself and one of her sisters who entered a convent.[38] In everything from the vows taken by individual family members who entered religious orders to the courtship letters written by Constance, these poets and letter writers demonstrated their shared concerns, returning to similar ideas and phrases throughout the middle decades of the seventeenth century. Yet participants in this Catholic coterie also collected and responded to poetry by authors who did not share their doctrinal commitments, including clergymen of the English church. In Constance's miscellany, poems by Ben Jonson, Henry King, Katherine Thimelby, Lady Dorothy Shirley, and many others are gathered together, and Donne appears by name and allusion. The quotations and adaptations of Donne in the miscellany and the family letters underscore the importance of communal literary practice to the reception of individual authors and reveal how Catholic women participated in defining the significance of this most canonical of seventeenth-century poets.

Katherine includes a reference to Donne as a postscript in a letter that also elaborates on Constance's examination of human and divine love.[39] She first describes Herbert's absence as "a deprivation" that "will make us graunt a diference twixt Heavins constant joys and our uncertaine, this makes me content to sofer not to se you, not to here from you, for all things else I vow I would loose for you but that."[40] Katherine thus makes explicit what seemed at first to be absent in Constance's letters: Herbert's future wife values his love above everything *except* the joys of heaven. She follows this revisionary statement with an echo of Constance's early reflection on the respective worth of Aston and a potential beloved: Herbert, according to Katherine, "esteme[s] too much of the unworthy"—herself—but she will not follow him in this for

> I must pay all mine to the worthest which I will alow you are
> though you have erd for my hapines by bestowing love where no
> meret exaacts the lest but so you have exprest the bounty of your
> nature by making that a fre guift which would have bin calld a
> duty where meret livd to have peyd it, beleve I valew all you bestow
> at his full hight though I am ~~un~~ by it made unable to defrey my
> debts thus for my selfe you make me rich but porer for you. (34r)

Katherine elaborates upon Constance's economic metaphors of value, gifts, and debt by suggesting that she does not "meret" Herbert's love: she "pay[s]" while he offers "a fre guift." In a complex rendering of the difference between individuals as distinct economic actors and the couple as an economic unit, Katherine concludes that her relationship makes her richer as an individual but that her value to Herbert diminishes, since he offers what she cannot repay.

As Katherine traces the limits of one particular human relationship, the material form of her letter makes visible the multiple networks within which that relationship was embedded. The letter's primary devotional and emotional content, like so many of the letters written by members of this community, is framed within postscripts and additions that extend the scope of the letter beyond its named author and addressee. Among many other notes, she asks "why did you forget my brother Hary in your leter to me" and "why is your sister Gartrude so angry with me," while extending her "trew honors to [Herbert's] sister" and father ("I am infinitly sory my Lords so ill") (34v). Embedded within conversational references to their family network, Katherine quotes Donne's "The Legacy" to map her own emotional landscape. "How infinite a time will it seme tell I se you," she writes, "for lovers houres are full eternity Doctor dun sayd this but I think it" (34v). In order to delineate her commitment to Herbert, she not only contextualizes their relationship within a series of family associations but also locates it within a broader cultural exploration of the discourse of love. In other words, this paratextual reference to Donne explicitly engages with early modern poetics and builds upon the more allusive and elusive Southwellian reverberations in Constance and Katherine's letters. Dated 13 August and likely written after Herbert's return to England in July 1638 and before their marriage in the fall of that year (she signs her name "Katherine Thimelby" rather than "your hapy wife and servant, Katherin Aston"), this letter does not tell us whether Katherine was reading the printed 1633 or 1635 *Poems* or had access to manuscript collections of Donne's poetry (35v, 37r). But it does tell us that poetry mediated by women—and not just the devotional verse championed by Southwell—was a common language for this nonconformist community.

While Southwell forms an implicit backdrop to Katherine's and Constance's explorations of the possible conflicts between heavenly and earthly love, Donne appears by name in multiple letters and poems written by members of the family. Katherine's quotation of "The Legacy" could seem a strange choice for a member of the minority religion from which John Donne converted in order to become the "Doctor Donne" who preached from the pulpit of St. Paul's and rejected Catholicism in prose works such as *Ignatius his Conclave* and *Pseudomartyr*. Yet the poem's conceits—absence figured as death and hearts exchanged between bodies—chime with the content of the letters and poetry created and collected within the Aston-Thimelby family. In Constance's miscellany, for example, multiple poems explore absence and presence, from an anonymous poem contemplating "exile" in an "accorsed clime" to Henry King's "The Exequy," which Constance titles "D K on the Death of his Wife."[41] The latter inverts the metaphor of absence as death in the first two lines of "The Legacy," which read "When I dyed last, and, Deare, I dye / As often as from thee I goe."[42] King instead figures death itself as a form of temporary geographical separation. The speaker refers to his beloved's death as "thy Exile" and imagines the passage of time in his daily life as a journey toward her: "At night when I betake to rest / Next morne I rise neerer my west / of life: allmost by eight howrs saile."[43] It is perhaps no surprise that Constance, for whom writing letters to distant loved ones was a primary mode of authorship, collected poems that figured absence in a variety of ways.[44] But these poems further reveal that seventeenth-century Catholics' interest in the tropes associated with love lyric was not limited to a devotional rejection of "the follies and fayninges of love." Instead, the metaphors they developed through their authorial and editorial practice figured love in ways that complicated the binary of religious and secular devotion suggested by Southwell's poetic theory: the speaker in King's poem sails toward the beloved but does so cognizant of "Heauens will" (63). He retains the "hope" of one day sitting beside her, which "bids mee goe one / And waite my dissolution / with feare and comfort" (113–15). King's speaker is able to treat death as a temporary separation from his beloved *because* of his faith: he maintains love for his wife and love for God. King himself was a Protestant and the eventual bishop of Chichester, but this seems to have bothered Constance no more than Donne's doctrinal affiliation bothered Katherine. Both of these Catholic women drew on poetry written by clergymen in the English church, and I am suggesting that they did so because of a shared metaphorical vocabulary that offered ways of thinking through ideas and issues already central to the women's own writing.

Tropes crossed confessional and gender lines, and the complex responses to both Southwell and Donne revealed by metaphorical echoes and adaptations in the writings of Constance Aston Fowler, Katherine Thimelby Aston, Gertrude Aston Thimelby, and Winefrid Thimelby demonstrate Catholic women's active role in the dissemination and digestion of what we now read as canonical English literature. An anonymous poem in Constance's collection takes their centrality for granted: "To My Honer'd Sister G.A." celebrates Gertrude for her poetry and points to a connection between the poet/speaker (probably Herbert), his sister, and Donne.[45] The speaker opens the poem with an invocation, asking the muses to help him "sing your great Queenes prayse; in uerse as high, / As strong lin'd donne; the soule of of poetry / Exprest his progresse; and Anatomy" (4–6). Though the speaker imagines Gertrude as queen of the muses, she is nonetheless initially positioned as the object of his Donne-like praise rather than a writing subject and poet in her own right. But as the poem progresses, it becomes clear that instead of standing in for Elizabeth Drury, the woman whose death offered the occasion for Donne's "An Anatomy of the World," Gertrude in fact supplants Donne as her brother's ideal poet:

> no subIect's fitt
> For you to write of but your selfe, no witt
> Able to comprehend you but your owne;
> To write none worthy but your selfe alone:
> I doe confesse that this my contemplation
> Is not my owne; tis but an inspiration,
> which I receaue from you; tis you that giue
> my lines the worth they haue; by you they liue.
> You are the soule of them; and of all uerse. (39–47)

The speaker no longer wishes to be like "strong lin'd donne"; instead, he looks to his sister to infuse his lines—and all verse—with value. This poem demonstrates that the male poetic models for the letters and poems I have been discussing were part of a conversation sustained and often directed by women like Gertrude, whose "witt, and skill / . . . tye / Eternall luster to our familye" (97–102). Ultimately, the speaker disavows his own authorship in favor of his sister's—"all prayse to you is due / For tis not I haue written this tis you"—thereby suggesting an understanding of poetic authorship that might include letter-writing, editorial collection, and the stimulating effects one writer could have on another within or beyond her immediate community (127–28).

The family letters tie together the strands of writing, collection, and influence that comprised this recusant community's authorial practice. While not all the letters are extant, the surviving materials offer a compelling representation of collaborative authorship, from the elaborate metaphors of Constance Aston Fowler and Katherine Thimelby Aston to the incorporation of poems in and among more quotidian details of seventeenth-century life. Sometimes, the scraps of poetry scrawled on the verso of letters communicating family news seem unmotivated: Herbert Aston, for example, copies and then rewrites the first stanza of Donne's "A Feuer" on the back of a letter written to him by his sister-in-law, Winefrid. Like Katherine, who quoted Donne before their marriage not only to describe her own emotional state but also to suggest a difference between poetry ("Doctor dun sayd this") and individual experience and cognition ("but I think it"), her husband explores the limits of Donne's poetry:[46]

> Dr Donne to his wife
> Oh Doe not Dy for I shall hate
> All women so when you are gone
> That you I shall not celebrate
> When I remember you wer one

> By another to his [illeg.]
> Oh doe not Dy, for I shall love
> All women so cause you were one
> Till ~~That~~ I ~~must needs~~ ^{to you} unconstant prove
> <u>& be in Love with every one</u>
> & thinke ~~theas~~ many what you were alone
> & fix some Idoll in your throne
> Thus I a reprobate ~~may~~ ^{shal} doe prove
> & fix sum Idoll in her[overwritten: yr] throne
> Then I perhaps ^{Apostate} unconstant prove
> & fix[47]

Herbert's adaptation of Donne could arguably be traced to biographical circumstances: Winefrid Thimelby began corresponding with Herbert after Katherine's death in 1658, so he had experience with the loss of a wife when he reworked "hate" into "love." But reading this poetic experiment as a straightforward reflection of his life as a widower does little to acknowledge the extent to which poetry could enable explorations of identity, emotion, and faith that arose from a web of textual associations that motivated, preceded, or even replaced lived experience and action. To fully understand Herbert's revision of Donne, we must look again to echoes and repetition, asking what might have prompted him to write *this* poem on the back of *this* letter—for it is not one of the many letters written by family members in the immediate wake of Katherine's death, urging Herbert not to allow grief to overcome him.[48]

The letter is brief: in it Winefrid expresses her "quiet hope-full expectation," occasioned by "such joyes as your last promised, long before ther tyme, . . . to temper the discomfort of our present seperation" (69r).[49] Though she does not name these joys, the reference to their "present" separation suggests a future proximity, and Winefrid describes the paradoxical tension between her pleasure at this possibility and her "great impatience" for the event itself (69r). How, she asks, "shall I reckone the houres, how shall I fall out with tyme for ever, now as too slowe, then I am sure too quicke, after that scarce to bee indured" (69r). Winefrid, like her sister before her, counts hours that move too slowly in anticipation of a future reunion with Herbert. Her language echoes and expands upon Katherine's quotation of Donne on the "infinite" nature of anticipatory time and the feeling that "lovers houres are full eternity" (34v). While it is unlikely Winefrid had access to Katherine's letter, she nonetheless shares a vocabulary with her sister—and their common language explores a set of concerns that would have been familiar to many recusant Catholic families separated due to religious vocations that necessitated exile from home and homeland.[50]

But Herbert did have access to his wife's earlier letter, which was collected along with Winefrid's and found among the family papers at Tixall.[51] What would it mean, then, to imagine that Winefrid's similar understanding of separation reminded him of Katherine's quotation of Donne? While we cannot know with certainty why Herbert copied and adapted Donne's "A Feaver" on the back of Winefrid's letter, the material history of the poem may offer another strand in the textual web created by members of this family network, for "A Feaver" not only addresses the death of a beloved—it also appears immediately after "The Legacy" in Donne's 1633 and 1635 *Poems*.[52] Did reading Winefrid's letter prompt Herbert to return to what Katherine thought about absence, leading him to seek out the full poem in which Donne "sayd" what she felt?[53] If so, upon opening a printed volume of Donne's poetry to read "The Legacy," he would have seen "A Feaver" on the facing page. This reconstruction of Herbert's reading and writing practices, while necessarily speculative, is also consistent with what we have seen of the textual network in which he was embedded. Male and female authors in these recusant families were bound by ties of affection, intermarriage, and shared faith. Together, they created a collaborative writing community, visible today in their responses not only to one another but also to English literary culture and early modern poetic theory, which appeared in materials ranging from original letters and poetic compositions to heterogeneous manuscript compilations. Poetic language in the letters of the Aston-Thimelby circle reveals more than the expression of individual emotion, which has too often been used to dismiss Catholic women's writings as adolescent, inappropriately erotic, or disappointingly personal. Instead, figures, allusions, and paradoxes enabled these writers to negotiate the demands of human ties and religious devotion. The letters and lyrics of the Aston-Thimelbys thus demonstrate how Catholic women grappled with the concerns at the heart of seventeenth-century devotional lyrics in their development of literary communities. Yet it remains difficult to recognize their contributions to the broader discourses in which early modern poetry was embedded: as sophisticated and playful as their texts may be, they are not treated as necessary for a more nuanced understanding of our contemporary canon—an oversight that renders opaque the complexities and contradictions of much early modern literature.

The Vanishing Nuns of Appleton House

The manuscripts of the Aston-Thimelby family suggest a canon in which Southwell and Donne share space with women like Gertrude Aston and Winefrid Thimelby, and collaborative literary communities with monastic associations are recognized as literary arbiters throughout the seventeenth century. Yet female communities in early modern literature are more often represented as dangerous vectors of misdirected devotion, unproductive sexuality, and empty rhetoric than as sites of complex engagement with questions of faith, love, and language. Andrew Marvell's *Upon Appleton House* crystallizes this contradiction in its history of the cloister that preceded the country house. The poem's monastic interlude functions like a romance narrative: the beautiful Isabel Thwaites has been seduced into the convent, only to be rescued by triumphant masculinity in the form of her betrothed, William Fairfax, whose violent disruption of the monastic community simultaneously anticipates, echoes, and compacts English history. This section of the poem, which begins "opportunely" with a glimpse of "that neighbour-ruin" and ends with the claim that "The wasting cloister with the rest / Was in one instant dispossessed," brackets a vibrant collective life within ruined walls and contains events that occurred over years or decades within the speaker's experience of the estate's grounds at a particular moment.[54] Marvell treats the dissolution as if it were coterminous with Thwaites's removal from the temptations of the cloister—collapsing dispossession into a continuous "instant" that follows "thenceforth" from the actions of "the glad youth [who] away her bears / And to the nuns bequeaths her tears" earlier in the same stanza (269, 265–66)—despite the fact that Fairfax and Thwaites married two decades before the Cistercian priory at Nun Appleton was dissolved in 1539.[55]

These formal strategies of containment and erasure place monasticism in the distant past: as England's landscape is transformed and its religious practices reformed, so too religious life within a female community is revealed to be mere fantasy, an "enchantment" with no power left to draw young women or frustrate young men (269).[56] *Upon Appleton House* thus worked a magic of its own, rendering the vitality of female communities in the seventeenth century invisible to generations of readers and scholars,[57] despite the fact that Marvell's portrait of the pre-Reformation convent suggests, in its violent conclusion, the pressing need to continue enacting the dissolution in service of solidifying England's still-contentious religious identity and diminishing the imaginative force of the convents on the continent.[58] This extended, seductive narrative, shoehorned as it is into the midst of a country house poem that drops the "Nun" from "Nun Appleton," makes evident the strain necessary to efface the continued relevance and appeal of faith-based female communities. Even as *Upon Appleton House* contributed to a literary culture that rendered networks of readers and writers associated with the convent inconsequential, it offered a glimpse of countercanonical possibilities that were expressed more fully a decade and a half later, in Margaret Cavendish's *The Convent of Pleasure*. By approaching Marvell's poem with the ongoing lyric engagements of the Aston-Thimelby family in mind, the localized and historicized English monasticism it portrays in 1651 can be understood as a partial reaction to contemporary recusant and monastic networks that spanned England and the continent, offering crucial points of contact and expressions of English identity for recent royalist exiles.

As the continent came to be associated not only with Catholicism-in-exile but also with the court-in-exile, representations of the English monasteries as institutions safely located in the past offered an alternative to an uncertain present of diasporic consciousness. Marvell's poem may touch on only one pre-Reformation convent in its praise of Thomas Fairfax, his family, and his estate, but it is part of a broader interest in the history of England's monasteries, exemplified by Roger Dodsworth's *Monasticon Anglicanum*, a collection of antiquarian materials compiled under Fairfax's patronage and first published after Dodsworth's death by William Dugdale, in 1655.[59] By articulating monastic history in literary terms, *Upon Appleton House* turned away from the threat of contemporary English monasticism abroad even as it invoked a very specific understanding of the feminine embodiment and vocalization of that threat in the person of a rhetorically powerful nun. While Isabel Thwaites remains silent, Marvell lingers over the words of her interlocutor, a nun whom Anne Cotterill describes as "like a persuasive poet": she "weaves a spell of rich plenty but only to disguise poverty and sterility, enchantment and theft."[60] The nun, in other words, uses the tropes of seduction lyrics to draw Thwaites away from, rather than into, heterosexual union and dynastic reproduction. Scholars such as Melissa Sanchez, James Holstun, and Elena Levy-Navarro have shown how the convent in *Upon Appleton House* thus suggests an alternative to "the Protestant ideal of married, procreative sexuality,"[61] focusing especially on the erotic implications of the community's positioning as "a timeless and sinless lesbian idyll."[62] But Marvell's poem does not simply implicate female monasticism in "the polemically familiar inversions and sensualities of Roman Catholicism"[63]—indeed, as Sanchez astutely observes, "Marvell's treatment of the convent as a hotbed of lesbian sex was unusual in early modern England, when religious houses were more commonly satirized as sites of illicit *heterosexual* liaisons."[64] Instead, the conjunction of female community and sociable artistic production in *Upon Appleton House*—including embroidery, singing in the choir, collective prayer, and reading aloud—shows how the temporal distancing and disparagement of female monasticism in the absence of corrupt priests can reveal concerns about precisely the type of female-centered networks of literary production explored earlier in this chapter.

Unlike the ruined abbey in *The Duchess of Malfi*, which prompts Antonio to reflect on the disease of the church and imagine the voice of his dead wife, the convent in *Upon Appleton House* is full of life even in decay. The ruins of the "nunnery" gave "birth" to the current house in a metaphor that, as Alison Shell argues, "brilliantly combines a sense of genealogical inevitability and an anti-Catholic sneer at nuns' bastards": "for," the speaker claims, "virgin buildings oft brought forth" (85–86).[65] But this pejorative metaphor also suggests the vitality of subsequent stanzas, which focus not on architectural ruins but rather on the productivity and pleasure of communal life prior to the dissolution. After invoking "this gloomy cloister's gates," the speaker turns his attention to how "the blooming virgin Thwaites" came to enter the convent (89–90). Marvell's use of internal and end rhyme in this couplet draws attention to a striking shift in tone: the gloomy gates are replaced by the blooming Thwaites, who "oft . . . spent the summer suns / Discoursing with the subtle nuns" (93–94). Alliterative gloom is thus dispelled by an image of a young woman as flower and by the sibilant—and seductive—warmth of the summer sun in which she sits.

While participating in this collective conversation, Thwaites is introduced to the many group activities available in the convent, a space where creative production is interwoven with discourse and lived devotional practice. " 'When we have prayèd all our beads,' " the nun explains, " 'Someone the holy legend reads; / While all the rest with needles paint / The face and graces of the saint. / But what the linen can't receive / They in their lives do interweave' " (121–26). The expressive work of embroidery arises from communal prayer and reading, practices which form the foundation for lives organized by faith and representation.[66] As one nun reads from the "holy legend"—likely Jacobus de Voragine's *Golden Legend*, a collection of saints lives—community members create images in response to the narrative. The nun's use of a definite rather than indefinite article to identify the object of representation ("the saint") suggests that the nuns' embroidery depicts the very saint whose life is being read to them. So, too, that saint serves as a model for the community, as the remnants of representation are woven into their lives. These activities have literary implications, which Marvell foregrounds by associating the nun's seduction lyric itself with needlework: "in these words one to her weaved" (95).[67] While "one" nun weaves the words of seduction, she does so on behalf of the community, positioning her appeal in the first person plural through the insistent repetition of "we," "our," and "us" in this section of the poem.[68] By offering her poetic persuasion in a collective voice, the nun thus creates a connection between the forms of communal labor practiced in the convent and a collective mode of poetic authorship akin to that practiced by members of the Aston-Thimelby family.

Yet the nun eventually turns away from the community's devotional, intellectual, and creative work, and focuses instead on Thwaites as exceptional icon rather than egalitarian community member. She uses conventional poetic appeals—to the "fire" that inspires her speech and the "glory" of Thwaites's beauty—to seduce, rather than to confront the complexities of love and religious worship (137, 143). As a result, she succumbs to the very dangers that Constance and Katherine guard against in their epistolary expressions of love and devotion: rather than interrogating the tropes associated with love poetry, the nun embraces them, thereby revealing the hypocrisy of a religious community that offers to "bend" its "strictly penned" rule to suit the individual (156, 155). The idolatrous implications of the nun's suggestion that Thwaites herself could serve as a model for the embroidered representations of the Virgin Mary thus subsumes the possibility that the convent might serve as a space of creative production in women's control: now, instead of using reading as a spur to representation, community members will simply copy Thwaites's "features" as they sew (134). Sarah Monette has argued that "the nun's speech is disruptive to history . . . for she seeks to woo Thwaites away from the historical world of heterosexual reproduction into an entirely feminine world, where the only things produced are altar cloths."[69] Certainly, Marvell's bracketing of this community and its material and intellectual compositions within a poem that reduces the convent to "quarries," producing only the building blocks of a country house and a Protestant dynasty, suggests that what happened inside monastic walls was of no consequence (88). But the embedded scene of the community at work is nonetheless significant, for to represent a "production economy of the nunnery," even in opposition to the "historical world of heterosexual reproduction" that the poem ultimately supports, is to suggest that such an economy—both "entirely female and entirely in the realm of representations"—might exist in a monastic context.[70] As we have seen, depictions of nuns controlling the materials and modes of representation are unusual in canonical early modern literature, and although Marvell treats both the products of nuns' labor and the conditions of collective production as impediments to the dynastic future that the reader knows Thwaites will fulfill, his poem also acknowledges that an alternative path was once available for literary history.

Yet in locating that alternative literary history firmly in the past and transforming the female community from "nuns" into "gypsies," *Upon Appleton House* denies the possibility that such a path could still exist in seventeenth-century England: no longer central to their country's religious identity, nuns are pushed to the margins of history and associated with wandering, foreignness, and deceit (266–68).[71] To underscore this transformation, Marvell emphasizes the similarities between Thwaites and the young Maria Fairfax, showing how the latter has fulfilled her ancestor's promise without replicating her mistakes.[72] Maria will follow Thwaites into an appropriate marriage, but she will do so without a dilatory interlude amidst a female community that celebrates pleasure and nondynastic modes of reproduction. It is thus no surprise that Maria enters the poem only after the lengthy story of Nun Appleton's monastic history, nor that she is first referred to as "the virgin Nymph" (301).[73] By marking her as a virgin, Marvell associates Maria with Thwaites and the convent that once was: "the blooming virgin Thwaites" (90), who spent her youth within "virgin buildings," among "virgin Amazons" who offered her a new "fresh and virgin bride" each night (86, 106, 186), is supplanted by the "virgin Nymph" who "seems with the flowers a flower to be" (301–2). Maria's superlative virginity displaces the poem's other virgins, both true and false; as the speaker claims in the poem's final stanzas, "all virgins she precedes" (751). She, in other words, "surpass[es] in quality or degree" or "take[s] precedence over" all other virgins.[74] But there is also a shadow logic at work here, in which she "exist[s] before" or is "earlier than" all other virgins.[75] In a poem concerned with temporality—with what is past, what is present, and what is yet to come—this moment suggests hierarchy and succession conspiring to nullify the monastic life: it is not simply past but never truly was, as its foundational virginity is given the lie by Maria's precedence.

The project of writing Catholic women's communities out of literary history was partially dependent on such idealized representations of individual Protestant femininity, as we saw in Puttenham's celebration of Elizabeth and Spenser's representations of her.[76] Maria's exceptional status is contingent upon not only her future marriage and her peerless virginity but also her separation from a space of collective literary production. Rather than participating in prayer, reading, and needlework, Maria creates reflections in "the limpid brook" and in those who gaze upon her (701). She does not write poetry of her own; instead, she inspires it in others only to hinder its expression:

Blest Nymph! that couldst so soon prevent
Those trains by youth against thee meant;
Tears (wat'ry shot that pierce the mind);
And sighs (Love's cannon charged with wind);
True praise (that breaks through all defence);
And feigned complying innocence;
But knowing where this ambush lay,
She 'scaped the safe, but roughest way. (713–20)

While the speaker claims that Maria can "prevent" the "tears," "sighs," and "true praise" of her suitors, *Upon Appleton House* nonetheless represents the poetic language by which they attempt to seduce her. The speaker's parenthetical glosses thus mock the very tropes that Southwell revitalized, suggesting that these figures for love, once supercharged with meaning, have now collapsed under the weight of signification. Where Southwell interrogated the intersections of devotion, seduction, and wounding in his poetry, suggesting both the dangers of the "follies and faynings of love" and the promise of a revitalized poetics of religious love centered on women, Marvell treats such language as a lie. It is a trap from which knowing young women should escape—not an arena for their own poetic and linguistic experiments.

Indeed, even as the poem represents Maria as a source of poetic inspiration for both the fictive youths and the speaker himself, she resists entrance into a discursive community: she can "converse / In all the languages as hers" and yet she never speaks (707–8). Instead, she values the acquisition of languages "for that wisdom, not the noise"—and "affect[s]" that wisdom only "as 'tis heaven's dialect" (710–12). Maria, in other words, possesses both "knowledge" and "virtue," but these qualities are explicitly coded as unproductive: she will not write poetry, read saints' legends, embroider altar cloths, or use her facility in language to seduce (735–36). Instead, she will "with graces more divine / Suppl[y] beyond her sex the line," producing children who will continue the Fairfax dynasty (737–38).[77] Thomas Fairfax broke the entail upon his estates in order to allow his daughter and her heirs to inherit, and the final stanzas of *Upon Appleton House* acknowledge the complexities surrounding Maria's marriage and birthright: "goodness doth itself entail / On females, if there want a male" (727–28). This substitutive logic follows from the rest of the poem, and culminates in the claim that "Fate" will "find a Fairfax for our Thwaites" (747–48). Maria is not only a replacement for the son her father should have had but also a perfected version of the ancestor who mistakenly entered a female community rather than willingly accepting her reproductive fate.

Upon Appleton House thus places the threat of female community squarely in the past, only to repeatedly pull that past into the poem's imaginative present: Maria, the "sacred bud," must be "cut" from her family tree (742), "the Fairfacian oak" (740), in order to be regrafted in marriage—a metaphor that suggestively recalls the "rend[ing]" of the cloister that the poem treated as a direct result of Thwaites's marriage (270).[78] These substitutions and echoes reveal the difficulty of erasing female monastic community from the landscape of England and the homes of men like Fairfax. Rending and cutting leaves its scars, even as our own critical ability to read and recognize those scars has faded with historical distance. When Marvell wrote his poem, for example, the full name of Fairfax's estate of Nun Appleton retained the memory of the nunnery once located there, just as its ruined buildings made that memory tangible.[79] In naming his poem *Upon Appleton House* rather than, say, *To Nun Appleton*, Marvell performed a tenacious act of literary erasure. In comparison to earlier examples of the country house genre, the body of the poem is similarly remarkable for Marvell's refusal to call Fairfax's estate by name: Jonson and Lanyer mention Penshurst and Cookham in the first lines of their respective poems, while Carew waits only until the fifth to invoke Saxham. The title of Marvell's poem reified the project of erasure embedded in its content: monastic associations disappear as the country house poem invokes a history of female community only to repeatedly deny its efficacy or its longevity, thereby negating the continued importance of the convent not simply as an alternative to marriage but as a space, both real and imaginative, that helped to enable women's participation in seventeenth-century literary culture.

Pleasure Meets Piety: Literary Culture in the Convent

Over the past three decades, scholars have shown how women—even those with various forms of privilege (social, educational, religious)—confronted both explicit proscriptions on publication and the more pernicious gendering of print.[80] More recent critics have demonstrated that these impediments to women's writing, while certainly active in early modern culture, have too often been taken as determinative—much like the hyperbolic rhetoric of the anti-Catholic materials I surveyed in earlier chapters.[81] We now know that admonitions to be chaste, silent, and obedient constituted just one of many ways of thinking about women in the early modern period, for even as the recovery of women's writing continues, we already have ample evidence of its richness and variety. Yet literary coteries that centered on women, whether Catholic or Protestant,[82] were rarely represented in imaginative literature, regardless of their importance to the production and dissemination of that literature.[83] And while female poets, including members of the Aston-Thimelby circle such as Katherine Thimelby Aston and Lady Dorothy Shirley, illuminated the conditions of poetic exchange within their manuscript verses to one another, the complexity of collective female literary engagement rarely appeared in print.[84] As a result, competing representations overshadowed the significance of the convent and the literary networks to which its members contributed, just as Marvell's idealized portrait of Maria Fairfax as virginal paragon took precedence over Isabel Thwaites's sojourn in a female community. Margaret Cavendish, duchess of Newcastle, provides an exception to this general rule and to its specific illustration in *Upon Appleton House*.

Cavendish was not the only one of her contemporaries to explore the possibility of female community in print, but she did so with a difference: rather than proposing an educational institution, like Mary Astell's Protestant nunnery, or writing lyrics to female friends, like Katherine Philips, Cavendish offered compelling depictions of female community as the impetus for intellectually engaged and generically heterogeneous literary production.

Many critics have addressed Cavendish's generic flexibility and her representation of communities of women, but few have recognized that her interest in all-female spaces—convents, single-sex churches, solitary anchorholds—is deeply inflected with Catholicism.[85] While on the continent during the 1640s and 1650s, first as a maid of honor to Henrietta Maria, England's Catholic queen, and then as the wife of William Cavendish, Margaret Cavendish encountered not only the flourishing baroque aesthetic of the post-Tridentine church but also previous generations of English exiles living in Paris and Antwerp. The Cavendishes spent most of their exile—a period that overlapped with both Marvell's writing of *Upon Appleton House* and the ongoing epistolary exchanges of the Aston-Thimelby family—in Antwerp, where they lived next to the English Carmelite convent.[86] Her proximity to contemporary women who had withdrawn from the world to practice their faith may have inspired her fascination with the figure of the anchoress, expressed in her stated desire to "inclos[e] my self like an Anchoret"—a surprising point of reference for a late seventeenth-century Protestant Englishwoman.[87] Jennifer Summit has noted how "the appeal of the anchoress lies in her isolation, which Cavendish reproduces as the condition of her own writing," and yet I would suggest that Cavendish represents something quite unlike the condition of her own writing in her fictional texts.[88] Rather than the solitary writing woman invoked in her self-presentation, Cavendish's female author figures are surrounded by other women. In *The Convent of Pleasure*, Lady Happy authorizes the creation of a convent and the literary productions that take place within its walls, from domestic satire to pastoral interlude. She does so as part of a community of women who participate in the convent's literary culture, housed within an enclosure that redeems condemnations of monastic excess in its celebration of luxurious comfort as the basis for female pleasure and self-determination. This play thus reveals that the centrality of Catholic women to English literary culture was recognized by contemporary Protestant writers—and not only in the attempts to imagine it away or imagine it otherwise.

When Lady Happy creates a monastery devoted to Nature—not "a Cloister of restraint, but a place for freedom"—Cavendish provides her with a series of interlocutors who question her intentions.[89] Madame Mediator and the men who had hoped to compete for Lady Happy's hand in marriage suggest that the convent is a flawed model for a pleasurable retreat from the world, both because it is fundamentally a religious institution, and because it excludes men, "whose conversation is thought the greatest Pleasure" (220). These are mild critiques compared to the pamphleteers' vitriolic attacks on nuns' faith and chastity and Marvell's suggestions of idolatry and a flexible rule, but they are rooted in similar assumptions about appropriate female roles and desires in Protestant England: women should remain under the authority of a father or husband in order to ensure female chastity and patriarchal stability, and the benefits of companionate marriage are such that they should want nothing else. Cavendish's play exploits the fear that women might have other desires and pleasures, and in so doing transforms the accusations of religious hypocrisy ubiquitous to monastic satire into the material inspiration for her non-Catholic convent. Where pamphleteers such as Lewis Owen depict nuns financing the rich appetites of male monastics, claiming that "Jesuites, Monks, and Friers. . . . worke upon the flexible nature of women, to perswade them to wilfull povertie, that they may bee enriched with their Gifts and Legacies, and have their Colledges and Cloisters augmented with their Lands and Revenues," Cavendish inverts this gendered power dynamic in her portrait of a motley assortment of younger sons desperate for the wealth Lady Happy encloses within her walled community.[90] Instead of relinquishing her property, Lady Happy offers sumptuous descriptions of the pleasures associated with it, many of which sound as if they were borrowed from the Protestant propaganda of authors like Owen, who expounded at length on monastic luxury:

All these former Orders, or Sects of *Monks* and *Friers*, doe abound
in riches, and doe more resemble Princes than Religious men. . . .
Haue they not all the pleasures that the Country can afford? Doe
they not feed on the choisest meat and drink, yea carouse of the
purest wine (in bowles and goblets of gold and siluer) that can
be got for money? Haue they not their Orchards stored with the
delicatest fruits that can be had? Oh how are their Gardens
contriued with pleasant walkes, and furnished with infinite varietie
of sweet and medicinable herbes and roots, and with most curious

and costly fountaines, springs, statues, groues and thickets? Doe
they not rest vpon beds of downe, and pure sweet linnen? How are
their Celles hanged with cloth of Arras, and other curious and
costly tapistrie? Haue they not their white Island dogges, munkies,
parots, and other prating birds, to sport and recreate themselues
withall? . . . . Haue they not their Monasteries, Orchards, Gardens,
walkes, groues, fountaines, and fish-ponds compassed about with a
high thicke stone or bricke wall, to the end that none may discouer
their secret knaueries, or participate of their pleasant walkes? . . . .
And is this (judge you) to forsake the world, to mortifie the flesh,
and to spend the time in holy meditations and prayers? Or is it not
to carry the world, and all the pompe, pleasures and concupis-
cences thereof with them into their Cloisters and Monasteries?[91]

The features of the monastic landscape that Owen enumerates are repeated
almost exactly by Madame Mediator, when she explains to the frustrated
younger sons why Lady Happy has no need of visitors to the convent: "she
has so much compass of ground within her walls, as there is not only room
and place enough for Gardens, Orchards, Walks, Groves, Bowers, Arbours,
Ponds, Fountains, Springs, and the like; but also conveniency for much Pro-
vision" (223). Madame Mediator's list is more extensive than Owen's, and
Lady Happy further elaborates upon this description of self-sufficiency:

I have such things as are for our Ease and Conveniency; next for
Pleasure, and Delight. . . . in the Spring, our Chambers are hung
with Silk-Damask. . . . In the Summer I have all our Chambers
hung with Taffety, and all other things suitable to it, and a Cup-
board of Purseline, and of Plate, and all the Floore strew'd every
day with green Rushes or Leaves, and Cisternes placed neer our
Beds-heads, wherein Water may run out of small Pipes made for
that purpose. . . . In the Winter our Chambers must be hung with
Tapestry, and our Beds of Velvet, lined with Sattin. . . . and our
Sheets, Pillows, Table-Clothes and Towels, to be of pure fine
Holland, and every day clean. . . . and my Gardens to be kept
curiously, and flourish, in every Season of all sorts of Flowers, sweet
Herbs and Fruits, and kept so as not to have a Weed in it, and all
the Groves, Wildernesses, Bowers and Arbours pruned. . . . Also,
we will have the choisest Meats every Season doth afford . . . and

all our Drinks fresh and pleasing: Change of Garments are also
provided, of the newest fashions for every Season, and rich Trim-
ming; so as we may be accoutred properly, and according to our
several pastimes: and our Shifts shall be of the finest and purest
Linnen that can be bought or spun. (224–25)

The excerpts I have provided here offer only a small sample of the variety,
extent, and ingenuity of Cavendish's material imagination. In representing
her ideal female community, it is as if she sought out the most derisive depictions of monastic excess only to reject the paucity of the pamphleteers' vision.
Why simply use the best of everything, when you can do so with seasonal
variation: the best, multiplied by four?

As we have seen, critiques of Catholic excess were everywhere in early
modern English culture, but Cavendish did not shy away from associating
her convent of pleasure with either the monastic luxuries condemned in Protestant propaganda or the materiality of baroque aesthetics. Yet while a handful of recent critics have examined how Cavendish's time on the continent
shaped her fascination with Catholicism's material culture, often such readings
work to distance Cavendish from an interest in devotional practice or the
continuing tradition of English Catholicism. In an important reading of
Cavendish's encounter with "Catholic sensibilities on the continent," for example, Sara Mendelson argues that "Cavendish responded to the medium
rather than the message, the sensual and aesthetic appeal of Baroque Catholicism. What attracted her was the cultivation of luxury, magnificence,
and conspicuous display."[92] Both she and Julie Crawford address convents
"established to cater to the comfort and entertainment of a wealthy well-
educated elite" as possible inspirations for *The Convent of Pleasure*.[93] Crawford
focuses on two former convents, St. John's Abbey and Welbeck Abbey, that
were transformed into the homes of the Lucas and Cavendish families, as
well as Henrietta Maria's new foundation in Chaillot, but her call for a criticism that examines "the specific role of the *convent* as a site for these female
coteries" nonetheless elides the English convents on the continent that were
sites of female literary communities during the period when Cavendish was
living and writing in Antwerp.[94] Nicky Hallett's work corrects this critical
tendency by pointing out that the Cavendish residence in Antwerp was "only
a garden away from the English Carmelite convent" and that Margaret
Cavendish participated in the monastic clothing ceremony of one young
Englishwoman.[95] Hallett is primarily interested in the sensory experience of

convent life as expressed in the nuns' writing, and thus does not address how Cavendish's proximity to a contemporary English convent and her interaction with a future nun shaped her interest in female withdrawal from the world, but the attention Hallett draws to "these two spatially connected, at times radically divergent, sensory and intellectual worlds" is essential to understanding the significance of Cavendish's imaginative representation of life within convent walls—a life nominally devoted to "physical and material pleasure" but in fact deeply invested in community formation, social critique, and literary engagement.[96]

When Lady Happy describes the pleasures associated with her new convent, neither literary materials nor books of any kind are included in her exhaustive list of bedclothes, wall hangings, linens, food, pictures, flowers, gardens, and clothing. These luxuries, which we have seen Protestant pamphleteers contend were part of the hypocrisy of monastic life, provide the structure for Lady Happy's foundation, where all things are ordered for "Ease and Conveniency; next for Pleasure, and Delight" (224). In embracing physical comforts, Lady Happy explicitly rejects the religious ideology that her interlocutors claim must accompany female enclosure, but leaves space for a more flexible form of worship. Madame Mediator contends that "those that incloister themselves, bar themselves from all other worldly Pleasures" and associates monasticism with devotional asceticism: "when the Mind is not imployed with Vanities, nor the Senses with Luxury; the Mind is more free, to offer its Adorations, Prayers and Praises to the gods" (219). Lady Happy disagrees, arguing that such sacrifices are "not for the gods sake, but for opinion's sake" (219). She believes that "when the Senses are dull'd with abstinency, the Body weakned with fasting, the Spirits tir'd with watching, the Life made uneasie with pain, the Soul can have but little will to worship: only the Imagination doth frighten it into active zeal, which devotion is rather forced then voluntary" (219). Such deprivations lead to a parody of devotional lyric: "their prayers rather flow out of their mouth, then spring from their heart, like rain-water that runs thorow Gutters, or like Water that's forced up a Hill by Artificial Pipes and Cisterns" (219). This is tears poetry *in extremis*, and Lady Happy claims that it suggests gods who "take pleasure in nothing but in the torments of their Creatures"; in her theology, on the contrary, "the gods are bountiful, and give all, that's good, and bid us freely please our selves in that which is best for us: and that is best, what is most temperately used, and longest may be enjoyed, for excess doth wast it self, and all it feeds upon" (220). Far from a simple rejection of divinity or faith, Lady Happy offers an alternative to religious ideologies that deny aesthetic pleasure and devotional joy. This "Doctrine," as Madame Mediator calls it, is neither Protestant nor Catholic: despite her interest in Catholic aesthetics and her denial of an association between monasticism and either abstinence or excess, Cavendish is not making a case for a particular post-Reformation religious affiliation (220). Instead, she argues for the possibility of a female community void of neither aesthetic delights nor religious devotion—an idealized portrait of monastic life that nonetheless approaches the practice of recusant literary coteries.

Lady Happy's rationale for her convent reveals that physical comforts are not the end of her foundation but its means: wealth and the luxuries it can afford enable a female community that produces multiple forms of pleasure, including social, devotional, and intellectual. And yet her detailed argument for female community, which ranges from a theological justification for the pursuit of joy to a critique of the gender system whose hierarchies mean that "Men are the only troublers of Women," concludes with a lyric that returns to the variety of material delights available within the convent: "*each Season shall our Caterers be, / To search the Land, and Fish the Sea; / To gather Fruit and reap the Corn / That's brought to us in Plenty's Horn*" (220–21). In her celebration of how "*Variety each Sense shall feed,*" Lady Happy implies that the senses she is most concerned with are "the faculties of corporeal sensation considered as channels for gratifying the desire for pleasure and the lusts of the flesh" (221).[97] But this country house poem in miniature begins by suggesting a more capacious understanding of the senses: "*For every Sense shall pleasure take, / And all our Lives shall merry make: / Our Minds in full delight shall joy, / Not vex'd with every idle Toy*" (220–21). The physical senses are here joined with the "faculties of the mind or soul," those incorporeal senses that perceive and create.[98] This is the first of many literary interpolations within *The Convent of Pleasure*, and its exploration of variety and the senses offers an important supplement to the dialogue between Lady Happy and Madame Mediator regarding the convent's mission. By broadening the definition of the senses to include those faculties that produce mental delight, this poem reveals that literature contributes to the imaginative variety of the convent, even though Lady Happy never mentions its importance to her foundation. Her choice of genre, though, is telling: the country house poem offers a catalogue of physical delights in praise of a patron and the bounty of his or her estate, written by a poet who is marginal to the social milieu he or she describes—as we saw in Marvell's *Upon Appleton House*. Yet Lady Happy is both patron

and poet, producing not only corporeal pleasures but also the lyric that celebrates them, and her authorial position reveals that the play as a whole is
fundamentally concerned with literature itself as a product of the convent
and one of its chief pleasures.

For Cavendish, the pleasure of literature lies not only in its aesthetic
beauty, which Southwell critiqued when devoid of religious truth, nor in its
ability to entertain its audience. Instead, following classical and contemporary
literary theory, Cavendish represents literature's ability to delight and instruct.
Soon after the Princess, who will later be revealed to be a Prince, arrives at
the convent, s/he is greeted with a series of vignettes labeled "a Play" whose
epilogue reveals a didactic thrust (231): "*Marriage is a Curse we find, | Espe-
cially to Women kind: | From the Cobler's Wife we see, | To Ladies, they unhap-
pie be*" (233). While the lessons included in this play produced and performed
by members of the convent may seem like a radical departure from the sensual delights featured in Lady Happy's country house poem, these vignettes
are in fact sensible elaborations upon her lyric celebration of variety. The nine
scenes feature characters identified only as "Woman," "Lady," "Maid," or
"Gentleman," and there is no apparent logic to their organization. While plot
elements in one scene sometimes resurface in another (a woman cries out for
a midwife in Act 3 Scene 7, and we learn in Act 3 Scene 9 that a midwife has
arrived to help a woman because her previous patient died in childbirth), the
play as a whole is more concerned with sketching a broad portrait of life as a
woman in the seventeenth century than with presenting a linear narrative:
the female characters are plagued by drunken, gambling, adulterous and
spendthrift husbands; death in childbirth; the death of children; criminal
sons; runaway daughters; and threats of rape or divorce. Variety is prominent
here, but these are all variations on a single theme: Lady Happy's foundational claim that "Men are the only troublers of Women" (220). And rather
than inspiring delight, the play provokes censure: when Lady Happy asks
the Prince/ss how s/he "like[s]" the play, s/he does not use the language of
pleasure or liking in response (233). "I cannot in conscience approve of it,"
s/he replies, "for though some few be unhappy in Marriage, yet there are
many more that are so happy as they would not change their condition" (233).
In one sense, this is an appropriate response: the Prince/ss offers an intellectual and moral consideration of the play's didacticism. But by flattening the
many issues represented in the vignettes to a simple dichotomy of happy
and unhappy marriages, the Prince/ss rejects not only the lesson of the play
but also its form. This is not a dialogue, offering two sides of a single issue,

and the Prince/ss's either/or formulation denies the heterogeneity of these loosely connected vignettes. The variety represented by this play builds upon Lady Happy's monastic vision while simultaneously suggesting a generic range and a literary project only hinted at in her authorial imagination. This play within the play is the first of many "Sports and Recreations" written, directed, and performed by other members of the convent community, and its juxtaposition with Lady Happy's country house poem demonstrates how literature feeds the senses with variety.[99] The women of the convent embrace the sensual and the intellectual, creating lyric encomiums to material pleasures alongside dramatic domestic satires critiquing the early modern gender system (239).

In *The Convent of Pleasure*, Cavendish represents a literary practice akin to that of the Aston-Thimelby circle: women writing across multiple genres, influenced by both secular and religious traditions, and contributing to a communal literary culture. While the literature produced by denizens of the Convent of Pleasure is resolutely not devotional, its generic variety—country house poem, domestic satire, pastoral, masque—matches a similar diversity in the writings of early modern Catholic Englishwomen. In this book alone, I have examined life writing, letters, polemic, lyric poetry, spiritual devotions and prayers—a small sample of the generic range on display in Caroline Bowden's field-defining *English Convents in Exile, 1600–1800*, a six-volume set of primary materials written in and about the convents.[100] The extent to which English nuns and recusant women were engaged in literary culture appears only obliquely in *The Convent of Pleasure*, which avoids any explicit mention of Catholicism or intervention into doctrinal controversies. But Cavendish nevertheless points to convents not only as places of female community and refuge from men but also of literary creation. By recognizing that the convent could be an intellectually productive space for women and not confining it to the past, Cavendish reveals that the depraved monastic communities discursively created in the pages of Protestant propaganda (and subsequently dismantled in texts created at the convents) were not the only representations available to early modern authors.[101]

But Cavendish's vision of the convent as a utopian literary community is only a brief interlude in a patriarchal system that replaces collective female authorship with the heroic couplets of a fool. Following the explicit social critique of the convent's first play, subsequent performances are increasingly oriented around a courtly culture centered on Lady Happy and the Prince/ss. Critics have identified a strain of "respectful nostalgia for the feminocentric

Caroline court culture" underlying the pastoral interlude and masque of Act 4, and Henrietta Maria's influence as a patron offers an important analogue for Lady Happy's role within the convent community.[102] Yet the tenor of these later productions suggests a movement away from the convent's founding principles: while the other women within the convent continue to participate in the creation and performance of lyrics, their searing critique of married life is replaced by a pastoral song "In honour of our dancing Queen and King" (238). As Erin Lang Bonin argues, "the players discard separatist discourse to stage a pastoral scene that enacts heterosexual paradigms for desire. . . . The pastoral production obliterates the 'Varieties' of pleasure that animate earlier moments in the play."[103] The masque, which features the Prince/ss as Neptune and Lady Happy as an unnamed Sea Goddess, moves still further away from the remarkable heterogeneity of the satirical vignettes: a dialogue between Neptune and the Sea Goddess replaces the profusion of voices and characters in the earlier play, and the only other woman to speak is a sea nymph who sings a song on behalf of the community: "*We Watery Nymphs Rejoyce and Sing / About God* Neptune *our Sea's King*" (242). The Prince/ss first joins and then replaces Lady Happy as the center of the convent community. While the entertainments themselves may be modeled on the masques of Henrietta Maria performed at the Stuart court, Cavendish nevertheless discards a feminocentric model of collective authorship in favor of masculine authorization for women's speech.

This shift in focus is confirmed in Act 5, when the Prince/ss is revealed to be a Prince and his marriage proposal and threat of violence, should it not be accepted, are directed at "the Councellors of this State" rather than Lady Happy herself (243). The barely submerged autocratic implications of the Duke's proposal to Isabella in *Measure for Measure* here rise to the surface, only to be smoothed over by the matrimonial ending Shakespeare never grants his audience. Lady Happy becomes a Princess, and though the convent arguably remains intact after the wedding, her property is no longer under her control. Instead, the Prince and the fool Mimick conclude the play by bantering about the appropriate organization for the community.

> *Mimick.* I have an humble Petition to your Highness.
> *Princ.* Rise; What Petition is that?
> *Mimick.* That your Highness would be pleased to divide the
>   *Convent* in two equal parts; one for Fools, and th' other for
>   Married Men, as mad Men.

Princ. I'le divide it for Virgins and Widows.

Mimick. That will prove a *Convent of Pleasure* indeed; but they will
    never agree, especially if there be some disguised Prince amongst
    them; but you had better bestow it on old decrepit and bed-rid
    Matrons, and then it may be call'd the *Convent of Charity*, if it
    cannot possibly be named the *Convent of Chastity*. (246)

The Prince resists the fool's petition, but he does offer him an unnamed present in exchange for performing the epilogue. The variety and invention of
Lady Happy's convent is thus reduced to a final poem by a Mimick, who
tropes on tears in precisely the way Lady Happy rejected early in the play: as
the signs divorced from meaning that Marvell mocked in his representation
of Maria Fairfax's suitors. Despite his claims of *"Grief"* and *"sorrow"* in the
epilogue, Mimick composes it only after deciding that "words are nothing,
and then an *Epilogue* is nothing, and so I may speak nothing; Then nothing
be my Speech" (247, 246). The poem's image of *"Floods of Tears, that Through
[his] Eyes will flow"* if the play receives no praise thus aligns him with those
whom Lady Happy critiqued for prayers that "rather flow out of their mouth,
then spring from their heart, like rain-water that runs thorow Gutters" (247,
219). As in *Upon Appleton House*, this is anti-Southwellian tears poetry: it
reverses Southwell's modification of Petrarchism by emptying his most
powerful metaphor of its emotional heft and spiritual significance. Lady
Happy's dream of a space for women not impeded by counterfeit devotion,
where literature flows freely as the expression of feelings, is thus expunged in
a final lyric that simultaneously denies the power of recusant poetics and of
female community.

Mimick's poem illuminates the twinned losses of *The Convent of Pleasure*'s conclusion: the loss of a separate, pleasurable space for women and of
the exhilarating literature produced by those women. As such, it reveals a
play at odds with itself. The central acts of *A Convent of Pleasure* depict female community as an engine of literary creation, and while that vision
erodes over the course of the play, the women's literary endeavors—especially
their vignettes depicting women, marriage, childbirth, and family—remain
indelible even after the final scene's celebration of marriage. The play is thus
not simply a paean to or elegy for the possibility of life without men; it is also
an important intervention into a contemporary conversation regarding what
convents were, are, and could be. Cavendish writes in the wake of condemnations of the convent as either prison or brothel, and decades before Mary

Astell's call for "a *Monastry* . . . being not only a Retreat from the World for those who desire that advantage; but likewise, an institution and previous discipline, to fit us to do the greatest good in it."[104] Yet even Cavendish's celebratory representation of female monasticism, which may have been inspired by the convents she encountered on the continent, falls short of the dynamic devotional and literary practice of seventeenth-century English nuns and recusant women. In their own writing and in texts written about them, Mary Champney, Margaret Clitherow, the sisters of Syon, Gertrude More, Barbara Constable, Constance Aston Fowler, Katherine Thimelby Aston, Gertrude Aston Thimelby, Winefrid Thimelby, and many others reveal contradictions and complexities that help to enrich our understanding of early modern English Catholicism, female monasticism, and the many alternative paths through literary history.

Epilogue.
Failures of Literary History

One Crucifixion is recorded – only –
How many be
Is not affirmed of Mathematics –
Or History –

—Emily Dickinson

In attending to poetry and prose, to print culture and manuscript archive, to country house and cloister, the boundaries between center and margin in English literary history no longer obtain. A more capacious narrative of early modern literature, grounded in Catholic women's prolific manuscript and print texts and their shaping influence on canonical authors, necessitates a reevaluation not only of individual plays and poems but also of the forms and genres that constitute that literature. This Epilogue traces one prominent early modern subgenre, the Passion poem, in order to show how the recognition of Catholic women's crucial perspectives on early modern literary culture enables a reciprocal recognition of how the multiple perspectives embedded in canonical literature point to a more expansive and inclusive literary history. In Passion poems written over the course of the seventeenth century, the simultaneity of divinity and humanity in the body of Christ prompted explorations of the limits and possibilities of poetic sympathy. By probing the divine mystery of incarnation, poets confronted the incomprehensible and attempted to make it available through representation. This enabled the recognition and inhabitation of other forms of difference: authors such as John Donne, George Herbert, and an anonymous author in Constance Aston Fowler's manuscript miscellany approached Christ's death from a variety of lyric subject positions, creating poems in which confessional and gender identities are less significant than the spatial and temporal perspectives from which one is able to view, and attempt to comprehend, the crucifixion.

Where is the poetic speaker located? Does he or she look to the past, the present, or the future? And how does the speaker imagine his or her relationship to the witnesses of Christ's death? Building on Louis Martz's foundational reading of the importance of Ignatian meditation and especially its "composition of place" to seventeenth-century religious lyric, I show how early modern poets responded to and reoriented this practice in poems that reveal the necessity of multiplying the contexts and perspectives that shape our readings of early modern literature.[1] As Emily Dickinson would later intimate, the multiplicities of Christ's crucifixion are not accessible through math or history, yet the final lines of her poem suggest that even beyond Christ's "Compound Witness" there are "newer – nearer Crucifixion / Than That – " (13, 15–16). In attempting to create this sense of immediacy and nearness to Christ's sacrifice, Dickinson's poetic predecessors mapped circuitous paths to the truths only partially available to history and science, guided by flexible understandings of gender and confessional identity that contemporary scholarship has only recently begun to recollect.[2]

Passion poems explore the possibility of access to the ineffable in an appropriately paradoxical fashion, offering the promise of entrance into a divine mystery only to deny the reader a singular and complete understanding of even Christ's sufferings on the cross. The genre reached an apotheosis in John Milton's famously incomplete "The Passion," which repudiates the tradition by adamantly refusing either access to the divine or separation from a singular poetic perspective. More than one critic has claimed that "The Passion" is a poem about failure and poetry, suggesting that Milton "is concerned to depict not the Passion but the psychological state of a speaker who is attempting—without success—to become inspired about that event."[3] Such a reading is tempting. Milton's explanatory note certainly points us in this direction: "*This subject the author finding to be above the years he had when he wrote it, and nothing satisfied with what was begun, left it unfinished.*"[4] And treating "The Passion" as a poetic exploration of the limits of human imagination and especially of the imaginative spiritual exercises that helped to shape earlier Passion poems helps explain the speaker's manifest difficulty in depicting the details of Christ's crucifixion—or, rather, his refusal to do so.[5] Yet it also does too much to create coherence where the material of the poem actively resists it, alleviating the discomfort attendant upon even self-proclaimed authorial insufficiency. What if we instead recognize "The Passion" as a failure? Not simply a deliberate failure—though certainly the choice to print the poem in 1645 and 1673 was deliberate—nor a poem about failure, but a genuine and emblematic failure of literary history?

For in proclaiming his poem a failure, Milton effaced the nuances of a poetic tradition that suggested not a simple, readily available truth but many truths—and one that worked to cultivate not complete knowledge of the divine but human sympathy and separation from the narcissistic demands of the self. This Epilogue will survey how seventeenth-century poetry approaches the crucifixion within space, time, and from a variety of lyric subject positions in order to suggest that Milton's denial of a thriving poetic genre has proved persistent in part because we have followed him in valuing the singular, the central, and the coherent above the multiple, the marginal, and the divergent. Reading Milton's poem in relationship to not only Donne and Herbert but also the very type of poem most critics have claimed it fails in order to critique—one situated within a specifically Catholic devotional context that locates, witnesses, and responds to the suffering of the crucifixion—reveals how the failure of a particular poem or genre relates to larger failures of literary history. Milton's poem suggests a theologically motivated crisis of representation that comments on both failure and poetry through an aesthetic and formal interrogation of the poetics of multiplicity and transformation shared by authors and manuscript compilers across confessional divides. While Milton's speaker acknowledges and incorporates the tradition of which he should be a part, he does so without accepting the radical displacement of self in space, in time, and in subjectivity that was central to the seventeenth-century manifestations of that tradition, thereby shattering the prismatic light shed on the others who participated in it. This poetic failure thus succeeds in denying a place to the multiple perspectives on religion and poetry that earlier Passion poems embraced and inhabited, including the perspectives of women associated with Catholic devotional practice.

*   *   *

The title of Donne's "Good Friday, 1613. Riding Westward" suggests that the details of temporal and spatial location are essential to understanding poetic responses to the Passion. Donne's speaker is located precisely in time—not just on the day commemorating Christ's crucifixion, but in a specific year—while his physical location is in flux: he moves from east to west, with his back turned on the location and person of God. The transitional nature of Donne's speaker is at the heart of this poem, which opens with the conceit of man's soul as a sphere, moved by "pleasure or business" rather than by its "first mover" (7–8).[6] The speaker moves away from God rather than allowing himself to be moved by him, and this itinerant perspective results in a lack of vision: the speaker "should see" the image of Christ's crucifixion, which is figured first metaphorically, as "a Sun, by rising, set, / And by that setting endless day beget" (11–12), and then literally: "But that Christ on this cross did rise and fall / Sin had eternally benighted all" (13–14). But despite the poem's doubled depiction of the event, the speaker nonetheless claims not to *see* it. Indeed, he dares "almost be glad I do not see": for to see God would be death, and even if it were not, it would surpass the limits of human perception (15).

The middle section of the poem proceeds as a series of questions: "Could I behold," the speaker asks "those hands which span the poles . . . . Could I behold that endless height which is / Zenith to us, and our antipodes, / Humbled below us?" (21–25). These are questions with implied answers, but the speaker does not offer them, and his silence suggests that there are no satisfying solutions to the problems his questions pose. To ask "What a death were it then to see God die?" contains a paradoxical answer within itself: it is both death and life to see God die. So, too, the questions about whether the speaker can behold God's hands and height: face, hands, and height are all equally unseeable and unknowable, and these questions together point to the impossibility of actually comprehending God, even with the Ignatian "eyes of the imagination" that should enable meditation on his suffering (18).[7] Like Milton's "The Passion," then, Donne's "Good Friday" is in some sense about failure: about what we cannot perceive, understand, or know, even if we face the incarnation and sacrifice directly, which this speaker repeatedly claims he will not do.

Instead, he considers an indirect perspective on the crucifixion: if the speaker "durst not look" on Christ, might he instead "Upon his miserable mother cast mine eye, / Who was God's partner here, and furnished thus / Half of that sacrifice which ransomed us?" (29–32). This is the poem's final question and, like those that precede it, it receives no direct response. Yet it differs from those earlier questions in a way that suggests the importance not only of temporal and spatial location but also the significance of alternate subjectivities. The question about Mary is not a question of whether the speaker is *capable* of beholding the Virgin, but a question of whether he dares "cast [his] eye" upon her. He can physically turn his eyes to her—which he knows he should do toward Christ, even though such a turn would not enable him to behold him fully—but does he dare? A turn to Mary is possible, but is it acceptable, meaningful, efficacious? The possible answers to this question are multitude, but our speaker abandons it and all questions in its wake. Mary, and the problem of whether to look to her in order to gain perspective on Christ's suffering, puts an end to the speaker's troubled attempt to reconcile the incommensurability of his sacrifice.

Thus, in the final lines of the poem, the speaker casts aside his internal debate and returns to his own physicality and mobility: "Though these things, as I ride, be from mine eye, / They're present yet unto my memory" (33–34). It is as if his question about Mary has reminded him of the reality of his current situation, disrupting his unproductive interrogation of the limits of human sight in favor of the possibilities of memory. He is only able to move beyond a frustrated reflection on his own incapacity as witness after reflecting on Mary as God's partner and "half of that sacrifice" (32). Mary is not imagined as an intercessor here; instead, her humanity enables the speaker to remember his own relation to Christ: she is one of "these things" that his memory "looks towards" when his sight fails (33, 35). These final lines of "Good Friday" reveal that the sight of the Passion is not what is required of the speaker; instead, he must abandon himself to Christ's gaze in order to be remade in his image. Only then will he "turn" his face—a conversion enabled by trying and failing to view the crucifixion from multiple perspectives.

Herbert's "The Sacrifice" addresses the central problem of Donne's poem—how might one properly see, remember, and respond to Christ's Passion?—in its opening lines. Here, the speaker is Christ, and he calls on an unseeing humanity: "*Oh all ye*, who passe by, whose eyes and minde / To worldly things are sharp, but to me blinde; / To me, who took eyes that I might you finde" (1–3).[8] These lines read almost like a condemnation of Donne's speaker for precisely what he recognizes in himself: a movement from point A to point B (here, passing by; there, riding away) and a focus on "worldly things" such as pleasure or business, both of which prevent proper recognition of Christ's dual nature and the immensity of his sacrifice. This is the three parts of "Good Friday" condensed into three lines: moving away from God, being blind to his true nature, and recognizing the importance of Christ's gaze on humanity. Herbert thus offers what seems like a more focused poem on the Passion, spoken not by a fallen individual desperate to find a perspective from and with which to view the sacrifice, but by Christ himself. And yet the singularity suggested by the choice of Christ as speaker is everywhere frustrated within the poem: instead of narrowing our focus, Herbert widens it in his consideration of what Christ can see and know.

And so, over the course of the poem, the reader is inundated with the many different reactions to Christ offered by (and this is by no means an exhaustive list) "The Princes of my people," "Mine own Apostle," "my Disciples," "one ruler to another," "Herod," "Pilate," "my own dear people," "the soldiers," "Angels," etc. As Christ moves through the stations of the cross, he critiques and encompasses both those who interact with him and those who look away. This is a singular speaker capable of inhabiting multiple perspectives simultaneously, and Herbert makes this clear when Christ shifts from first person to third, explaining that "The Priest and rulers all false witnesse seek / 'Gainst him, who seeks not life, but is the meek / And readie Paschal Lambe of this great week," only to return to his insistent first-person refrain "Was ever grief like mine?" (57–60). Christ is both inside and outside, able to view his sacrifice as both God and man—and as multiple other men—simultaneously. This multiplicity of perspective produces the irony for which the poem is known: the gap between what Christ knows and what his interlocutors, accusers, and torturers know is revealed through his ability to ventriloquize them and condemn them simultaneously. In a particularly potent example, he describes how "Servants and abjects flout me; they are wittie: / *Now prophesie who strikes thee*, is their dittie. / So they in me denie themselves all pitie" (141–44). The rhyme of witty/ditty/pity suggests that these abjects can sink still lower: for the sake of an empty witticism, they lose the possibility of future grace and mercy. But it is the "they in me" that necessitates pause: Christ emphasizes his incorporation of humanity within himself at the moment of suffering and beyond it. All the "they" in this poem are in him, which suggests that Christ himself reveals the impossibility of attempting to understand the Passion from a single perspective or subject position.

What, then, of those authors or compilers we might expect to be more directly indebted to the Ignatian tradition of meditating on the crucifixion? "On the Passion of our Lord and saviour Jesus," an anonymous poem recorded in Fowler's manuscript miscellany, follows Catholic guides to meditation in its imaginative depiction of numerous scenes leading up to and including Christ's death on the cross. It begins at a specific temporal moment, "when that æternall word, with sacred love / In nature's robes came clothed from a bove," but shifts almost immediately from the past into the present tense, collapsing the time between the incarnation and the "now" of Christ's Passion (1–2).[9] The first-person speaker is barely present in the poem's first twenty lines—just one of many who share "our shape" with Christ—but the vivid depiction of Christ in the garden is interrupted by her startled interjection: "But o where are my sences!" (21). The speaker disrupts what Martz calls the "practices of 'composition' or 'proposing'" that "lie behind the vividly dramatized, firmly established, graphically imaged openings" of early modern poetry (31), and thus calls the reader's attention to those very practices by questioning the location of her sensory perception. Yet unlike Donne's speaker, who is acutely aware of his own location but questions the possibility of beholding Christ, this dislocated speaker reinforces the efficacy of her devotional practice. Even as her senses are unmoored from any precise location, "what strange sight / my soule beholds" (21–22). This is a poem of beholding, as emphatic in witnessing Christ's suffering as Donne's poem was in interrogating the human capacity to do so.

If I were to end here, the relationship among these poems might suggest a doctrinal continuum: from the Catholic devotional lyric of Fowler's miscellany, which draws upon Ignatian spiritual practices,[10] to what Michael Schoenfeldt has identified as a far more conflicted Protestant poetics of the Passion. He argues that "whereas the goal of Catholic meditational writers is to imagine the self in the scenario of the Passion in order to cultivate the extreme passions it arouses, Donne, Herbert, and Milton discover the difficulty of that act of the imagination, and stumble upon the corollary truth that the fitting object of sacrifice is the tacitly arrogant self that would claim to be able to respond appropriately to this event."[11] Schoenfeldt's argument, following Debora Shuger, is that Passion poems enable seventeenth-century authors to "discover a kind of Reformed subjecthood," one in which the psychological effects of the Passion take priority over its emotional impact.[12] And Donne, Milton, and Herbert do confront what Schoenfeldt calls "the idea that the sacrifice inevitably defeats human response," but such an idea is not unique to Protestant poets or compilers in the seventeenth century—and it is certainly not unique to canonical male poets or their male speakers.[13] The affinities among these Passion poems, especially their shared attention to a multiplicity of gendered and confessional perspectives, go beyond the composition of place in locational, emotional, or even psychological terms. Instead, theirs is an affinity achieved through the incorporation of difference.

Like the poems of Donne and Herbert, "On the Passion of our Lord and saviour Jesus" contemplates Christ's sacrifice from multiple subject positions, leading the speaker to acknowledge the necessity of her own sacrifice of self. After recognizing what "my soule beholds," the speaker calls on the reader to "Behold him" and "heere behold" (22, 27, 31). We are on the outside looking in, but this external perspective on the Passion shifts after the speaker turns to Mary: "His poore Afflicted Mother hee had left / Widow'd of all her comforts, and bereft / Of her deere soone; O see her sadly weepe / prepard with teares his funerall to keepe" (57–60). The speaker does "see" Mary, but, as in "Good Friday," Mary initiates a shift in the poem's perspective: for Donne's speaker, Mary returns him to himself, and the realization that Christ must look on him and make him new. In this poem, Mary pulls the speaker deeper into the scene of the crucifixion: she is no longer an external witness, but instead enters into the perspectives of Christ and his apostles. The line immediately following the description of Mary describes how "Hee saw Th'Inraged Jews," and subsequent verbs of sight are attributed to Christ or those who surround him: "griev'd at the sight hee approacheth neere," "seinge their prey so neere," "they looke behinde." When the speaker returns to herself, it is with a new sense of perspective:

> Now I behold, and see my selfe most cleere
> Agent in all that happened to him heere
> My costly clothinge made him naked goe
> My easy lodgings forst his scourginge soe
> My curious Diett Hungar to him brought
> My foolish Joyes presented him sad thoughts
> My pleasures in vaine glory breed his scorns
> My often curlinge weav'd his crown of Thorns. (179–86)

This scene of self-recognition, poised between Christ's trial and his journey to the site of the crucifixion, suggests the importance not just of seeing and witnessing Christ but of recognizing one's own participation in Christ's suffering. Here, that participation is figured in ambiguously gendered terms: the speaker's "often curlinge" of her hair is both the culminating practice identifying her as an "agent in all that happened to him heere" and the poem's primary intimation of the gender of its speaker. By suggesting an embodied female self not associated with Mary or the other women present at Christ's death and waiting until after the poem's midpoint to do so, this anonymous author encourages his or her readers, male and female, to inhabit a subject position rarely available in canonical early modern literature, even as the poem acknowledges that this is only one way of beholding Christ.

"Good Friday," "The Sacrifice," and "On the Passion" are complete in their very recognition of the incomplete comprehension of a fragmented self, displaced in space, time, and subjectivity—a fragmented self that corresponds to the fragmentary and multiple nature of early modern English literature and its many confessional perspectives. By situating Milton's attempt to re-figure the Passion tradition in relationship to these poetic treatments of perspective, we see that Milton rejects not only the possibility of finding a proper perspective from which to view Christ but also the dissolution of self and recognition of others essential to contemplating his sacrifice. Milton's speaker seems incapable even of articulating his relationship *to* Christ. Stanza three of "The Passion" depicts his physical appearance on the cross, but does so without any sense of perspective: who is viewing "He sov'reign priest stooping his regal head" (15)? Verbs of sight are entirely absent from the early stanzas of the poem: the speaker does not suggest that he will behold Christ's suffering but only that he will attempt to sing it. And even when he labels the imagery of stanza three in the first line of stanza four as "scenes" that "confine [his] roving verse," the focus remains on the act of writing poetry rather than witnessing Christ's crucifixion from a particular location, time, or subject position (22). As many critics have pointed out, the first five stanzas of the poem are almost entirely about poetic inspiration and vocation: a self-reflexive exercise that suggests that Christ's supposed centrality is entirely beside the point. But stanza six offers a striking intervention into this solipsistic project: "See, see the chariot and those rushing wheels," the speaker exclaims (36). Sight initiates a displacement of spirit from body, and the soul is transported to "where the towers of Salem stood" to "sit / In pensive trance, and anguish, and ecstatic fit" (39, 41–42). This parody of the "composition of place" indicates that Milton's poem critiques the Passion poem tradition, but it is an unfinished and unstable critique that fails to acknowledge the extent to which displacement—riding east, inhabiting multiple perspectives on the Passion, and turning to one's own fallen humanity—is not a simple matter of location. Marshall Grossman has shown that "unlike the meditative poems of Crashaw and Herbert, which contemplate the intensity of Christ's suffering so as to appreciate the depth of his gift to man and man's need of that gift, Milton's poem dwells on the poet's choice of a place to stand."[14] But, as I have shown, *all* these poets consider the importance of a place to stand—but they do so to radically different ends.

In seventeenth-century Passion poems, even a multiplicity of perspectives enables only a limited recognition of Christ: the depths of his suffering and the mystery of his incarnation are never fully articulated, even when he is the poetic speaker. Milton's "The Passion" sees, recognizes, and critiques this limitation through its parodic and solipsistic focus on poetic inspiration and "a place to stand." But Milton's speaker refuses the turn that Donne, Herbert, and the anonymous poet all make essential: "The Passion" is indeed unfinished, for it refuses to turn Christ's gaze on us or to imagine ourselves from his perspective. By maintaining a singular subject position even as he attempts to view Christ's sacrifice from a variety of physical locations, Milton's speaker rejects the radical attention to perspective that is central to seventeenth-century Passion poems and thereby establishes a pejorative stance from which to view his literary predecessors. This is thus not simply a poem about failure or a poem about poetry and the limits of representation but rather a poem that presents its readers with a genuine failure of imagination: Milton's speaker can offer images of suffering and grief, but he cannot stand outside of himself and offer his fallen humanity to the gaze of Christ or recognize others who would do the same. The speaker is everywhere in this poem dominated by first-person pronouns, but he is ultimately invisible, unwilling to render himself to Christ and the reader for judgment and mercy.

* * *

In the final lines of "The Passion," the speaker turns his gaze more directly on contemporary poetics, breaking the poem off after an image that invokes the tears poetry of Southwell, William Alabaster, and Richard Crashaw: "I (for grief is easily beguiled) / Might think th'infection of my sorrows loud, / Had got a race of mourners on some pregnant cloud" (54–56).[15] These lines may be disassociated from Milton and the taint of failure if they are read as a parodic critique of his fellow poets. Schoenfeldt, for example, suggests that "Milton here sounds like Crashaw on a bad day," before claiming that Milton "could have completed a comparatively slight lyric on the highly conventional subject of the Passion if he had wanted to."[16] Schoenfeldt implies that this unwritten poem would have been far superior to the poem Milton actually wrote, despite the slightness of the genre—and certainly superior to the work of a poet like Crashaw. This critical move recuperates even the flawed poetry of authors upon whom we have conferred canonicity and participates in the continued exile of alternative perspectives from English literary history based on aesthetic judgments that are in fact grounded in early modern religious politics, as Richard Rambuss, Alison Shell, Molly Murray, and others have aptly demonstrated in their arguments for Crashaw as part of the early modern poetic canon.[17]

This important work of returning underappreciated male poets to the canon and recognizing their shaping influence on early modern literature has, though, had an unfortunate side effect: in disputing characterizations that dismiss Crashaw as a bit too Catholic and a bit too feminine, for example, the standard by which we judge literary significance changes very little.[18] Crashaw's canonicity is often supported through likeness. He is comparable to other convert poets, even if his poetry embraces hermaphroditic figures— "mixing and multiplying"—more readily than theirs.[19] His *Steps to the Temple* is not just an homage to Herbert's posthumous volume but "has more in common with Milton's *Poems* than with Herbert's *Temple*."[20] Indeed, "when we read Crashaw against a broader Bernadine tradition, the poet becomes as native to English literary piety as Donne and Herbert."[21] These are powerful and convincing arguments, and the use of similitude as a shield against accusations of poetic failure and floridity is understandable in a literary and critical tradition that has too often associated difference with marginality. But what if we instead celebrate difference as a sign of early modern literature's vitality and potency? To do so would be to acknowledge the extent to which the formation of our canon and our subsequent readings of that canon have reproduced the limited perspectives and value judgments inscribed by certain early modern authors: for the "florid divagations" and "feminine perspectives" of an author like Crashaw, like the perspectival multiplicity of early modern Passion poems, illuminate the very aspects of English literary history foregrounded in the writings and representations of Catholic women that Milton's "The Passion" rejected and attempted to expel.[22]

Catholic women unsettle and disrupt narrative, form, and genre, forcing us to bring renewed attention even to those poems and plays that seem not at all concerned with them. We will not find representations of nuns in every text or every genre, but the literary effects and affects associated with the women who wrote from exilic, enclosed, recusant, and conformist perspectives enable recognition of a more flexible and fluid early modern canon. Indeed, the Virgin Mary's significance in "Good Friday" and "On the Passion" reveals not a particular confessional identity but rather how women associ-ated with Catholic devotional practices helped shape English literature, and Milton's bad Crashaw tells us more about our own critical understandings of gender and Catholicism than it does about the relative merits of two early modern religious poets. By taking a circuitous path through literary history, guided by the remarkable contributions of Catholic women, we thus discover fresh paths and perspectives new, even in the work of our most canonical authors.

NOTES

INTRODUCTION. GENDER, RELIGION, AND ENGLISH LITERARY HISTORY

Epigraph: Emily Dickinson, "Tell all the Truth but Tell it Slant," in *The Poems of Emily Dickinson: Variorum Edition*, ed. R. W. Franklin, 3 vols. (Cambridge, Mass.: Belknap Press of Harvard University Press, 1998), poem 1263, lines 1–2.

1. See Caroline Bowden, "'A distribution of tyme': Reading and Writing Practices in the English Convents in Exile," *Tulsa Studies in Women's Literature* 31.1/2 (2012): 99–116; Genelle Gertz, "Barbara Constable's *Advice for Confessors* and the Tradition of Medieval Holy Women," in *The English Convents in Exile, 1600–1800: Communities, Culture and Identity*, ed. Caroline Bowden and James E. Kelly (Farnham: Ashgate, 2013), 123–38; Jaime Goodrich, "'Ensigne-Bearers of Saint Clare': Elizabeth Evelinge's Early Translations and the Restoration of English Franciscanism," in *English Women, Religion, and Textual Production, 1500–1625*, ed. Micheline White (Farnham: Ashgate, 2011), 83–100 and "Nuns and Community-Centered Writing: The Benedictine Rule and the Brussels Statutes," *Huntington Library Quarterly* 77.2 (2014): 287–303; Nicky Hallett, *The Senses in Religious Communities, 1600–1800* (Farnham: Ashgate, 2013) and "Shakespeare's Sisters: Anon and the Authors in Early Modern Convents," in Bowden and Kelly, *The English Convents in Exile, 1600–1800: Communities, Culture and Identity*, 139–55; and Victoria Van Hyning, "Expressing Selfhood in the Convent: Anonymous Chronicling and Subsumed Autobiography," *British Catholic History* 32.2 (2014): 219–34.

2. See Jennifer Summit, *Lost Property: The Woman Writer and English Literary History, 1380–1589* (Chicago: University of Chicago Press, 2000) for a foundational analysis of how the figure of the woman writer was essential to the formation of an English literary tradition.

3. For example, Kimberly Anne Coles, *Religion, Reform, and Women's Writing in Early Modern England* (Cambridge: Cambridge University Press, 2008); Katharine Gillespie, *Domesticity and Dissent in the Seventeenth Century: English Women Writers and the Public Sphere* (Cambridge: Cambridge University Press, 2004); Catharine Gray, *Women Writers and Public Debate in Seventeenth-Century Britain* (New York: Palgrave Macmillan, 2007); and Hilary Hinds, *God's Englishwomen: Seventeenth-Century Radical Sectarian Writing and Feminist Criticism* (Manchester: Manchester University Press, 1996).

4. There have been a number of studies of the Catholic queens Anna of Denmark and Henrietta Maria as literary patrons and imaginative influences on the culture of their period, including: Leeds Barroll, *Anna of Denmark, Queen of England: A Cultural Biography* (Philadelphia: University of Pennsylvania Press, 2000); Karen Britland, *Drama at the Courts of Queen Henrietta Maria* (Cambridge: Cambridge University Press, 2009); Erin Griffey, ed. *Henrietta Maria: Piety, Politics and Patronage* (Aldershot: Ashgate, 2008); Laura Lunger

Knoppers, *Politicizing Domesticity from Henrietta Maria to Milton's Eve* (Cambridge: Cambridge University Press, 2014); and Claire McManus, *Women on the Renaissance Stage: Anna of Denmark and Female Masquing in the Stuart Court (1590–1619)* (Manchester: Manchester University Press, 2002). The longstanding recognition of Catholic convert Elizabeth Cary's literary accomplishments has recently been complemented by work on her daughters' monastic writings. See the essays in Karen Raber, ed., *Elizabeth Cary* (Farnham: Ashgate, 2009) and Heather Wolfe, ed., *The Literary Career and Legacy of Elizabeth Cary, 1613–1680* (New York: Palgrave Macmillan, 2007).

5. For the strand of literary criticism variously identified as new formalism or historical formalism, see the essays in Mark David Rasmussen, ed., *Renaissance Literature and Its Formal Engagements* (New York: Palgrave, 2002), especially Stephen Cohen, "Between Form and Culture: New Historicism and the Promise of a Historical Formalism," 17–41, and Douglas Bruster, "Shakespeare and the Composite Text," 43–66. Marjorie Levinson queries the associations of new formalism in "What Is New Formalism?" *PMLA* 122.2 (2007): 558–69. For the turn to religion, see Ken Jackson and Arthur Marotti, "The Turn to Religion in Early Modern English Studies," *Criticism* 46.1 (2004): 167–90.

6. Mark David Rasmussen, "Introduction: New Formalisms?" in *Renaissance Literature and Its Formal Engagements*, 1–14, 9.

7. Sasha Roberts, "Feminist Criticism and the New Formalism: Early Modern Women and Literary Engagement," in *The Impact of Feminism in English Renaissance Studies*, ed. Dympna Callaghan (New York: Palgrave Macmillan, 2007), 67–91, 70.

8. Elizabeth Scott-Baumann, *Forms of Engagement: Women, Poetry, and Culture 1640–1680* (Oxford: Oxford University Press, 2013), 3.

9. Frank Whigham and Wayne A. Rebhorn point out that "a sense of the social and political reference of English Renaissance rhetoric and poetry has become a commonplace, but Puttenham is the first contemporary writer to bind them together explicitly to that goal." The introduction to their edition of *The Art* offers an analysis of Puttenham's ambitions and omissions: George Puttenham, *The Art of English Poesy*, ed. Frank Whigham and Wayne A. Rebhorn (Ithaca, N.Y.: Cornell University Press, 2007), 1–72, 60, cited parenthetically by page number.

10. As Sasha Roberts has noted, "the *Arte of Poesie* may be read in terms of its indelibly gendered tropes that serve to reduce women to their sexuality or, alternatively, to limit their rhetorical discrimination," but she maintains that it "remains an ambivalent and conflicted text in relation to women, articulating their exclusion from humanist literary culture while assuming their participation and interest in it as writers and readers" ("Feminist Criticism and the New Formalism," 72). See also Summit on how Puttenham's representation of Elizabeth leads him to figure poetry as "a womanly art" (174). I follow Roberts and Summit in attending to the ambivalences of Puttenham's text, contending that those exclusions he makes visible—Scottish Queens, virgins' screams, and perverse ladies—suggest a submerged attention to other narratives of literary history.

11. Puttenham, 92. As Summit has argued, by naming Elizabeth as the "figurehead" of English poetry, Puttenham makes it "the basis of a new national literature" (202).

12. As Whigham and Rebhorn explain, "the term refers to a general polishing or refining of one's style rather than identifying a single rhetorical figure" (333n4). The Greek etymology, however, also reveals the relationship to ποῐεῖν and *poeta*: exergasia derives from the Greek ἐξ-εργάζομαι "to work out, make completely, finish off, bring to perfection" or "to accomplish,

perform, achieve a work." *An Intermediate Greek-English Lexicon* (Oxford: Clarendon, 1997), 272. This is making at its most accomplished.

13. For Mary Stuart's poetry, see Elizabeth Mazzola, "Who's She When She's at Home?: 'Manifest Housekeepers', Jealous Queens, and the Artistry of Mary Stuart," *Exemplaria* 15.2 (2003): 385–417. For a reading of Puttenham's practice of "riddling disclosure" in this passage, see Rosemary Kegl's " 'Those Terrible Aproches': Sexuality, Social Mobility, and Resisting the Courtliness of Puttenham's *The Arte of English Poesie*," *ELR* 20.2 (1990): 179–208. Summit reads this passage in terms of poetic and political dissimulation, and analyzes how poetry played a role in Elizabeth's attempts to manage Mary (174–202).

14. Barbara Lewalski, *Protestant Poetics and the Seventeenth-Century Religious Lyric* (Princeton, N.J.: Princeton University Press, 1979). For recent work on Protestant poetics and gender, see Coles, 75–112.

15. Whigham and Rebhorn, "Introduction," 23.

16. See Whigham and Rebhorn, 7–15.

17. Steven W. May describes the archival evidence related to Puttenham and *The Art* in "George Puttenham's Lewd and Illicit Career," *Texas Studies in Literature and Language* 50.2 (2008): 143–76; for Lady Windsor's Catholicism, see 148. See also Tim Stretton, "Misogyny and Male Honour in the Life of George Puttenham, Elizabethan 'Princepleaser'," in *Worth and Repute: Valuing Gender in Late Medieval and Early Modern Europe; Essays in Honour of Barbara Todd*, ed. Kim Kippen and Lori Woods (Toronto: Centre for Reformation and Renaissance Studies, 2011), 337–63.

18. Lady Windsor's *Articles into the Arches* are held in the Hampshire County Records Office, 44M69/F2/14/1, Bundles 1–2. Puttenham's sexual assaults are detailed in Bundle 2, viii.1, entitled "The cause of complayte wrong and Injuries sustayned by the La Elizabeth Windesor by George Puttenham her husband by the space of thes xv yeres last paste."

19. Ibid., Bundle 1, viii.7.

20. Heather Dubrow argues that "the open eroticism of some Continental epithalamia, like the open conflict of Catullus 62, represents a kind of negative identity for the Stuart epithalamium, a road not taken: one can cite some telling exceptions, but by and large that unabashed and uncontrolled sexuality is not the value Stuart poems wish to advocate but rather the threat they attempt to control" in *A Happier Eden: The Politics of Marriage in the Stuart Epithalamium* (Ithaca, N.Y.: Cornell University Press, 1990), 48.

21. *Articles into the Arches*, Bundle 2, viii.1.

22. Jacques Lezra offers a compelling reading of the implications of this passage in " 'The Lady Was a Litle Peruerse': The 'Gender' of Persuasion in Puttenham's *Arte of English Poesie*," in *Engendering Men: The Question of Male Feminist Criticism*, ed. Joseph A. Boone and Michael Cadden (New York: Routledge, 1990), 53–65. "Reason, aligned with the 'wise man,' is set into opposition to a 'little perverseness,' aligned with the noble woman who is in want of reformation. The perlocutionary force of the example is to 'reforme her selfe by hearinge reason'—a goal that then allows the category of *form* itself to be aligned with both reason and the male figure. The pedagogical formalism of the *Arte of English Poesie* is specifically figured, in this sense, as a constitutively male attribute of the text; and its examples would then tend to become the pedagogical instrument with which reason is beaten into the ignorant (female) head" (59). Stretton suggests that this passage "bears strong parallels" to Puttenham's representation of Lady Windsor (357).

23. May, 170.

24. Whigham and Rebhorn, 24.

25. Champney, Champneys, and Champnes were common variations on the same family name.

26. *The Life and Good End of Sister Marie*, British Library, Additional MS 18650, fol. 2r; cited parenthetically by folio. Mesaghan was a convent in Brabant. The nuns of Syon lived there between 1568 and 1572, when they fled to Antwerp. For a timeline of their movements, see the translation of the nuns' illuminated Spanish manuscript in Christopher de Hamel, *Syon Abbey: The Library of the Bridgettine Nuns and Their Peregrinations After the Reformation* (Otley: Roxburghe Club, 1991), 30–34. My second chapter offers a thorough history of the exilic book culture associated with Syon Abbey after the Reformation.

27. Ann M. Hutchison suggests that the manuscript was "intended for circulation among, and the edification of, English Catholics—and thus devoid of names of living people and places," yet the lack of identifying features may in fact suggest the possibility of a wider audience—or at least concerns that the manuscript might be read by the authorities. "Syon Abbey Preserved: Some Historians of Syon," in *Syon Abbey and Its Books: Reading, Writing and Religion, c. 1400–1700*, ed. E. A. Jones and Alexandra Walsham (Woodbridge: Boydell, 2010), 228–51, 232. The anonymous author has not been identified, but internal evidence suggests that he or she was present at Champney's deathbed.

28. The legal documents state that Puttenham "did likewise take and moste wickedly abuse" Champneys "imediatly after" he arranged the marriage of another young woman he "did take and moste wickedly use," *Articles into the Arches*, Bundle 2, viii.1. May dates this marriage to September 6, 1564 (151).

29. May offers evidence to support the possibility that Puttenham traveled to the continent three times: in 1563, 1565/66, and 1567. In 1567, Queen Elizabeth granted a license for Puttenham and a Windsor daughter to travel for illness, which refers to a previous trip "beyonde the seas for the better cure of certen diseaes of himselfe and of a daughter of his wife's." See Hampshire County Records Office, 44M69/M6/7/24 for a typescript copy of the original license: "Licence from Queen Elizabeth to George Putenham." The supposed daughter is not named, and May suggests that "it is scarcely believable that Lady Windsor would have allowed her minor daughter, Elizabeth, to accompany her wayward husband on his overseas travels, and even less likely that the elder daughter, Mary . . . would have done so" (152). Instead, it seems plausible that the daughter on either the earlier trip or the 1567 trip was in fact the pregnant Champneys.

30. Champney "must have first been introduced to Abbess Palmer more than a year earlier, since there needed to be time for renewal of the request to join the Order (usually three months) and for probation (usually a year)" (Hutchison, "Syon Abbey Preserved," 231).

31. May, 148. These materials may also have belonged to George, but "there is no evidence that he adhered to Catholicism, as his wife and Richard Puttenham's wife, Mary, certainly did. In all likelihood, the contraband belonged to one or both of them."

32. The manuscript describes her "first calling" at twelve: a dream vision of being clothed in a habit (2r).

33. For work that addresses this period in Syon's history, see Jones and Walsham, eds., *Syon Abbey and Its Books*, especially Claire Walker's "Continuity and Isolation: The Bridgettines in the Sixteenth and Seventeenth Centuries," 155–76.

34. Not all responses to the nuns' travels were so positive: one contemporary letter suggests that "many of the wisest sort hath fownde great fault wth the sendinge over of the younge nonnes, whome God of his aboundante mercy hath delivered from a thousand periles

of body and sowle," T. F. Knox et al., eds., *The First and Second Diaries of the English College, Douay* (London: David Nutt, 1878), 149. The convent was based in Mechlin (also known as Mechelen in Dutch and Malines in French), just outside Antwerp, from 1573. The community fled to Rouen in 1580, when violence in the Low Countries escalated and the prince of Orange took the city.

35. Hutchison identifies this countryman as George Gilbert, a Catholic layman who supported the Jesuits in England. See Ann M. Hutchison, "Mary Champney a Bridgettine Nun Under the Rule of Queen Elizabeth I," *Birgittiana* 13 (2002): 3–32, 20, and "The Life and Good End of Sister Marie," *Birgittiana* 13 (2002): 33–89, 48n47, 75n133. The manuscript describes how the priest at her deathbed suggests "that all their portable bookes for theyr private use ar so rudelye written, that it pytyethe me to see them, & none of their service bookes were ever yet in prynte, & most comodious it were for all their order, that they should as well, as the service of many other orders. Will yow therefore beare the charge (quoth he) of the pryntynge of them, for purchase of virgins prayers, and of the Scale of Perfection, which is an other of their bookes, as needefull to be renewed, for the mendynge of the old prynte, And geve them a hundred powndes besides to ther poore Covent, agaynst any daye of grete charges for any companye of fitt yonge virgins thereto wantinge ayde to be receyved, and professed amonge them, for renewinge of their decayed number" (14v).

36. For its hagiographical pattern, see Hutchison, "Mary Champney," 22: "In following a hagiographical pattern, the narrative adheres particularly to appropriate details surrounding Mary's death: the fact it has been foretold, her age (thirty-three), the beginning of her death pains at nones (the hour of the crucifixion), and so on. In some quite striking respects, 'The Life' resembles the *vita* of St. Birgitta." See also Nancy Bradley Warren's reading of the manuscript in terms of suffering and embodiment in *The Embodied Word: Female Spiritualities, Contested Orthodoxies, and English Religious Cultures, 1350–1700* (Notre Dame, Ind.: University of Notre Dame Press, 2010), 104–12.

37. Hutchison takes the discontinuous narrative structure as evidence of the manuscript's literary aspirations, but her focus is on the reader's response rather than the text's internal tensions: "the author exploits the technique of the flashback primarily to provide necessary background information, but with the added effect of whetting the reader's interest in the development of the story's present by temporarily interrupting its progress" ("Mary Champney," 25).

38. For the lives of other early modern nuns, see vols. 3 (ed. Nicky Hallett) and 4 (ed. Katrien Daemen-de Gelder) of Caroline Bowden, ed., *English Convents in Exile, 1600–1800*, 6 vols. (London: Pickering & Chatto, 2012–13).

39. See my ODNB entry on Elizabeth Sander, and Betty S. Travitsky, "The Puzzling Letters of Sister Elizabeth Sa[u]nder[s]," in *Textual Conversations in the Renaissance: Ethics, Authors, Technologies*, ed. Zachary Lesser and Benedict S. Robinson (Aldershot: Ashgate, 2006), 131–45.

40. For Lucrece and the "narratological connection between rape and republican liberty," see Stephanie H. Jed, *Chaste Thinking: The Rape of Lucretia and the Birth of Humanism* (Bloomington: Indiana University Press, 1989).

41. Frances E. Dolan, *Whores of Babylon: Catholicism, Gender, and Seventeenth-Century Print Culture* (Ithaca, N.Y.: Cornell University Press, 1999). Dolan's study of Catholicism, gender, and print culture is a crucial forerunner for my own project: she explores pejorative representations of Catholic women, particularly the "connection between Catholicism and disorderly women" that pervaded anti-Catholic polemic (8).

42. John Bossy was not the first historian to recognize that women were important to post-Reformation English Catholicism, but his assertion that "the Catholic community owed its existence to gentlewomen's dissatisfaction at the Reformation settlement of religion" inspired subsequent historians to pursue further work in the field. *The English Catholic Community 1570–1850* (London: Darton, Longman & Todd, 1975), 158. See also Patricia Crawford, *Women and Religion in England 1500–1720* (London: Routledge, 1993); and Marie B. Rowlands, "Recusant Women 1560–1640," in *Women in English Society 1500–1800*, ed. Mary Prior (London: Methuen, 1985), 112–35. Claire Walker's study of the English convents in exile broadened the scope of these early histories to include early modern nuns: *Gender and Politics in Early Modern Europe: English Convents in France and the Low Countries* (New York: Palgrave Macmillan, 2003).

43. Caroline Bowden's six-volume *English Convents in Exile 1600–1800* offers an essential starting point for work in the field. Individual manuscripts have also been edited for volumes published by the Catholic Record Society and the *Analecta Cartusiana* series.

44. Since Eamon Duffy's *The Stripping of the Altars: Traditional Religion in England 1400–1580* (New Haven, Conn.: Yale University Press, 1992), numerous revisionary histories have shown the gradual nature of religious change, including Christopher Haigh, *English Reformations: Religion, Politics and Society Under the Tudors* (Oxford: Clarendon, 1993); Michael Questier, *Conversion, Politics and Religion in England, 1580–1625* (Cambridge: Cambridge University Press, 1996); and Alexandra Walsham, *Church Papists: Catholicism, Conformity and Confessional Polemic in Early Modern England* (London: Royal Historical Society, 1993). For a recent summary of the field, see Eamon Duffy, "The English Reformation After Revisionism," *Renaissance Quarterly* 59.3 (2006): 720–28.

45. See, for example, Haigh; Questier, *Conversion, Politics and Religion*; and Walsham, *Church Papists*.

46. Recent work on Spanish and Italian convents does suggest important cross-cultural relationships. For Italy, see K. J. P. Lowe, *Nuns' Chronicles and Convent Culture in Renaissance and Counter-Reformation Italy* (Cambridge: Cambridge University Press, 2003); Elissa B. Weaver, *Convent Theatre in Early Modern Italy: Spiritual Fun and Learning for Women* (Cambridge: Cambridge University Press, 2007); and Mary Laven, *Virgins of Venice: Enclosed Lives and Broken Vows in the Renaissance Convent* (London: Viking Penguin, 2002). For Spain, see Elizabeth A. Lehfeldt, *Religious Women in Golden Age Spain: The Permeable Cloister* (Aldershot: Ashgate, 2005). For the act expelling priests and Jesuits, see 27 Eliz. I, c. 2. *The Statutes at Large* (London: Bonham Norton and John Bill, 1618), 2.285–6.

47. Claire Walker counts twenty-two contemplative cloisters founded after 1591 that survived the seventeenth century (*Gender and Politics*, 17). In "Combining Martha and Mary: Gender and Work in Seventeenth-Century English Cloisters," *Sixteenth Century Journal* 30.2 (Summer 1999): 397–418, 398, she puts the total number of houses at thirty-six by 1700. For Mary Ward's order of unenclosed nuns, see Laurence Lux-Sterritt, *Redefining Female Religious Life: French Ursulines and English Ladies in Seventeenth-Century Catholicism* (Aldershot: Ashgate, 2005) and David Wallace, *Strong Women: Life, Text, and Territory, 1347–1645* (Oxford: Oxford University Press, 2011).

48. As Claire Walker has shown, "the restoration of conventual life for English women occurred during a renaissance of female religiosity" in Europe, and she establishes that the number of professions at the new English cloisters grew steadily from the 1590s, with an initial peak in the 1620s and continued steady professions in the 1650s–1690s (*Gender and Politics*, 9, 20).

49. During the same period, Stuart queens including Anna of Denmark and Henrietta Maria had significant cultural influence, but I focus here on those women who have not been imagined as central to England's political, religious, or literary culture. For an important reading of Henrietta Maria and the imaginative construction of female Catholicism, see Dolan, *Whores of Babylon*.

CHAPTER 1. FRACTURED DISCOURSE:
RECUSANT WOMEN AND FORMS OF VIRGINITY

1. I borrow this phrase from Susan Frye, *Elizabeth I: The Competition for Representation* (New York: Oxford University Press, 1993), in which she "focuses on the struggle for meanings embodied in the queen's body by treating Elizabeth I as a discursive agent, as a woman engaged in a continual, fluid struggle for the images she became" (6).

2. Heather Dubrow offers a helpful overview of these ambiguities: "the authors of marriage manuals and of other treatises on wedlock contradict one another—and often themselves—on many issues that are especially germane to marriage and its celebration. In particular, the conventional wisdom would have us believe that the value of marriage was firmly established in Stuart England: in contrast to and reaction against the Catholic distrust of sexuality and privileging of celibacy, the Reformers and their followers celebrated the married state. . . . But unqualified tributes to marriage at the expense of celibacy are not the norm: instead, both the Protestant conduct books and other Elizabethan and Jacobean discussions of wedlock testify to a continuing and uneasy debate on the relative virtues of those two states" (*A Happier Eden*, 16).

3. Helen Hackett analyzes Marian devotion and Elizabeth's iconography in *Virgin Mother, Maiden Queen: Elizabeth I and the Cult of the Virgin Mary* (Houndmills: Macmillan, 1995).

4. Kathryn Schwarz calls virginity "a strangely permeable ideology, not so much contested or subverted as porous to unexpected positions of articulation." See "The Wrong Question: Thinking Through Virginity," *differences* 13.2 (2002): 1–34, 7.

5. Kathleen Coyne Kelly and Marina Leslie, "Introduction: The Epistemology of Virginity," in *Menacing Virgins: Representing Virginity in the Middle Ages and Renaissance*, ed. Kathleen Coyne Kelly and Marina Leslie (Newark: University of Delaware Press, 1999), 15–25, 18.

6. Susan Frye argues that Elizabeth's "chastity was never a fixed idea but was always evolving and unstable, and thus continually open to repossession," "Of Chastity and Rape: Edmund Spenser Confronts Elizabeth I in *The Faerie Queene*," in *Representing Rape in Medieval and Early Modern Literature*, ed. Elizabeth Robertson and Christine M. Rose (New York: Palgrave, 2001), 353–79, 355. For a list of the poem's virgin characters, see David Scott Wilson-Okamura, "Belphoebe and Gloriana," *ELR* 39.1 (2009): 47–73, 47. Wilson-Okamura identifies "several characters who are virgins for life and who don't wish to get married or have sex ever," but Belphoebe, the female celibate at the center of his argument, does not take a religious vow of virginity and instead participates in a courtly love narrative.

7. See Schwarz, who recognizes "virginity's contested status in early modern narratives" but focuses her own analysis on Elizabeth ("The Wrong Question," 5).

8. Arthur F. Kinney, "Reading Marlowe's Lyric," in *Approaches to Teaching Shorter Elizabethan Poetry*, ed. Patrick Cheney and Anne Lake Prescott (New York: Modern Language Association, 2000), 220–25, 220.

9. Edmund Spenser, *The Faerie Qveene*, ed. A. C. Hamilton (London: Longman, 1977), 1.10.4.4; cited parenthetically by line number.

10. For a reading of how Spenser reclaims "bead" as prayer in this episode, see James Kearney, *The Incarnate Text: Imagining the Book in Reformation England* (Philadelphia: University of Pennsylvania Press, 2009), 128–35.

11. *Oxford English Dictionary*, 2nd ed., s.v. "chastity," definitions 2 and 1a (emphasis mine). For a more thorough explication of this shift in understandings of chastity in relationship to Queen Elizabeth, see Frye, "Of Chastity and Rape."

12. Jill Delsigne's reading of Britomart in the temple of Isis further illuminates how married chastity comes to replace celibacy. "Reading Catholic Art in Edmund Spenser's Temple of Isis," *Studies in Philology* 109.3 (2012): 199–224. Delsigne compares Britomart to the virgins in earlier romance and saints' lives: she is "one of these active virgins seeking her bridegroom, though her destiny is ultimately a secular marriage rather than the mystical marriage to Christ of a vowed woman" (224).

13. Spenser does mention a nun who conforms to her vow of virginity, but she does so for the wrong reasons. The Squyre of Dames, in his quest to find women who refuse his advances, discovers "an holy Nunne to chose, / Which would not let me be her Chappellane, / Because she knew, she sayd, I would disclose / Her counsell, if she should her trust in me repose" (3.7.58.6–9). The nun does not remain chaste because of her vow but for fear of discovery, and the Squyre of Dames suggests that if he were in a sexual relationship with her, he would perform the function of her chaplain or priest—a common claim in Protestant propaganda that I examine in more detail in Chapter 2.

14. Dubrow suggests that "not only literary texts but also political semiotics should be reinterpreted in light of the ambivalences about virginity in Protestant England. Thus Elizabeth's cult as the Virgin Queen emerges as a policy even more astute than scholars have recognized: confronted with subjects who found the closely related ideals of virginity and celibacy somewhat appealing but did not wish to be associated with the Catholic position on the subject, she provided them with a safe way to express their values" (*A Happier Eden*, 21).

15. Elizabeth I, *Collected Works*, ed. Leah S. Marcus, Janel Mueller, and Mary Beth Rose (Chicago: University of Chicago Press, 2000), 58.

16. See, for example, Roy Strong, *The Cult of Elizabeth: Elizabethan Portraiture and Pageantry* (London: Thames and Hudson, 1977), Philippa Berry, *Of Chastity and Power: Elizabethan Literature and the Unmarried Queen* (London: Routledge, 1989), and Stephen Hamrick, *The Catholic Imaginary and the Cults of Elizabeth, 1558–1582* (Farnham: Ashgate, 2009).

17. Ruben Espinosa, *Masculinity and Marian Efficacy in Shakespeare's England* (Farnham: Ashgate, 2011), 28.

18. Schwarz suggests that this continues to be the case: "we may get at some of the meanings of early modern virginity not so much by analyzing what early modern authors said about Elizabeth I as by looking at what we ourselves have done with her" ("The Wrong Question," 5).

19. Elizabeth I, 58.

20. Theodora A. Jankowski, *Pure Resistance: Queer Virginity in Early Modern English Drama* (Philadelphia: University of Pennsylvania Press, 2000), 12–13.

21. Elizabeth I, 57.

22. P. Crawford, *Women and Religion*, 30. Nuns' pensions were typically £2 or less.

23. Walker, *Gender and Politics*, 13. The nuns of Syon Abbey are a significant exception, and I will discuss the quite different position of seventeenth-century English nuns in my later chapters.

24. De Hamel, *Syon Abbey*, 31. This volume includes facsimile images of a seventeenth-century manuscript detailing Syon's exile and a translation of the text accompanying those images. I discuss the manuscript and Syon's post-Reformation book culture in Chapter 2.

25. Ibid.

26. For an overview of this literature, see Jankowski, 75–110.

27. Jankowski, 11. Jankowski correctly points out that "arbitrarily drawn lines between Catholic and Protestant thought are expected to reveal a blatant privileging of vowed virginity on the Catholic side and a similarly strong privileging of marriage on the Protestant side," but Catholic writers such as Vives and Erasmus nonetheless wrote works strongly in favor of marriage (90). She does not, however, acknowledge that marriage could offer Catholic women certain freedoms and opportunities that were unavailable to vowed virgins, particularly in the unique case of Protestant England.

28. *The Faerie Qveene*, 737.

29. Jessica C. Murphy, " 'Of the sicke virgin': Britomart, Greensickness, and the Man in the Mirror," *Spenser Studies* 25 (2010): 109–27, 120. For a divergent reading, see Andrew Hadfield's "Spenser and Religion—Yet Again," *SEL* 51.1 (2011): 21–46, in which he claims that "We never witness the marriage of Britomart and Artegall, but we know that it will happen" (40). Hadfield offers a nuanced analysis of how Calvin's treatment of marriage may have influenced Spenser.

30. As Jonathan Goldberg suggests in his reading of Spenser's letter to Ralegh, "It could be that the telos of the book is not its literal ending and not confined within a textual space at all, something glanced at when Spenser moves in the letter to Ralegh to reveal that the end of the book, were it ever to be reached, would have been its initial and initiating moment (the sending forth of the knights from the court of the Faerie Queen), a moment that might, or might not, ever have been planned to appear in the book." *The Seeds of Things: Theorizing Sexuality and Materiality in Renaissance Representations* (New York: Fordham University Press, 2009), 64. See also Dubrow, who argues that "the contradictions in Edmund Spenser's comparisons between celibacy and wedlock are sometimes traced simply to the political exigencies of flattering his monarch; but the conduct books indicate instead that the ambivalent comparisons of those two states which we find in Book III of *The Faerie Queene* reflect a deeper, recurrent pattern in the culture and in Spenser himself" (*A Happier Eden*, 20).

31. Patricia Parker defines romance as "that mode or tendency which remains on the threshold before the promised end, still in the wilderness of wandering, 'error,' or 'trial' " in *Inescapable Romance: Studies in the Poetics of a Mode* (Princeton, N.J.: Princeton University Press, 1979), 4. Andrew Zurcher explains that "romance is a genre prone to additivity, and its literary history demonstrates at large the complex networks of narrative deficiency and supplement to which it invited its authors" in his reading of a supplement to *The Faerie Queene* written by Ralph Knevet in "Deficiency and Supplement: Perfecting the Prosthetic Text," *SEL* 52.1 (2012): 143–64, 159. I would argue that the same logic is at work in Spenser's own treatment of deficiency and supplement in the 1596 book.

32. Many scholars have explored this relationship, including Gordon Teskey, *Allegory and Violence* (Ithaca, N.Y.: Cornell University Press, 1996); Katherine Eggert, "Spenser's Ravishment: Rape and Rapture in *The Faerie Queene*," *Representations* 70 (2000): 1–26; Michael

Slater, "Spenser's Poetics of 'Transfixion' in the Allegory of Chastity," *SEL* 54.1 (2014): 41–58; and Frye, "Of Chastity and Rape."

33. Rachel E. Hile, "The Limitations of Concord in the Thames-Medway Marriage Canto of *The Faerie Queene*," *Studies in Philology* 108.1 (2011): 70–85, 84.

34. In focusing on the tournament rather than the religious ceremony, Spenser arguably replicates the weddings critiqued for "pompe and pride" in contemporary pamphlets on marriage—though he does avoid "superfluous eating and drinking" (f. 58v). See Heinrich Bullinger, *The Christian State of Matrimony* (London: John Awdeley, 1575). Bullinger offers a brief description of what a marriage ceremony without such superfluities would look like on fol. 59.

35. I am indebted to Goldberg's compelling reading of this passage; as he points out, "Whether this 'band' is his bond to his nation or to his bride is not said" (94).

36. Goldberg, 94.

37. Ibid., 95.

38. *The Bible* (Geneva: Rouland Hall, 1560).

39. Murphy, 122.

40. For the latter reading, see John Leonard, "Marlowe's Doric Music: Lust and Aggression in Hero and Leander," *ELR* 30.1 (2000): 55–76.

41. Christopher Marlowe, *Hero and Leander: A Facsimile of the First Edition, London 1598* (New York: Johnson Reprint, 1972), E2v–E3r. Vincenzo Pasquarella offers a thorough editorial history in "The Implications of Tucker Brooke's Transposition in *Hero and Leander* by Christopher Marlowe," *Studies in Philology* 105.4 (2008): 520–32.

42. Marlowe, *Hero and Leander: A Facsimile*, E3r.

43. Ibid. In a lovely reading of this passage, Judith Haber explains that "the 1598 text confronts us once more with a frustrating series of false climaxes; we are once more led to ask, 'Are we there yet?'" (383). She convincingly argues that the editorial emendation "calls up the spectres of loss and displacement that it tries to dispel" (383–84). See "'True-loves blood': Narrative and Desire in *Hero and Leander*," *ELR* 28 (1998): 372–86. Stephen Orgel agrees that the original "makes a more interesting sense psychologically than the revision," but supports the editorial choice of revision based on the progression of Marlowe's metaphors. "A Note on the Text, and on Emendation, Modernization, and Annotation," in Christopher Marlowe, *The Complete Poems and Translations*, ed. Stephen Orgel (New York: Penguin, 2007), xxiv. Graham Hammill also examines the emendation, but offers a different reading of how it affects interpretation in "The Marlovian Sublime: Imagination and the Problem of Political Theology," in *The Return of Theory in Early Modern English Studies: Tarrying with the Subjunctive*, ed. Paul Cefalu and Bryan Reynolds (New York: Palgrave Macmillan, 2011), 143–66.

44. Christopher Marlowe, *The Complete Poems and Translations*, ed. Stephen Orgel (New York: Penguin, 2007), 1.162, 256. All future citations will be from this edition, which includes both Marlowe's and Chapman's *Hero and Leander*, divided into sestiads. Cited parenthetically by sestiad and line.

45. *Oxford English Dictionary*, 2nd ed., s.v. "coverture," definitions 1, 2, 3, and 6 for the literal; definitions 6 *fig.* and 7 *fig.* for the figurative. John Leonard also focuses on coverture, but his reading of this moment emphasizes the sexual and comic dimensions of Hero's movement under the bedclothes: "I am arguing that Marlowe creates a comic gap between Hero's own understanding of her act and the very different construction that might be placed upon it even by a sympathetic observer" (60).

46. John Rastell, *An Exposition of Certaine Difficult and Obscure Words, and Termes of the Lawes of this Realme* (London: Richard Tottell, 1579), 54.

47. John Calvin, *Sermons of M. John Calvine, upon the X Commandementes of the Lawe*, trans. J. H. (London: John Harison, 1579), fol. 67v–68r.

48. Ibid., 67v.

49. For an overview of women's property rights, see Amy Louise Erickson, *Women and Property in Early Modern England* (London: Routledge, 1993). Erickson distinguishes legal theory from everyday practice throughout her book, and the case of Catholic women reveals just one of the many paradoxes inherent in the doctrine of coverture: "no amount of equal inheritance could counteract the law of coverture and its legal 'fiction' that a husband and wife were one person—the husband—and therefore their property was his. However, in practice wives maintained during marriage substantial property interests of their own" (19).

50. See Walsham, *Church Papists*.

51. 3 Jac. I, c. 4. See *The Statutes at Large* (London: Bonham Norton and John Bill, 1618), 2.591.

52. Ibid., 596–97.

53. Bossy, P. Crawford, and Rowlands all examine the role of women in the English Catholic community.

54. Henry Hastings to William Cecil, 12 September 1576, British Library, Harley MS 6992, fol. 50.

55. For an analysis of Clitherow that situates her within the Catholic community's debates over church attendance and recusancy, see Peter Lake and Michael Questier, "Margaret Clitherow, Catholic Nonconformity, Martyrology and the Politics of Religious Change in Elizabethan England," *Past & Present* 185 (November 2004): 43–90. Megan Matchinske reads John Mush's narrative in terms of gender in *Writing, Gender and State in Early Modern England: Identity Formation and the Female Subject* (Cambridge: Cambridge University Press, 1998), 53–85.

56. See, for example, Richard Verstegan, *Theatrum Crudelitatum Hæreticorum Nostri Temporis* (Antwerpe: Adrian Hubert, 1587), 76–77 and Diego de Yepes, *Historia particular de la persecucion de Inglaterra* (Madrid: Luis Sanchez, 1599), 4.602–3.

57. Anne Dillon, *The Construction of Martyrdom in the English Catholic Community, 1535–1603* (Aldershot: Ashgate, 2002), 287. Dillon offers a fascinating analysis of how Mush "constructed Margaret as a model of heroic virtue within the demands of the new conventions of the Counter Reformation Church" (321).

58. John Mush, "A True Report of the Life and Martyrdom of Mrs. Margaret Clitherow," in *The Troubles of Our Catholic Forefathers, Related by Themselves*, ed. John Morris (London: Burns and Oates, 1877), 3.360–440, 432: "Her hat before she died she sent to her husband, in sign of her loving duty to him as to her head"; cited parenthetically as Mush.

59. As Frances Dolan has argued, the "domestic locations of Catholic education in England were the same locations at which women were relatively powerful," making women's teaching "pervasive and almost impossible to regulate" (*Whores of Babylon*, 140). A. C. F. Beales notes "the key position of the mother in Catholic education" in *Education Under Penalty: English Catholic Education from the Reformation to the Fall of James II: 1547–1689* (London: Athlone, 1963), 92.

60. 27 Eliz. I, c. 2. regulated against sending children "beyond the Seas" to Catholic seminaries or colleges. See *The Statutes at Large*, 2.286.

61. Lake and Questier explicate Clitherow's negotiation between temporal and spiritual authorities: "thus was the disobedience to prince, magistrate and husband of a (relatively) humble and (formerly) unlettered butcher's wife redescribed (and hence legitimated) as obedience to the equally patriarchal, but inherently superior, spiritual authority wielded in God's name by the Catholic Church and the priesthood. . . . In the process, of course, the formal distinctions and hierarchies, the power relations that usually pertained between clerical mentor and lay adept, confessor and confessant, between the lay patron and the clerical client, were not merely mixed and miscegenated but in the end entirely reversed" (53).

62. Christine Peters, "Religion, Household-State Authority, and the Defense of 'Collapsed Ladies' in Early Jacobean England," *Sixteenth Century Journal* 45.3 (2014): 631–57, 632.

63. Lake and Questier, 57.

64. Susannah Monta argues that "writers who wished to promote strict recusancy . . . used monastic or religious analogies to characterize, value, and ultimately order the domestic piety, devotion, and work of English wives, and that the insistence on the virtue of obedience and the figuring of marital fidelity as spiritual loyalty both reveal and attempt to mitigate Catholic communities' dependence upon wives and domestic spaces." See "Uncommon Prayer? Robert Southwell's *Short Rule for a Good Life* and Catholic Domestic Devotion in Post-Reformation England," in *Redrawing the Map of Early Modern English Catholicism*, ed. Lowell Gallagher (Toronto: University of Toronto Press, 2012), 245–71, 257. Clitherow shows that such analogies were not always persuasive within the Catholic community.

65. Lake and Questier make a similar argument, explaining that "either she was an obedient wife and mother, or else a disorderly woman who defied her husband and neglected her children, first by diverting the resources of her household to sustain a nest of disruptive and treasonous priests, and latterly abandoning them altogether for a suicidal 'martyr's' death" (76). Their analysis of Clitherow's life is one of the few to identify the complex political affiliations that underlie Mush's text and is an important influence on my work, but their focus on the intradoctrinal struggles of the Catholic community leads them to overlook the cultural and literary reverberations that may have arisen from Mush's representation of female recusancy.

66. As Dolan points out, "the charge that priests invariably seduced the penitents who confessed to them worked to discredit priests, women, and the intimacies between them" (*Whores of Babylon*, 90).

67. Lake and Questier, 86.

68. A contemporary manuscript belonging to the English Benedictine nuns of Cambrai describes the Tridentine restrictions on enclosure as follows: "They must have an extraordinarie great care of keeping their Inclosure, so much commended, and so severely commaunded by the Councell of Trent: so that none that are not Religious, or not of the Convent (of what sexe or condition soever they be) may enter into the limits of their Inclosure . . . but upon necessarie causes, and with licence heereafter to be specified, otherwise the person that entreth incurreth excommunication, according to the decree of the same Councell of Trent" (Archives Départmentales du Nord, Lille, Box 20H, MS 20 H 1, *Constitutions compiled for the better observation of the holie Rule of our most glorious Fa: and Patriarch S. Bennet: confirmed by the Regiment of the English Benedictine Congregation, and by it delivered to the English Religious Dames of the same Order and Congregation, living in Cambray, and to all their successors*, 13–14). See also Walker, *Gender and Politics*, 45–54; and Amy E. Leonard, "Female Religious Orders," in *A Companion to the Reformation World*, ed. R. Po-chia Hsia (Malden, Mass.: Blackwell, 2004), 237–54.

69. Alice Dailey suggests that "her silence—her refusal either to be tried or to explain her rejection of trial—acts as an open-ended signifier that can be interpreted in multiple, competing ways. In place of a clear subject—martyr or traitor, madwoman or suicide—the text inscribes a cipher, a subject who simultaneously occupies all and none of these positions." *The English Martyr from Reformation to Revolution* (Notre Dame, Ind.: University of Notre Dame Press, 2012), 143.

70. In the last two decades, critics have given more thought to the political aspects of *Hero and Leander*, following Patrick Cheney's *Marlowe's Counterfeit Profession: Ovid, Spenser, Counter-Nationhood* (Toronto: University of Toronto Press, 1997), in which he argues "that Marlowe was in the process of constructing a career model distinctly counter-Virgilian in its forms and goals" but nonetheless political in its scope (9). See Aaron Kitch, "The Golden Muse: Protestantism, Mercantilism, and the Uses of Ovid in Marlowe's *Hero and Leander*," *Religion and Literature* 38.3 (2006): 157–76.

71. Katherine Cleland suggests that Chapman's focus on the marriage ceremony might "shed light on Elizabethan marriage practices" (216). She interprets Hero and Leander's relationship as a spousal contract that is not sanctioned by the state in Marlowe's poem and argues that "the sex scandal that critics identify in *Hero and Leander* . . . does not derive from sex outside of marriage but rather from sex that takes place within a marriage that has yet to be solemnized by the church" (228). "'Wanton loves, and yong desires': Clandestine Marriage in Marlowe's *Hero and Leander* and Chapman's Continuation," *Studies in Philology* 108.2 (2011): 215–37.

72. Frye calls these qualities "'chaste,' according to [Elizabeth's] redefinition of the word" (*Elizabeth I*, 107).

73. Cheney, 247. Cleland also compares Hero to Elizabeth, but focuses on their parallel use of iconography in chaste courtship (224).

74. In his analysis of Leander's blazon, for example, Cheney argues that "this line subtly equates Hero with Queen Elizabeth, and Leander with a certain suitor. We do not have to look far to discover who this suitor might be; he is the lover of 'Fair Cynthia,' Sir Walter Ralegh. Thus, in another Ovidian narrative poem, *Ocean to Cynthia*, Ralegh identifies Elizabeth as Hero and himself as Leander" (246).

75. Ibid., 239.

76. Ibid., 258.

77. See Cleland, especially 227–37, for a reading of the "private, transactional pact" between Hero and Leander in Marlowe's poem and the emphasis on public ceremony in Chapman's continuation.

78. For the negative associations of the "coverture of Religion," see Anthony Munday, trans., *The Masque of the League and the Spanyard discovered* (London: I. Charlewoode, 1592), B4v and K2v. Protestant propagandists and preachers were swift to associate Catholicism with hypocrisy, dissembling, and other negative definitions of coverture; see, for example, Thomas Drant, *Two Sermons Preached* (London: John Daye, 1570): "ye kill these men if ye take away ye coverture of the Church of Rome. This Church is the ritch Arras that covereth all their faultes and follies."

79. Stephen Orgel, "Musaeus in English," *George Herbert Journal* 29.1/2 (2005/2006): 67–75, 70.

80. Compare Christopher Marlowe, *Hero and Leander* (London: Edward Blount, 1596), STC 17413, to Christopher Marlowe and George Chapman, *Hero and Leander* (London: Paul Linley, 1598), STC 17414.

81. Natasha Korda explores the implications of Shakespeare's choice of the Poor Clares in *Shakespeare's Domestic Economies: Gender and Property in Early Modern England* (Philadelphia: University of Pennsylvania Press, 2002), 159–91. See also Rosalind Miles, *The Problem of "Measure for Measure": A Historical Investigation* (London: Vision Press, 1976), who suggests that "since the naming of the order which Isabella is to join is one of Shakespeare's additions to his sources, it is clear that he expected an audience of 1604 to grasp the inference here" (222).

82. See Walker, *Gender and Politics*, 8–42, for an account of the new English foundations, including statistical data on the number of contemplative convents and female professions in the seventeenth century.

83. Ulrike Strasser explores "the political nature of virginity and its importance to the functioning of the polis" in *State of Virginity: Gender, Religion, and Politics in an Early Modern Catholic State* (Ann Arbor: University of Michigan Press, 2004), 4.

84. Debora Shuger, *Political Theologies in Shakespeare's England: The Sacred and the State in "Measure for Measure"* (New York: Palgrave, 2001), 1.

85. Julia Reinhard Lupton positions *Measure for Measure* in a hagiographical tradition, specifically associating it with "the medieval legends of the saints" in *Afterlives of the Saints: Hagiography, Typology, and Renaissance Literature* (Stanford, Calif.: Stanford University Press, 1996), 111; Sarah Beckwith reads the play in relationship to the sacrament of penance in *Shakespeare and the Grammar of Forgiveness* (Ithaca, N.Y.: Cornell University Press, 2011), 59–81; Alison Findlay compares Isabella to both Mary Ward, founder of an unenclosed apostolic order for women, and Margaret Clitherow in *A Feminist Perspective on Renaissance Drama* (Oxford: Blackwell, 1999); Natasha Korda offers an exceptional reading of the monastic context for the play, but repeatedly refers to it as a "pre-Reformation setting" (*Shakespeare's Domestic Economies*, 176); and Jessica Slights and Michael Morgan Holmes provide a thorough overview of the place of the convent in post-Reformation England, suggesting that "monasticism in *Measure for Measure* ought to be examined in light of the remarkable tenacity with which sympathy for Roman Catholicism endured in post-Reformation England" in "Isabella's Order: Religious Acts and Personal Desires in *Measure for Measure*," *Studies in Philology* 95.3 (1998): 263–92, 268–69. Others, such as Darryl J. Gless, have associated *Measure for Measure* with anti-Catholic propaganda, critiquing Isabella for "the wrong-headed faith symbolized visually by her costume." *Measure for Measure, the Law, and the Convent* (Princeton, N.J.: Princeton University Press, 1979), 211. See also Huston Diehl, " 'Infinite Space': Representation and Reformation in *Measure for Measure*," *Shakespeare Quarterly* 49.4 (Winter 1998): 393–410, who suggests Isabella's vocation is identified "with a false—or counterfeit—righteousness" (395); Anna Kamaralli, "Writing About Motive: Isabella, the Duke and Moral Authority," *Shakespeare Survey* 58 (2005): 48–59, who calls Isabella "outrageously radical" (48); Maureen Connolly McFeely, " 'This day my sister should the cloister enter': The Convent as Refuge in *Measure for Measure*," in *Subjects on the World's Stage: Essays on British Literature of the Middle Ages and the Renaissance*, ed. David G. Allen and Robert A. White (Newark: University of Delaware Press, 1995), 200–216; and Kimberly Reigle, "Staging the Convent as Resistance in *The Jew of Malta* and *Measure for Measure*," *Comparative Drama* 46.4 (2012): 497–516.

86. The financial penalties for recusancy that had been imposed during Elizabeth's reign were expanded significantly in James's first decade on the throne; while fewer Catholics were executed under the Stuart monarch, the recusant populace faced a variety of new economic sanctions. But only in 1610, following a series of debates on how to penalize Catholic women for recusancy, did Parliament pass "An Act for administering the Oath of Allegiance, and ref-

ormation of married women Recusants," which confined recusant women to prison unless their husbands paid ten pounds per month to secure their freedom (7 Jac. I, c. 6. *The Statutes at Large*, 2.666–67).

87. Thomas Robinson, *The Anatomy of the English Nunnery at Lisbon* (London: Robert Mylbourne and Philemon Stephens, 1622), 8; and Lewis Owen, *The Running Register: Recording a True Relation for the State of the English Colledges, Seminaries and Cloysters in all forraine parts* (London: Robert Milbourne, 1626), 103.

88. *Measure for Measure*, 1.4.4–5 in *The Riverside Shakespeare*, ed. G. Blakemore Evans and J. J. M. Tobin (Boston: Houghton Mifflin, 1997). Cited parenthetically by line number. Korda explores "the divergence between the theory and practice of pious poverty" in her reading of Isabella's desire for a more strict restraint (173).

89. Clitherow's daughter Anne did, in fact, become a nun at the Augustinian convent in Louvain.

90. At its most basic level, Sanford Budick identifies chiasmus as "a diagram of the simultaneous occurrence of opposition and reciprocity, as in the pattern AB:BA." "Counter-Periodization and Chiasmus: The Case of Wordsworth and 'the days of Dryden and Pope,'" in *The Challenge of Periodization: Old Paradigms and New Perspectives*, ed. Lawrence Besserman (New York: Routledge, 1996), 107–32, 108. Patricia Parker explores antimetabole in Shakespeare and suggests that "if such uses were to be followed up and into the larger questions of particular plays, they would begin to adumbrate other important relations of reversal—reversals of direction, of cause and effect, of logical and ideological sequence." *Literary Fat Ladies: Rhetoric, Gender, Property* (London: Methuen, 1987), 91.

91. See, for example, Molly Murray, *The Poetics of Conversion in Early Modern English Literature: Verse and Change from Donne to Dryden* (Cambridge: Cambridge University Press, 2009); and Susan Stewart's reading of Crashaw's reversals in *Poetry and the Fate of the Senses* (Chicago: University of Chicago Press, 2002). For earlier work on chiasmus, see A. B. Chambers, "Crooked Crosses in Donne and Crashaw," in *New Perspectives on the Life and Art of Richard Crashaw*, ed. John R. Roberts (Columbia: University of Missouri Press, 1990), 157–73.

92. As Kathryn Schwarz argues, "Isabella cannot be abstracted into the symbolic, any more than she can be reduced to instrumental use; she negotiates a meeting point between corporeal and social states" (169). See her chapter on *Measure for Measure* in *What You Will: Gender, Contract, and Shakespearean Social Space* (Philadelphia: University of Pennsylvania Press, 2011).

93. James A. Knapp's reading of embodied chiasmus in *Measure for Measure* has helped shape my own understanding of the play's formal properties. See "Penitential Ethics in *Measure for Measure*," in *Shakespeare and Religion: Early Modern and Postmodern Perspectives*, ed. Ken Jackson and Arthur F. Marotti (Notre Dame, Ind.: University of Notre Dame Press, 2011), 256–85.

94. In moving beyond the AB:BA pattern of chiasmus, Budick describes how the figure can create multiplicity: "Instead of a formula of exclusion, A not B, or even a cross drawn in only two lines of a chiasmus, we experience a continuous circulation of relations both direct and inverse: namely, AB, BA', A'B', B'A, AA', BB', each of which may be encountered separately and in combinations, forward and reverse. We can begin to describe the X experiences in chiasmus only by this illimitable circulation. By virtue of the cross-reading it sets in motion, chiasmus uncovers endless changes in its component antitheses, sometimes to discomposing effect" (109).

95. Budick argues that "chiasmus itself entails recreating an emptiness or obliviousness within language. This emptiness results in the reachings out of language, from its incompleteness or obliviousness, towards symmetry with other language" (109).

96. In a reading of this moment in terms of "the epistemological problem nagging theological debates over the relation of world and Word," Knapp suggests that the chiasmus reveals that Angelo's "disembodied thought and prayer are set against the bodily chewing mouth and lecherous intention" (277).

97. Kirsten Hastrup has described the social formulations through which "a female is not fully specified as a woman until she has been sexually associated with a man. . . . it is only through intercourse with a man that a woman becomes wholly a woman, and thus enters into the pure female category." "The Semantics of Biology: Virginity," in *Defining Females: The Nature of Women in Society*, ed. Shirley Ardener (New York: Wiley, 1978), 49–65, 58. But in the wake of the Reformation, as Strasser explains, "the spiral of Protestant discourse and Catholic counterdiscourse resulted in the sexualization of virginity and gendering of the nun as female" (76).

98. Isabella arguably returns to this more traditional association of women with matter when she says "we are soft as our complexions are, / And credulous to false prints," but Slights and Holmes suggest that "as the subject of Isabella's sentence shifts from 'they' (women) to the collective—or at least gender-ambiguous—'we' (socially constructed selves), her figurative image evolves into a metaphoric association of imprintable selves with the soft metal of coins that take the print of sovereigns. Isabella's final punning homonym drives her dual point home: Angelo's identity is a constructed one, and men and women alike must be wary of both 'false prints' in general and the false prince to whom she is speaking in particular" (283–84).

99. Ibid., 283.

100. Immediately before turning his own formulation of less and more against him ("If he be less, he's nothing; but he's more, / Had I more name for badness"), Isabella poses the following chiasmus:

> 'Tis not impossible
> But one, the wicked'st caitiff on the ground,
> May seem as shy, as grave, as just, as absolute
> As Angelo. Even so may Angelo,
> In all his dressings, caracts, titles, forms,
> Be an arch-villain. (5.1.53–58)

101. Knapp, 259. For Knapp, chiasmus helps reveal "Angelo's and Isabella's movement toward penitential ethics," which relies on recursive reading to initiate temporal progress.

102. Mario Digangi analyzes the distinctions between "maid," "widow," and "wife" in "Pleasure and Danger: Measuring Female Sexuality in *Measure for Measure*," *ELH* 60.3 (1993): 589–609, 591–92.

103. Although the Duke's ideology of marriage treats it as "public and measured answer to a private and immoderate sin, a way of harnessing Vienna's sexual appetites to strengthen, rather than weaken, the society," it is never clear that Isabella or her playwright conceptualizes it in these terms and, as we have seen, marriage was open to as many conflicting interpretations as chastity in the decades after the Reformation. Stacy Magedanz, "Public Justice and Private Mercy in *Measure for Measure*," *SEL* 44.2 (2004): 317–32, 327.

104. Ellison, *"Measure for Measure and the Executions of Catholics in 1604," ELR* 33.1 (2003): 44–87, 74. Ellison argues that Shakespeare "took the opportunity to update and extend the iconoclastic message" of the Reformation in order to critique radical Puritanism as well as Catholicism (74).

105. Interpretations of this final interaction abound, from those who believe Isabella "preserves her virginity and does not marry" to those who claim that she "renounces the sterile bondage of her rule and gains a liberty of love." For the former, see David Beauregard, "Shakespeare on Monastic Life: Nuns and Friars in *Measure for Measure*," in *Shakespeare and the Culture of Christianity in Early Modern England*, ed. Dennis Taylor and David Beauregard (New York: Fordham University Press, 2003), 311–35, 313. For the latter, see Gless, 212.

106. Korda, 162. She further suggests that "Although the play's interruption of Isabella's initiation into the order at the precise moment when a Clarissan novice would have invested her property in her spiritual bridegroom (Christ) appears to preserve it for her world suitor (the Duke), the circuit of transmission remains incomplete due to Isabella's silence. The indeterminacy produced by Isabella's destiny at the end of the play resists this forced solution and, in so doing, echoes the divergent destinies of the inhabitants of dissolved nunneries in post-Reformation England" (189).

107. Though she does not offer a formal reading of this moment, Barbara Baines similarly argues that Isabella "chooses silence as a form of resistance to the patriarchal authority and to the male discourse within which this authority operates. In her silence to the Duke's proposal, Isabella thus adheres to the rules of the sisters of St. Clare: she shows her face but remains silent, perhaps with the key to the convent still in her pocket," in her work on chastity as "a site and mode of secular power." "Assaying the Power of Chastity in *Measure for Measure*," *SEL* 30.2 (1990): 283–301, 299, 284. See also Slights and Holmes, who point out that "At *Measure for Measure*'s end Isabella communicates in the same way that her Clarist sisters do, by *not* speaking" (289).

108. Lady Cecilia Heywood, "Records of the Abbey of Our Lady of Consolation at Cambrai, 1620–1793," in *Publications of the Catholic Record Society*, vol. 13, *Miscellanea VIII*, ed. Joseph Gillow (London: Ballantyne, Hanson, 1913), 1–85, 73.

109. Anthony Copley, *A Fig for Fortune* (London: Richard Johnes, 1596), 82–84.

CHAPTER 2. TO THE NUNNERY: ENCLOSURE AND POLEMIC IN THE ENGLISH CONVENTS IN EXILE

1. The first new English convent was founded in Brussels in 1598, and the peak in foundations occurred in the 1620s. See Walker, *Gender and Politics*, especially 8–42 and the chart on 20.

2. The revenge tragedies that proliferated under James I targeted Catholicism as an object of horror, scorn, and wrath, evoking what Alison Shell has called "the apocalyptic image-clusters of sixteenth- and seventeenth-century anti-Catholic polemic." *Catholicism, Controversy and the English Literary Imagination, 1558–1660* (Cambridge: Cambridge University Press, 1999), 23.

3. With one notable exception, which I address in my reading of *A Game at Chess* in Chapter 3.

4. Lewis Owen, *The Unmasking of All Popish Monks, Friers, and Jesuits* (London: J.H. for George Gibs, 1628), 159.

5. Forced professions were not as common in post-Reformation England as on the continent, given the legal and geographical barriers to entry into a convent. For the continental context see Jutta Gisela Sperling, *Convents and the Body Politic in Late Renaissance Venice* (Chicago: University of Chicago Press, 1999).

6. See Huston Diehl, *Staging Reform, Reforming the Stage: Protestantism and Popular Theater in Early Modern England* (Ithaca, N.Y.: Cornell University Press, 1997); Rory Loughnane, "The Artificial Figures and Staging Remembrance in Webster's *The Duchess of Malfi*," in *Arts of Remembrance in Early Modern England: Memorial Cultures of the Post-Reformation*, ed. Andrew Gordon and Thomas Rist (Farnham: Ashgate, 2013), 211–27; Thomas Rist, *Revenge Tragedy and the Drama of Commemoration in Reforming England* (Aldershot: Ashgate, 2008); Todd Borlik, "'Greek Is Turned Turk': Catholic Nostagia in *The Duchess of Malfi*," in *The Duchess of Malfi: A Critical Guide*, ed. Christina Luckyj (London: Continuum, 2011), 136–52; and John C. Kerrigan, "Action and Confession, Fate and Despair in the Violent Conclusion of *The Duchess of Malfi*," *Ben Jonson Journal* 8 (2001): 249–58.

7. Webster's possible source texts include Thomas Beard, *The Theatre of Gods Judgements* (London: Adam Islip, 1597) Simon Goulart, *Admirable and Memorable Histories*, trans. Edward Grimeston (London: George Eld, 1607); William Painter, *The Second Tome of the Palace of Pleasure* (London: Henry Bynneman, 1567); and George Whetstone, *An Heptameron of Civill Discourses* (London: Richard Jones, 1582).

8. Painter, 176v; cited parenthetically. As we saw in Chapter 1, the marital doctrine of coverture sometimes allowed women to subvert religious, political, and cultural norms.

9. This warning nonetheless points to the appeal of the Duchess's romance with Antonio, and the possibility that it might encourage rather than prevent similar faults.

10. For readings of social mobility in *The Duchess of Malfi*, see Frank Whigham, *Seizures of the Will in Early Modern English Drama* (Cambridge: Cambridge University Press, 1996), 188–226; and Barbara Correll, "Malvolio at Malfi: Managing Desire in Shakespeare and Webster," *Shakespeare Quarterly* 58.1 (2007): 65–92.

11. Beard condemns the Cardinal in harsher terms, but nonetheless imagines him as an instrument of divine justice: "And this was a true Cardinal-like exploit indeed, representing that mildnesse, mercifulnesse, and good nature which is so required of every Christian, in traiterous murthering a man so many yeres after the first rancour was conceived, that might well in halfe that space have been digested, in fostering hatred so long in his cruell heart, and waging ruffians and murtherers to commit so monstrous an act: wherein albeit the Cardinals crueltie was most famous, as also in putting to death the poore infants, yet Gods justice bare the sway, that used him as an instrument to punish those, who under the vaile of secret marriage, thought it lawfull for them to commit any villany. And thus God busieth sometime the most wicked about his will, and maketh the rage and fury of the devill himselfe serve for meanes to bring to passe his fearefull judgements" (323).

12. A number of critics have noted that this is one of Webster's significant deviations from the source material: the Duchess's eldest son with Antonio inherits the dukedom in the play, rather than the son by her first marriage identified by Painter. Michelle M. Dowd suggests that "Webster consistently reworks Painter's narrative so as to expose rather than to suppress the indeterminacy of patrilineality" (502). "Delinquent Pedigrees: Revision, Lineage, and Spatial Rhetoric in *The Duchess of Malfi*," *ELR* 39.3 (2009): 499–526.

13. Leah Marcus points out that Cariola's assessment of the Duchess's marriage might also be interpreted in a negative light and compares her to Painter, before exploring the com-

plications in this reading. "The Duchess's Marriage in Contemporary Contexts," in Luckyj, *The Duchess of Malfi: A Critical Guide*, 106–18.

14. John Webster, *The Duchess of Malfi*, ed. René Weis (Oxford: Oxford University Press, 1996), 1.1.47–49; cited parenthetically by line number.

15. L. Owen, *The Running Register*, B1v. Julian Yates addresses such identifications in "Parasitic Geographies: Manifesting Catholic Identity in Early Modern England," in *Catholicism and Anti-Catholicism in Early Modern English Texts*, ed. Arthur F. Marotti (Houndmills: Macmillan, 1999), 63–84.

16. L. Owen, *The Running Register*, 102.

17. Leonard Lessius and Fuluius Androtius, *The Treasure of Vowed Chastity in secular persons. Also the Widdowes Glasse*, trans. IWP (1621), A1r–v.

18. Ibid., A1v.

19. See Dympna Callaghan's essay on "*The Duchess of Malfi* and Early Modern Widows," in *Early Modern English Drama: A Critical Companion*, ed. Garrett A. Sullivan, Jr., Patrick Cheney, and Andrew Hadfield (Oxford: Oxford University Press, 2006), 272–86. See also Christy Desmet, "'Neither Maid, Widow, nor Wife': Rhetoric of the Woman Controversy in *Measure for Measure* and *The Duchess of Malfi*," in *In Another Country: Feminist Perspectives on Renaissance Drama*, ed. Dorothea Kehler and Susan Baker (Metuchen, N.J.: Scarecrow Press, 1991), 71–92; and Margaret Lael Mikesell, "Catholic and Protestant Widows in *The Duchess of Malfi*," *Renaissance and Reformation/Renaissance et Réforme* 7.4 (1983): 265–79.

20. See Arthur Marotti, "Alienating Catholics in Early Modern England: Recusant Women, Jesuits and Ideological Fantasies," in Marotti, *Catholicism and Anti-Catholicism*, 1–34.

21. For a persuasive analysis that draws out the relationship between Ferdinand's incestuous desire for his sister and his strict policing of class boundaries, see Whigham, who reads "Ferdinand as a threatened aristocrat, frightened by the contamination of his supposedly ascriptive social rank, and obsessively preoccupied with its defense" (*Seizures of the Will*, 191). Leonard Tennenhouse also notes "that women must be punished excessively when they have blurred within their bodies the distinction between what is properly inside and what must be kept outside the aristocratic community" in *Power on Display* (New York: Methuen, 1986), 116.

22. Thomas Robinson, *The Anatomy of the English Nunnery at Lisbon*, 9.

23. For a parallel reading of the Duchess's marital choices, see Frances E. Dolan, "'Can this be certain?': The Duchess of Malfi's Secrets," in Luckyj, *The Duchess of Malfi: A Critical Guide*, 119–35. Dolan argues that "the Duchess asserts independence of conscience as well as a capacity to consecrate her choices without the sanction of clergy" (130).

24. Curtis Perry and Melissa Walter also suggest that "Webster's pervasive, metadramatic interest in the conventions governing the representation of secret interiors finds expression in a conceptual battle between the Duchess and her brother over the meanings of the spaces they both inhabit" in a reading of the play that focuses on the political implications of "corrosive scrutiny that royal privacy generates" (98, 89). "Staging Secret Interiors: *The Duchess of Malfi* as Inns of Court and Anticourt Drama," in Luckyj, *The Duchess of Malfi: A Critical Guide*, 87–105.

25. See Judith Haber, "'My Body Bestow upon My Women': The Space of the Feminine in *The Duchess of Malfi*," *Renaissance Drama* 28 (1999): 133–59, for "the Duchess's attempt to construct and control her own body, to create a circular, 'feminine' space that is free from invasion" (138). There are many parallels in our readings, but Haber is ultimately interested in

mapping the "space of sexual difference, a space in which 'woman' can exist," while I see the Duchess's understanding of enclosure developing through her conversations with male interlocutors (Ferdinand, the Cardinal, Antonio, Bosola).

26. Whigham, too, notes the Duchess and Antonio's turn to enclosure in his important work on the play, but reads it as a failure of liberation rather than a willing redefinition of interiority: "the marital inversion, conceptually a liberated move outward into the wilderness, takes the ironic practical form of a secret unwilling withdrawal that grows more and more claustrophobic. This effective quarantine encloses her gesture of liberation" (*Seizures of the Will*, 208).

27. See, for example, Ellen Caldwell, "Invasive Procedures in Webster's *The Duchess of Malfi*," in *Women, Violence, and English Renaissance Literature: Essays Honoring Paul Jorgensen*, ed. Linda Woodbridge and Sharon Beehler (Tempe: Arizona Center for Medieval and Renaissance Studies, 2003), 149–86, who explores the relationship between interiority and subjectivity; Lisa Hopkins, "With the Skin Inside: The Interiors of *The Duchess of Malfi*," in *Privacy, Domesticity, and Women in Early Modern England*, ed. Corinne S. Abate (Aldershot: Ashgate, 2003), 21–30, who believes that "to the Duchess, interiors represent safety" (22); and Theodore B. Leinwand, "'Coniugium Interruptum' in Shakespeare and Webster," *ELH* 72.1 (2005): 239–57.

28. Sir Thomas Edmondes to King James I, 14 September 1612, Edmondes Papers vol. 8, British Library, Stowe MS 173, fol. 118v. This document is the draft of a letter from Edmondes to King James I; cited parenthetically by folio.

29. The earliest English convents in exile were located in the Low Countries: the Brussels house of English Benedictines, founded in 1598, was followed in 1608 by the Poor Clares at Gravelines and in 1609 by the Augustines of Louvain and Mary Ward's new order in St. Omer. Syon Abbey had settled in Lisbon in 1594. All these were Spanish territories.

30. As Claire Walker points out, English convents "would become focal points for worship and community identity among the exiled recusants" (*Gender and Politics*, 15). In a 1628 pamphlet, Lewis Owen claimed that there "are in *France* at this instant more *Monks, Friers, Jesuits*, and *Nuns*, by three thousand, then there were when the last King was murdered; yea, within *Paris* and the Suburbs thereof, or neere thereunto, there is betweene thirty and forty Monasteries and Colleges of *Monks, Friers, Jesuits* and *Nuns*, built since that Kings death" (*Unmasking*, 92). Henry IV of France was killed in 1610, suggesting that Edmondes's fears about the popularity of monasticism were realized in the following decades.

31. For a crucial clarification of the relationship between privacy and domesticity in the early modern period that reveals the political implications of the Duchess's family life, see Wendy Wall, "Just a Spoonful of Sugar: Syrup and Domesticity in Early Modern England," *Modern Philology* 104.2 (2006): 149–72.

32. As Kate Aughertson argues in an essay on the play's male characters, "patriarchalism is literally enacted in the story of the authoritarian brothers who rule church, state and sister." "Roaring Boys and Weeping Men: Radical Masculinity in Webster's *The Duchess of Malfi*," in *Literary Politics: The Politics of Literature and the Literature of Politics*, ed. Deborah Philips and Katy Shaw (New York: Palgrave Macmillan, 2013), 45–63, 53.

33. L. Owen, *The Running Register*, 101.

34. Huston Diehl has argued convincingly that Webster "depicts [the Duchess's] responses to torture as essentially those of the Protestant martyr," but too readily glosses over what is strange in Webster's choice to "cast an Italian duchess as a Protestant martyr" (*Staging Reform*, 197–98).

35. Margaret E. Owens, "John Webster, Tussaud Laureate: The Waxworks in *The Duchess of Malfi*," *ELH* 79.4 (2012): 851–77, 863–64. Rory Loughnane has explored the "blend of Catholic and Protestant detail" in relationship to the waxworks (218).

36. As Marcus puts it, "Ferdinand shows a predilection for manipulating ritualized fragments that may, for contemporary audiences, have suggested the Catholic reverences for images" (111).

37. Marriage was a sacrament in the Catholic Church, but not in the reformed faith.

38. See Borlik for a compelling reading of Webster's "complex response to the old faith" (137). While I do not find "poignant defenses of the old faith's ceremonialism" in Webster's plays, I agree that attention to religious ideas and iconography can help reveal a more richly textured response to contemporary Catholicism—here, a critique of its institutional structures in relationship to women (148). Thomas Rist follows Diehl in reading the Duchess as a Protestant figure with "Reformist contempt for venerating the dead" (137).

39. Beard, 321, 323–24.

40. Ibid., 323.

41. Ibid., 324.

42. John Gee, *New Shreds of the Old Snare* (London: Robert Mylbourne, 1624), 14.

43. L. Owen, *The Running Register*, A3v.

44. Though we differ in the specifics of our readings, I agree with Christina Luckyj's argument that "throughout *The Duchess of Malfi* and particularly in the final act, the subplot involving Julia functions as an interpretive key to the main action." *A Winter's Snake: Dramatic Form in the Tragedies of John Webster* (Athens: University of Georgia Press, 1989), 76.

45. Sir Edward Hoby, *A Letter to Mr. T. H. Late Minister: Now Fugitive* (London: Ed. Blount and W. Barret, 1609), A2v. This pamphlet was one of many Protestant responses to Theophilus Higgons, *The First Motive of T. H. Maister of Arts* (1609), a tract explaining his reasons for converting to Catholicism. While Higgons did not address women in his pamphlet, Hoby claims that the *Motive* "hatched, or harboured in the bosome of those (therin *unfortunate*) Ladies, unto whom it was by your factious factors so cunningly vented" (2).

46. As Christine Peters has shown, "In his choice of the word collapsed Hoby was being innovative: the *O.E.D*, although not necessarily an exhaustive source, cites this as the first usage in any application. Just as Alexandra Walsham's observation that the emergence of the language of church papist in the early 1580s crystallized Protestant concerns in late Elizabethan England, so too does the emergence of the collapsed lady in the early years of James's reign suggest a new anxiety" ("Religion, Household-State Authority," 641).

47. John Gee, *The Foot out of the Snare*, 3rd ed. (London: Robert Milbourne, 1624), 64.

48. Ibid.

49. For other contemporary references to "collapsed ladies," see L. Owen, *The Running Register*, 6, 13; L. Owen, *Unmasking*, 159; Daniel Featley, *The Grand Sacrilege of the Church of Rome* (London: Robert Milbourne, 1630), 281; and William Loe, *A Stil Voice, to the Three Thrice-honourable Estates of Parliament* (London: John Teage, 1621), 56.

50. L. Owen, *The Running Register*, A3r.

51. One of the Cardinal's most immediate literary predecessors is Edmund Spenser's Errour, the monstrous figure who appears when the Red Cross Knight wanders from the correct path in Book One of *The Faerie Queene*. Errour "spew[s] out of her filthie maw / A floud of poyson horrible and blacke, / . . . Her vomit full of bookes and papers" (1.1.20.1–6).

52. Robert Burton, *The Anatomy of Melancholy* (Oxford: Henry Cripps, 1621), 731. Like Henry Hastings, the earl of Huntingdon (see Chapter 1, page 38), Burton aligns gender

(female) and class (lower) in his depiction of those who will be most vulnerable to the manipulations of priests.

53. James I to Sir Thomas Edmondes, 22 September 1612, Edmondes Papers vol. 8, British Library, Stowe MS 173, fol. 127r; cited parenthetically by folio.

54. As Luckyj puts it, "the similarities between them suggest the vulnerability of women in a hostile masculine world" (*A Winter's Snake*, 90).

55. As Dympna Callaghan has argued, *The Duchess of Malfi* "demonstrates Webster's interest in women at the center of the tragic predicament, a perspective that serves both to focus and to exacerbate issues about power, sexuality, and the transmission of property that were being worked out in the everyday practices of households as well as in the political arena" (273). While Callaghan is specifically interested in the play's representation of widowhood as "an intensified condition of early modern femininity," she provides a useful framework for thinking about other aspects of "womanhood *in extremis*" in the play, and her understanding of how "a woman in crisis is rendered as symptomatic of cultural crises" is foundational to my reading (273, 284).

56. Diehl also notes this connection, but her reading of the Duchess-as-monument focuses on theater and iconoclasm. "The Duchess is constructed in terms of art. . . . Her attempt to escape the aestheticized and fetishized images men construct of her—to shatter their images, play the iconoclast—culminates, ironically, with the theatrical display of her strangled body" (*Staging Reform*, 211). Sara Eaton addresses the Duchess as a "fetishised female body" (184). "Defacing the Feminine in Renaissance Tragedy," in *The Matter of Difference: Materialist Feminist Criticism of Shakespeare*, ed. Valerie Wayne (Ithaca, N.Y.: Cornell University Press, 1991), 181–98.

57. Five new contemplative cloisters had opened by 1622, and Syon had settled permanently in Lisbon. Another nine opened by 1650. Mary Ward opened her first school in 1609 or 1610, and her unenclosed order became increasingly well known in the subsequent decades. See Walker, *Gender and Politics*, for a thorough history of the early cloisters.

58. Books that cited Robinson include John Gee's *New Shreds of the Old Snare* (1624); Peter Heylyn's *Mikrokosmos* (1625); William Vaughan, *The Golden Fleece* (1626); Lewis Owen, *The Running Register* (1626) and *The Unmasking of All Popish Monks, Friers, and Jesuits* (1628); William Prynne's *Philanax Protestant* (1663); and John Williams, *A Vindication of the History of the Gunpowder-Treason* (1681).

59. For an excellent example of the former, see Frances E. Dolan's analysis of Robinson's denial of nuns' agency in "Why Are Nuns Funny?" *Huntington Library Quarterly* 70.4 (2007): 509–35, especially 526–28. Nancy Bradley Warren offers sensitive readings of Robinson's rhetorical and political strategies in *Women of God and Arms: Female Spirituality and Political Conflict, 1380–1600* (Philadelphia: University of Pennsylvania Press, 2005), 164–67 and *The Embodied Word*, 224–30. In a recent collection on the history of Syon Abbey, both Claire Walker and Caroline Bowden effectively call into question Robinson's "veracity." Walker, "Continuity and Isolation," 166; and Bowden, "Books and Reading at Syon Abbey, Lisbon, in the Seventeenth Century," in Jones and Walsham, *Syon Abbey and Its Books*, 177–202, 185.

60. Thomas Robinson, *The Anatomy of the English Nunnery at Lisbon*, 17; cited parenthetically by page number. Both Stephen Orgel and Sasha Roberts cite this passage when examining early responses to Shakespeare's narrative poems. Stephen Orgel, "Mr. Who He?" *London Review of Books*, 8 August 2002, reprinted in *A Companion to Shakespeare's Sonnets*, ed. Michael Schoenfeldt (Oxford: Blackwell, 2007), 137–44; Sasha Roberts, *Reading Shakespeare's*

Poems in Early Modern England (Houndmills: Palgrave Macmillan, 2003), 79, and "Shakespeare 'creepes into the womens closets about bedtime': Women Reading in a Room of Their Own," in *Renaissance Configurations: Voices/Bodies/Spaces, 1580–1690*, ed. Gordon McMullan (Houndmills: Palgrave, 2001), 30–63.

61. Lukas Erne argues for "Latin title page epigraphs" as "an obvious paratextual feature with which to suggest . . . literary cachet." See *Shakespeare and the Book Trade* (Cambridge: Cambridge University Press, 2013), 100.

62. Virgil, *The Aeneid*, trans. Robert Fitzgerald (London: Harvill, 1984), 16.

63. Margaret Ferguson summarizes these narratives in *Dido's Daughters: Literacy, Gender, and Empire in Early Modern England and France* (Chicago: University of Chicago Press, 2003), 19–20.

64. I borrow this phrase from Ferguson, who suggests that "Dido's fate as a maker, receiver, and subject of narrative turns out to be intricately tied up with debates about the history and legitimacy of the Roman empire . . . she became a focus for enduring debate about history and fiction, about licit and illicit sexual behavior, about masculine and feminine social roles, and about the dangers of speaking and listening to strangers" (1). The same could be said of the post-Reformation English nun, with "church" substituted for "empire."

65. The woodcut, by contrast, depicts a fairly literal interpretation of the pamphlet's titular metaphor of dissection and display: various scenes at the convent culminate in an image of Robinson pulling back the curtain on the priest's bedchamber. The poem describes the woodcut in detail, with an emphasis on female passivity: "a Nun doth kneele," "Friers have power silly Nuns to charme," "they collude, / And doe poore silly Novices delude." Both woodcut and poem are reproduced in Warren, *The Embodied Word*, 226–27.

66. Walker summarizes their travels in "Continuity and Isolation," 157.

67. For information on Syon Abbey in England see David Knowles, *Bare Ruined Choirs: The Dissolution of the English Monasteries* (Cambridge: Cambridge University Press, 1976), 96–103; David N. Bell, *What Nuns Read: Books and Libraries in Medieval English Nunneries* (Kalamazoo, Mich.: Cistercian Publications, 1995); Christopher de Hamel, "The Library: The Medieval Manuscripts of Syon Abbey, and their Dispersal," in De Hamel, *Syon Abbey*, 48–133; James Hogg, ed., *Studies in St. Birgitta and the Brigittine Order*, Analecta Cartusiana 35:19, vol. 2 (Salzburg: Universität Salzburg, 1993); and Jones and Walsham, *Syon Abbey and Its Books*. For a fascinating early account of Syon's history, see John Rory Fletcher, *The Story of the English Bridgettines of Syon Abbey* (Devon: Syon Abbey, 1933).

68. L. Owen, *The Running Register*, 105.

69. For "las Monjas de Sion" see Carlos Dractan, trans., *Relacion que embiaron las Religiosas del Monesterio de Sion de Inglaterra* (Madrid: P. Madrigal, 1594), 58v. For "Sister Barbara, Abbess, and other English Sisters" see De Hamel, *Syon Abbey*, 26.

70. Edward Arber, *A Transcript of the Registers of the Company of Stationers of London; 1554–1640 A.D.* (London, 1877), 4.67. The manuscript response is dated 16 December 1622, which reveals how swiftly books traveled between London and Lisbon.

71. Including *The Life and Good End of Sister Marie*, which I address in the Introduction.

72. For an analysis of the letters and their circulation history, see Travitsky, "The Puzzling Letters of Sister Elizabeth Sa[u]nder[s]."

73. Robert Persons, *Relacion de Algunos Martyrios, que de nuevo han hecho los hereges en Inglaterra, y de otras cosas tocantes a neustra santa y Catolica Religion* (Madrid: Pedro Madrigal, 1590), fols. 42r–61v; Yepes, *Historia Particular de la Persecucion de Inglaterra*, 724–37.

74. Ann M. Hutchison describes the content of these volumes and their publication history in "Syon Abbey Preserved: Some Historians of Syon," in Jones and Walsham, *Syon Abbey and Its Books*, 228–51.

75. Dractan, 58v. This final page of the book indicates that the relation was completed in Lisbon on 30 July 1594.

76. Christopher Highley examines the nuns' strategies for maintaining "their unique institutional and national identity," but focuses on "the dangers of hispaniolization" in *Catholics Writing the Nation in Early Modern Britain and Ireland* (Oxford: Oxford University Press, 2008), 182–83.

77. Bowden points out that "the Bridgettines, like the other members of the English convents in exile, can be seen from evidence in manuscripts and from the books themselves as buyers, recipients of donations, librarians, readers, annotators, performers of texts, listeners, donors, translators, compilers and editors, authors, patrons, dedicatees, subjects, repairers and copyists of the books in their collection" ("Books and Reading," 180).

78. The manuscript history is transcribed and translated in De Hamel, *Syon Abbey*, which also includes facsimile copies of the manuscript's illuminations.

79. For a full account of the manuscript, see the "Introduction" by John Martin Robinson in De Hamel, *Syon Abbey*, 3–10.

80. John Martin Robinson explains that "the relation is a product of the brief moment when an Anglo-Spanish royal match seemed almost certain, during the short-lived rapprochement between the Protestant Stuarts and the Catholic Spanish Hapsburgs in the reign of James I. It can, from the historical evidence, be dated with confidence to the early 1620s, probably to the year 1623" (3). While this date is plausible for petition to the Infanta Maria, which refers to her father in the past tense, the same petition twice explains that "this account of the pilgrimage" was "presented" to Philip III, who died early in 1621 (De Hamel, *Syon Abbey*, 23, 26). Even if the nuns meant that they *intended* to present the petition to the former king, or had presented an earlier version to him, this suggests that some version of the relation and illuminations were at least in process before his death and before the publication of Thomas Robinson's pamphlet. See also Elizabeth Perry, "Petitioning for Patronage: An Illuminated Tale of Exile from Syon Abbey, Lisbon," in Bowden and Kelly, *The English Convents in Exile, 1600–1800*, 159–74.

81. De Hamel, *Syon Abbey*, 23.

82. Ibid., 24.

83. Thomas Scott, *Vox Populi or Newes from Spayne* (London, 1620), B2r.

84. Both Highley and Warren offer readings of this kind. Highley, 188–98; Warren, *Women of God and Arms*, 164–67; and Warren, *The Embodied Word*, 220–32.

85. De Hamel, *Syon Abbey*, 27.

86. "Papers Relating to the English Jesuits," British Library, Additional MS 21203, fols. 42–55, fol. 42v. Cited parenthetically by folio, as "Papers." John Rory Fletcher's early twentieth-century transcription of the manuscript has been edited by James Hogg in *Answer to an Attack on the Nuns of Sion*, Analecta Cartusiana 244 (Salzburg: Institut für Anglistik und Amerikanistik Universität Salzburg, 2006).

87. Because the manuscript is framed in collective terms, I use the plural for its author or authors. Ann Hutchison outlines the problem concerning the "authorship" of Syon's manuscripts in suggestive quotation marks, implying that we might reconsider our notion of early modern authorship when confronting multivocal texts. But Hutchison's tentative solution to the problem regarding *The Wanderings of Syon*—a history of the order in which early refer-

ences to the nuns in the first person plural ("us" and "we") are supplanted by later moments at which "the Sisters" function as objects of the narrative rather than its speakers—nonetheless conforms to the idea of an *individual* author, though couched in modifiers: "it seems *virtually* certain, as Fletcher suggested, that the narrative was composed under firm guidance of Father Seth Foster. I myself *wonder* if the occasional confusion of voice *may be* attributed to the strong *possibility* that the person actually recording the story and ultimately responsible for its final form was indeed one of the nuns" (Hutchison, "Syon Abbey Preserved," 249, emphasis added). As a point of historical fact, in other words, we cannot know with complete certainty which person (or persons) authored texts such as *The Wanderings of Syon*, the illuminated manuscript petition to the Infanta Maria, or the manuscript response to Protestant pamphleteer Thomas Robinson.

88. Marcy North, *The Anonymous Renaissance: Cultures of Discretion in Tudor-Stuart England* (Chicago: University of Chicago Press, 2003), 118.

89. *The New Testament of Jesus Christ* (Rhemes: John Fogny, 1582).

90. Jesse Lander, *Inventing Polemic: Religion, Print, and Literary Culture in Early Modern England* (Cambridge: Cambridge University Press, 2006), 31.

91. For an alternate reading of *The Friers Chronicle* that suggests its contemporary relevance, see Warren, *The Embodied Word*, 233–40.

92. Compare to the lines from *Measure for Measure* analyzed in Chapter 1: "When you have vow'd, you must not speak with men / But in the presence of the prioress: / Then if you speak, you must not show your face, / Or if you show your face, you must not speak" (1.4.10–13).

93. They thus anticipate Eamon Duffy's argument in *The Stripping of the Altars*.

94. This depiction aligns nicely with the illuminated manuscript, in which the nuns portray the Spanish kings as the "true descendants of their founders, the English Kings" (De Hamel, *Syon Abbey*, 33). Henry VIII, in other words, is not a "true descendant" of his predecessors.

CHAPTER 3. A GAME OF HER OWN: THE REFORMATION OF OBEDIENCE

1. Including Julian of Norwich's *Showings*. See Warren, *The Embodied Word*, 61–95.

2. In her recent review of early modern women's devotional writing, Susan M. Felch suggests that "one might be tempted to confine 'devotional writing' simply to prayers, metrical psalms, and meditations but might also extend it to include spiritual autobiography, exegesis, and even letters, taking 'devotional' as a marker for religious observance or acts of worship" (118). "English Women's Devotional Writing: Surveying the Scene," *ANQ: A Quarterly Journal of Short Articles, Notes, and Reviews* 24.1/2 (2011): 118–30.

3. Middleton sometimes quoted directly from his sources, which included Thomas Scott's *Vox Populi*; John Gee's *The Foot out of the Snare*; John Reynolds's *Vox Coeli*; and Thomas Robinson's *The Anatomy of the English Nunnery at Lisbon*. For the play's theatrical history, see the "Introduction" to T. H. Howard-Hill's Revels edition: Thomas Middleton, *A Game at Chess* (Manchester: Manchester University Press, 1993), 1–59.

4. Representative examples include Margot C. Heinemann, "Middleton's *A Game at Chess*: Parliamentary-Puritans and Opposition Drama," *ELR* 5 (1975): 232–50; Thomas Cogswell, "Thomas Middleton and the Court, 1624: 'A Game at Chess' in Context," *Huntington Library Quarterly* 47.4 (1984): 273–88; Jerzy Limon, *Dangerous Matter: English Drama and*

Politics in 1623/24 (Cambridge: Cambridge University Press, 1986); Paul Yachnin, "*A Game at Chess*: Thomas Middleton's 'Praise of Folly,'" *Modern Language Quarterly* 48.2 (1987): 107–23; Richard Dutton, *Mastering the Revels: The Regulation and Censorship of English Renaissance Drama* (Houndsmills: Macmillan, 1991), 236–48; Margot C. Heinemann, "Drama and Opinion in the 1620s: Middleton and Massinger," in *Theatre and Government Under the Early Stuarts*, ed. J. R. Mulryne and Margaret Shewring (Cambridge: Cambridge University Press, 1993), 237–65; Roberta Anderson, "'Well Disposed to the Affairs of Spain?' James VI & I and the Propagandists: 1618–1624," *Recusant History* 25.4 (2001): 613–35; and Richard Dutton, "Receiving Offence: *A Game at Chess* Again," in *Literature and Censorship in Renaissance England*, ed. Andrew Hadfield (Houndsmills: Palgrave, 2001), 50–74.

5. Her words are sometimes nearly indistinguishable from theirs. Compare, for example, More's assertion that "only living in Religion and pleasing our Superiors wil not advance us in the way of perfection, nor practising a blind Obedience which hath in it neither reason nor discretion" to Robert Burton's depiction of monastics who "performe canonicall and blinde obedience, to prostrate their goods, fortunes, bodies, lives, and offer up themselves at their superiors feet." Gertrude More, *The Spiritual Exercises of the Most Vertuous and Religious D. Gertrude More* (Paris: Lewis de la Fosse, 1658), A79–80; Burton, *The Anatomy of Melancholy*, 726.

6. For "blind faith," see More's sonnet on the opening page of *The Spiritual Exercises*. For "blind zeale," see Lewis Owen, *The Running Register*, 101.

7. In a poem "*To our most Holy Father Saint* Benedict," she frames this interpretive act as a return to the true intent of St. Benedict, explaining that "many praise Obedience, / and thy humility, / And yet conceave not as they should, / what either of them be" (More, B281).

8. For a review of sixteenth- and seventeenth-century political discourses of obedience, see Francis Oakley, "Christian Obedience and Authority, 1520–1550," 159–92; Robert M. Kingdom, "Calvinism and Resistance Theory, 1550–1580," 193–218; and J. H. M. Salmon, "Catholic Resistance Theory, Ultramontanism, and the Royalist Response, 1580–1620," 219–53, all in *The Cambridge History of Political Thought, 1450–1700*, ed. J. H. Burns (Cambridge: Cambridge University Press, 1991). Richard Rex focuses on the particulars of the English Reformation in "The Crisis of Obedience: God's Word and Henry's Reformation," *Historical Journal* 39.4 (1996): 863–94.

9. *Constitutions Compiled for the Better Observation of the Holie Rule of Our Most Glorious Fa: and Patriarch S. Bennet*, Archives Départmentales du Nord, Lille, Box 20H, MS 20 H 1, 33.

10. Ibid.

11. For a brief overview of the controversy, see Justin McCann, O.S.B, introduction to Peter Salvin and Serenus Cressy, *The Life of Father Augustine Baker, O.S.B. (1575–1641)*, ed. Justin McCann, O.S.B., Salzburg English & American Studies 20 (Salzburg: Institut für Anglistik und Amerikanistik, 1997), xxiii–xxviii.

12. Jos Blom and Frans Blom, eds., *Elizabeth Evelinge, II*, vol. 5 of *The Early Modern Englishwoman: A Facsimile Library of Essential Works*, Series I, Printed Writings, 1500–1640: Part 3 (Aldershot: Ashgate, 2002). The translation was originally attributed to Catherine Bentley, but Luke Wadding's catalogue of Franciscan authors suggests Evelinge was the translator. See Jaime Goodrich, "'Ensigne-Bearers of Saint Clare'."

13. Frances E. Dolan, ed., *Recusant Translators: Elizabeth Cary, Alexia Gray*, vol. 13 of *The Early Modern Englishwoman: A Facsimile Library of Essential Works*, Series I, Printed Writings,

1500–1640: Part 2 (Aldershot: Ashgate, 2000). See also Jaime Goodrich, "Nuns and Community-Centered Writing."

14. Caroline Bowden, ed., *English Convents in Exile, 1600–1800*. For convent rules, see especially vol. 2 on *Spirituality* and vol. 5 on *Convent Management*.

15. Hywel Wyn Owen and Luke Bell describe these manuscripts in their "The Upholland Anthology: An Augustine Baker Manuscript," *Downside Review* 107 (1989): 274–92.

16. Margaret Gascoigne, *Devotions*, Colwich Abbey, MS 18, 215. This volume also includes "A treatise of St. Richard of Hampole" translated by Augustine Baker, "A Similtude of a Pillgrime walking towards Jerusalem," and a loose quire of commentary on "The 4th degree of Hum."

17. See my article on Dame Barbara Constable's collections for an analysis of the implications for our understanding of authorship. "An English Nun's Authority: Early Modern Spiritual Controversy and the Manuscripts of Barbara Constable," in *Gender, Catholicism and Spirituality: Women and the Roman Catholic Church in Britain and Europe, 1200–1900*, ed. Laurence Lux-Sterritt and Carmen Mangion (London: Palgrave Macmillan, 2010), 99–114.

18. Augustine Baker, O.S.B., *The Life and Death of Dame Gertrude More*, ed. Ben Wekking, *Analecta Cartusiana* 119:19 (Salzburg: Institut für Anglistik und Amerikanistik Universität Salzburg, 2002), 147–48; cited parenthetically as *Life*.

19. Augustine Baker, "Concerning the Librarie of this howse," in *Vth Book of Collections*, Colwich Abbey, MS 9, 137–45, 137–38. For a partial transcription, see Anselm Cramer, O.S.B., " 'The Librairie of this Howse': Augustine Baker's Community and Their Books," in *"Stand up to Godwards": Essays in Mystical and Monastic Theology in Honour of the Reverend John Clark on His Sixty-Fifth Birthday*, ed. James Hogg, *Analecta Cartusiana* 204 (Salzburg: Institut für Anglistik und Amerikanistik Universität Salzburg, 2002), 103–10. Caroline Bowden offers an analysis of the times set aside for reading in " 'A distribution of tyme.' "

20. For a more detailed list of Baker's sources, see J. P. H. Clark, "Augustine Baker, O.S.B.: Towards a Re-Assessment," *Studies in Spirituality* 14 (2004): 209–24.

21. Heather Wolfe examines this process in "Reading Bells and Loose Papers: Reading and Writing Practices of the English Benedictine Nuns of Cambrai and Paris," in *Early Modern Women's Manuscript Writing*, ed. Victoria E. Burke and Jonathan Gibson (Aldershot: Ashgate, 2004), 135–56.

22. For Constable, see Heather Wolfe, "Dame Barbara Constable: Catholic Antiquarian, Advisor, and Closet Missionary," in *Catholic Culture in Early Modern England*, ed. Ronald Corthell, Frances E. Dolan, Christopher Highley, and Arthur F. Marotti (Notre Dame, Ind.: University of Notre Dame Press, 2007), 158–88; Gertz, "Barbara Constable's *Advice for Confessors*"; and my "An English Nun's Authority."

23. Catherine Gascoigne, "A Relation of the Lady Abesse her Spirituall Course," Colwich Abbey, MS 32, 208. See also Downside Abbey, Baker MS 33, 333–34. Gascoigne wrote these words in an account of her prayer submitted to the English Benedictine Congregation, which attempted to censor Cambrai's autograph Baker materials in the 1650s.

24. There is some confusion related to the title of More's book: it has been cited as either *The Spiritual Exercises* or *Confessiones Amantis* and has been incorrectly identified as the second edition of the 1657 *Ideots Devotions*. The difficulty derives from the title page, on which *The Spiritual Exercises* is typographically identifiable as the title, but "Ideots Devotions" and "Confessiones Amantis" are named as alternate titles used by More and Baker, respectively. Following Arthur Marotti's facsimile edition for the Early Modern Englishwoman series,

I use *The Spiritual Exercises* to refer to the printed book as a whole and "Confessiones Amantis" to refer to the devotional materials contained therein. Arthur F. Marotti, ed., *Gertrude More*, vol. 3 of *The Early Modern Englishwoman: A Facsimile Library of Essential Works*, Series II, Printed Writings, 1641–1700: Part 4 (Farnham: Ashgate, 2009).

25. For an analysis of the renewed controversy that examines manuscripts as property, see Claire Walker, "Spiritual Property: The English Benedictine Nuns of Cambrai and the Dispute over the Baker Manuscripts," in *Women, Property, and the Letters of the Law in Early Modern England*, ed. Nancy E. Wright, Margaret W. Ferguson, and A. R. Buck (Toronto: University of Toronto Press, 2004), 237–55.

26. See, for example, Colwich Abbey, MS 22, which includes "The Sixt Confession D.G." (123). This confession is found on B31 of the printed edition.

27. Gertrude More, *The Spiritual Exercises*, A4. Cited parenthetically as More. In order to differentiate between the two separately paginated sections of the book—the "Advertisement" and the "Confessiones Amantis"—I cite the "Advertisement" and prefatory material as section A and the "Confessiones Amantis" as section B.

28. "Introductory Note" in Marotti, *Gertrude More*, xvii.

29. Matt. 22:21, *The New Testament of Jesus Christ* (Rhemes: John Fogny, 1582).

30. Compare Matt. 22:21 to Luke 20:25. For scriptural dilation, see Roland Greene, "Anne Lock's *Meditation*: Invention Versus Dilation and the Founding of Puritan Poetics," in *Form and Reform in Renaissance England: Essays in Honor of Barbara Kiefer Lewalski*, ed. Amy Boesky and Mary Thomas Crane (Newark: University of Delaware Press, 2000), 153–70.

31. Matt. 22:15, 22:17.

32. *The New Testament of Jesus Christ*, 64. The Cambrai library held two copies of the 1582 Rheims New Testament, as well as multiple copies of the printings of 1600, 1621, and 1633. See J. T. Rhodes, ed., *Catalogue des livres provenant des religieuses angloises de Cambray: Book List of the English Benedictine Nuns of Cambrai c. 1739*, Analecta Cartusiana 119:32 (Salzburg: Institut für Anglistik und Amerikanistik Universität Salzburg, 2013), 145.

33. *The New Testament of Jesus Christ*, 64.

34. Warren analyzes this material in *The Embodied Word*, 97–102. See also Clark Hulse, "Dead Man's Treasure: The Cult of Thomas More," in *The Production of English Renaissance Culture*, ed. David Lee Miller, Sharon O'Dair, and Harold Weber (Ithaca, N.Y.: Cornell University Press, 1994), 190–225. Hulse suggests that "the perpetuation of the More family is the perpetuation of a central element of the Roman Catholic Church in England" (216).

35. Dorothy Latz, whose groundbreaking work on the writing of English nuns is an important forerunner of this book, attributed both parts of the poem to More, but the printer has created a clear typographic delineation: the sonnet authored by More is in italics and preceded by the lines "while she liv'd mortals among / Thus to her *Spouse Divine* she sung." See "Neglected Writings by Recusant Women," in *Neglected English Literature: Recusant Writings of the 16th–17th Centuries*, ed. Dorothy L. Latz (Salzburg: Institut für Anglistik und Amerikanistik, 1997), 11–48, 18. Latz also claims that the poem and picture of More are printed in the 1657 *Ideots Devotions*, which she refers to as the first edition of More's writings. This is not the case: neither the poem nor the picture is included in *Ideots Devotions* and it is not the first edition of *The Spiritual Exercises*. Marion Norman also attributes the invocation of Sir Thomas More to Gertrude More in "Dame Gertrude More and the English Mystical Tradition," *Recusant History* 13.3 (1976): 196–211, 203.

36. Warren, *The Embodied Word*, 100.

37. Sir Thomas More, *The Workes of Sir Thomas More Knyght* (London: John Cawod, John Waly, and Richarde Tottell, 1557), 1429.

38. Ethan Shagan, *Popular Politics and the English Reformation* (Cambridge: Cambridge University Press, 2003), 51.

39. *The Workes* appears in the Cambrai library catalogue, suggesting that More may have had access to it while in the convent (and likely would have had access to it in her family library, as well). The library also held copies of More's *A Dialogue of Comfort* (1573) and *The Apologye* (1533). See Rhodes, 98.

40. Thomas More, 1429. Ethan Shagan calls Gardiner's text "the quintessential conformist Catholic gloss on the royal supremacy" and "one of the most influential tracts of the early Reformation" (47). As Shagan makes clear, there was "no single 'Catholic' position on the royal supremacy but rather a wide spectrum of opinions ranging from passionate loyalism to passionate opposition, with all shades of ambiguity and expediency in between" (51).

41. Gardiner's *De Vera Obedientia* was first published in Latin in 1535. The English translation—"An oracion . . . touchinge true obedience"—is sometimes attributed to John Bale and was printed in 1553. For both the English and the Latin, see Pierre Janelle, ed., *Obedience in Church & State: Three Political Tracts by Stephen Gardiner* (Cambridge: Cambridge University Press, 1930), 107.

42. Oakley, 177. Lucy Wooding argues of Gardiner, "*De Vera Obedientia* has always been taken as an unprincipled attempt to work a way back into royal favour. But the intention behind the work does not impair its intellectual coherence. Gardiner developed an ideological context for the Supremacy which was intellectually viable and which in time seems to have become morally acceptable to him. It is important to remember, that obedience to the King was an essential part of religious duty, in itself a sacred obligation." See *Rethinking Catholicism in Reformation England* (Oxford: Oxford University Press, 2000), 69.

43. Cresacre More, *The Life and Death of Sir Thomas Moore* (1631). Cresacre borrows extensively from *The Workes* and cites Sir Thomas More's letters; one of the undated early printings (1631 or 1642) is also listed in the Cambrai library catalogue (Rhodes, 227).

44. Cresacre More, *The Life and Death*, 321. For an overview of "conscience" in early modern religious politics, see Edmund Leites, ed., *Conscience and Casuistry in Early Modern Europe* (Cambridge: Cambridge University Press, 2002).

45. As Jane Stevenson and Peter Davidson suggest, More was "highly conscious of her intellectual and spiritual heritage"; see *Early Modern Women Poets: An Anthology* (Oxford: Oxford University Press, 2001), 224.

46. For an overview of the parliamentary debate, see J. A. Guy, "The Origins of the Petition of Right Reconsidered," *Historical Journal* 25.2 (1982): 289–312.

47. Mihoko Suzuki explores women's echoes of the Petition of Right in "Daughters of Coke: Women's Legal Discourse in England, 1642–1689," in *Challenging Orthodoxies: The Social and Cultural Worlds of Early Modern Women; Essays Presented to Hilda L. Smith*, ed. Sigrun Haude and Melinda S. Zook (Farnham: Ashgate/Gower, 2014), 165–91.

48. Margaret More Roper, trans., *A Devout Treatise upon the Pater Noster*, by Desiderius Erasmus (London: Thomas Berthelet, [1526?]), E1v. Roper's translation is not listed in the Cambrai library catalogue, but More may have encountered it in her family library.

49. Jaime Goodrich, "Thomas More and Margaret More Roper: A Case for Rethinking Women's Participation in the Early Modern Public Sphere," *Sixteenth Century Journal* 39.4 (2008): 1021–40. "Read within the context of England's anti-Lutheran campaign, Margaret Roper's translation further reveals a political dimension in its positioning of Erasmus as an

orthodox Catholic and its continuance of his efforts to reconcile religious strife. The main thrust of the text's attack on Luther lies in Erasmus's argument that the hallmark of Christianity is obedience to divine will" (1032).

50. Goodrich, "Thomas More and Margaret More Roper," 1033.

51. Roper, D4v.

52. I touch on dissension within the Catholic community in York in my discussion of Margaret Clitherow in Chapter 1. For more thorough analyses of recusancy and church papistry in the sixteenth century and the Appellant Controversy at the turn of the century, see Michael Questier, *Catholicism and Community in Early Modern England: Politics, Aristocratic Patronage and Religion, c. 1550–1640* (Cambridge: Cambridge University Press, 2006); and Walsham, *Church Papists*.

53. See Walker, *Gender and Politics*, 43–44.

54. For an analysis of Jesuit direction of seventeenth-century contemplative convents, with particular reference to Brussels, see Walker, *Gender and Politics*, 134–47.

55. Jaime Goodrich, "Nuns and Community-Centered Writing," 298. Goodrich has also written on the Brussels dispute: "Translating Lady Mary Percy: Authorship and Authority Among the Brussels Benedictines," in Bowden and Kelly, *The English Convents in Exile, 1600–1800: Communities, Culture and Identity*, 109–22.

56. L. Owen, *The Running Register*, 102. As Arthur Marotti has pointed out, "the supposed political threats posed by Jesuits were often associated with their relations with women." *Religious Ideology and Cultural Fantasy: Catholic and Anti-Catholic Discourses in Early Modern England* (Notre Dame, Ind.: University of Notre Dame Press, 2005), 61.

57. Robert I. Lublin explores how costumes may have contributed to these identifications in *Costuming the Shakespearean Stage: Visual Codes of Representation in Early Modern Theatre and Culture* (Farnham: Ashgate, 2011), 163–80.

58. Thomas Middleton, *A Game at Chess*, ed. T. H. Howard-Hill, Revels Plays (Manchester: Manchester University Press, 1993), Induction.60; cited parenthetically by line number.

59. See, for example, John Loftis, *Renaissance Drama in England & Spain: Topical Allusion and History Plays* (Princeton, N.J.: Princeton University Press, 1987). Loftis writes, "an understanding of the primary thrust of Middleton's allegory, embodied in the main plot, requires only such knowledge of recent events as his audiences were likely to have had or as a modern editor can easily supply. The pawns' allegory, comprising the underplot, now seems obscure" (174–75).

60. T. H. Howard-Hill provides an overview of the allegorical identifications in "Political Interpretations of Middleton's 'A Game at Chess' (1624)," *Yearbook of English Studies* 21 (1991): 274–85.

61. T. H. Howard-Hill, ed., "Appendix I: Documents Relating to *A Game at Chess*," in Middleton, *A Game at Chess*, 192–213, 193; cited as "Appendix."

62. Other contemporary accounts describe a play about "Gondomar and all the Spanish proceedings" ("Appendix" 193), "all our spannishe traffike" (198), and "the whole Spanish busines" (202). In each instance, the pawns are overshadowed by Spain. Critical readings of the political significance of *A Game at Chess* have tended to follow Woolley in characterizing the pawns' plot as little more than background noise. In an early article suggesting a court-based sponsor for the play, Margot C. Heinemann dismisses the pawns silently, explaining that "although the play . . . is primarily an attack on Gondomar and Spain, it also contains a great deal of general anti-Catholic and anti-Jesuit satire without particular reference to nationality"

("Middleton's *A Game at Chess*," 236). The pawns are presumably the locus of this unspecified "general anti-Catholic and anti-Jesuit satire."

63. "Appendix," 208–10, 209.

64. Howard-Hill, "Political Interpretations," 284. See also David M. Holmes, who argues that "in the White Queen's Pawn plot we have a clear expression both of Middleton's personal alliance with the Church of England and of his concern for its security" in *The Art of Thomas Middleton: A Critical Study* (Oxford: Clarendon, 1970), 191.

65. Compare Thomas Robinson, who claims that the Jesuits will "dispossesse" women "of all worldly cares and vanities, and (like subtill Alchymists) refine them out of their silver and golden drosse, into a more sublime estate and condition, and will cherish and nourish them, even in their owne bosomes: such a burning zeale have they towards them" (9).

66. James Doelman explores the "politics of conversion" in relationship to the White Queen's Pawn, but does so in search of a "specific allegorical representation" that dismisses gender entirely. See "Claimed by Two Religions: The Elegy on Thomas Washington, 1623, and Middleton's *A Game at Chesse*," *Studies in Philology* 110.2 (2013): 318–49, 318.

67. See Chapter 2.

68. Gary Taylor, "Forms of Opposition: Shakespeare and Middleton," *ELR* 24.2 (1994): 283–314, 308. Jane Sherman suggests that Middleton "has perhaps even made a statement of political belief. Conservative writers had always stressed obedience as the prime duty of the third estate, as did James when dealing with his Commons. Yet it is the White Queen's Pawn's very susceptibility to the notion of absolute obedience that lands her in trouble." See "The Pawns' Allegory in Middleton's *A Game at Chesse*," *Review of English Studies* 29 (1978): 147–59, 159. For readings of the play as "opposition drama," see Margot C. Heinemann, *Puritanism and Theatre: Thomas Middleton and Opposition Drama Under the Early Stuarts* (Cambridge: Cambridge University Press, 1980); and Albert H. Tricomi, *Anticourt Drama in England, 1603–1642* (Charlottesville: University Press of Virginia, 1989).

69. Dorothy M. Farr, *Thomas Middleton and the Drama of Realism: A Study of Some Representative Plays* (Edinburgh: Oliver & Boyd, 1973), 100. Swapan Chakravorty, *Society and Politics in the Plays of Thomas Middleton* (Oxford: Clarendon, 1996), 178. Even Arthur Marotti, who identifies the Black Queen's Pawn with Mary Ward, focuses on how "this female Jesuit *assists* in the evil business" (emphasis mine). See "Alienating Catholics," 21.

70. Middleton, *A Game at Chess*, 152n148. The Oxford Middleton also includes "anger's" as a gloss for "blood's." *Thomas Middleton: The Collected Works*, ed. Gary Taylor and John Lavagnino (Oxford: Oxford University Press, 2007), 1866n149.

71. Roland Greene explores "blood" in *Five Words: Critical Semantics in the Age of Shakespeare and Cervantes* (Chicago: University of Chicago Press, 2013): "the fate of blood in the period belongs to a concept under revision and a word that exchanges allegorical for literal meanings" (108).

72. Gary Taylor, *Castration: An Abbreviated History of Western Manhood* (New York: Routledge, 2000), 89.

73. Caroline Bicks, "Staging the Jesuitess in *A Game at Chess*," *SEL* 49.2 (2009): 463–84, 477.

74. Taylor, *Castration*, 89; Bicks, 477.

75. This passage has also been read as fully individual: Swapan Chakravorty claims that the Black Queen's Pawn "wants to get back at the Jesuit for having deported and robbed *her*" (178, emphasis mine). Again, the community of women is elided and the Black Queen's Pawn is reduced to seeking only a very personal form of revenge.

76. In a letter of 1624, the Venetian ambassador to London described how *A Game at Chess* gave "several representations under different names of many of the circumstances about the marriage with the Infanta" ("Appendix," 204). Howard-Hill agrees that it is "a play about marriage," despite the fact that the only marriage explicitly represented in *A Game* is the impossible pairing of the White Queen's Pawn and the Black Bishop's Pawn. See Howard-Hill, *Middleton's "Vulgar Pasquin": Essays on "A Game at Chess"* (Newark: University of Delaware Press, 1995), 28.

77. Bicks is the exception to this general rule, and her reading of the Black Queen's Pawn as "the play's most unpredictable and effective stage director, as well as its most accomplished performer" offers a welcome corrective to critics who "focus on [the Black Queen's Pawn's] alliance with the Jesuits." Bicks and I differ, however, in our focus: I read *A Game at Chess* as a play that stages the interplay between female obedience and religious authority, while Bicks examines the parallel "conjunction of religious conversion and theater" in the relationship between the Black and White Queens' Pawns.

78. Thomas Robinson accused Henry Flood, "the chiefe Agent for the transporting of Nunnes" (8), of sending women with good dowries to Brussels, the convent at which the Black Queen's Pawn was a "probationer" (5.2.91), to "dispossesse them of all worldly cares and vanities" (9).

79. "Appendix," 205. These details are included in a letter from John Chamberlain to Sir Dudley Carleton dated 21 August 1624. Heinemann cites this letter as the basis for her analysis of Puritan interest in the play ("Middleton's *A Game at Chess*," 232) and Yachnin responds by emphasizing the fact that "Thomas Middleton's *Game at Chess* might have been a play for Puritans, but it certainly was not a play *only* for Puritans," using the same quote as his evidence ("*A Game at Chess*: Thomas Middleton's 'Praise of Folly,'" 107).

80. "Appendix," 197.

81. Ibid.

82. Many letters include some acknowledgment of this. See, for example, the letters of Winefrid Thimelby, abbess at Louvain: "it is not the first of mine, which hath miscaried. For really I have never mised any oportunitie which gave any hopes of aryving you. so carfull selfe love made me to soe my seede in hope to reape the pleasing fruit of your answers but when they fayled I never did admit a thought your love did so." Winefrid Thimelby to Katherine Thimelby Aston, 4 November, Aston Papers vol. 9: Private Correspondence 1613–1703, British Library, Additional MS 36452, 63r.

83. For an example of the latter, see *Defense of Lady Mary Percy*, British Library, Harley MS 4275. This manuscript reflects on the scandal over Jesuit instruction at Brussels and is polemically titled "Innocency justified and Insolency repressed, Or, A round yet modest answere, to an immodest and slaunderous Libell bearing this title . . . *A breefe and since Relation of the beginnings, grounds, and issue of the late Controversy betwixt the Lady Mary Percy Abbesse and her Religious*" (1r).

84. Of the Benedictine convent at Brussels, Walker says, "split into factions and openly warring, the cloister's problems became common knowledge—a fact reflected by the absence of professions in the 1630s and a single one in the 1640s" (*Gender and Politics*, 24).

85. This focus on intra-Catholic divisions elides the fact that similar struggles affected the English court, though Middleton does allude to the conflicting agendas of the White House when the White Knight and the White Duke secretly work together to prove the White Queen's Pawn's innocence and to infiltrate the Black House despite the White King's intransigence.

86. In his introduction to the play in the Oxford Middleton, Gary Taylor suggests that "*A Game at Chess* is an English history play—a play about history, which also made history," and I would argue that it registers a broader range of contemporary history than has previously been acknowledged (*Thomas Middleton: The Collected Works*, 1773).

87. Barbara Constable, *Considerations or Reflexions upon the Rule of the most glorious father St Benedict*, Downside Abbey, MS 82144/627 (1655), 6. Taylor suggests that "*A Game at Chess* anticipates the divisions that led to the English civil wars and the Glorious Revolution" in "Historicism, Presentism and Time: Middleton's *The Spanish Gypsy* and *A Game at Chess*," *SEDERI: Journal of the Spanish Society for English Renaissance Studies* 18 (2008): 147–70, 165.

CHAPTER 4. CLOISTERS AND COUNTRY HOUSES: WOMEN'S LITERARY COMMUNITIES

1. The plays in my second and third chapters participated in the creation of a persistent historical narrative, in which Catholicism is a religion dependent on the book as a material object: a talisman rather than truth. James Kearney troubles the easy distinction between "fleshy book" (Catholic) and "a turn to text" (Protestant) by demonstrating how "Christianity always enjoyed an ambivalent relationship to the book and . . . this ambivalence was exacerbated by the defining concerns of the Reformation" (*The Incarnate Text*, 7, 9). Without making the claim directly, Frances Dolan's *Whores of Babylon* reveals that Christianity's similarly ambivalent relationship to femininity was exacerbated by the defining concerns of the Reformation.

2. Debora Shuger, "Laudian Feminism and the Household Republic of Little Gidding," *Journal of Medieval and Early Modern Studies* 44.1 (2014): 69–94, 70. Shuger offers a compelling reading of both the community's feminism and its Laudianism, adopting Peter Lake's terminology in her identification of both as "avant-garde conformist" aspects of the community (90).

3. *The Arminian Nunnery* (London: Thomas Underhill, 1641), 3, 9. Shuger explains that "although John Ferrar's life of Nicholas foregrounds his brother's role in ordering and guiding the Little Gidding community, contemporary observers (particularly the hostile ones) tended to comment on its female government" (70).

4. Adam Smyth, " 'Shreds of holinesse': George Herbert, Little Gidding, and Cutting Up Texts in Early Modern England," *ELR* 42.3 (2012): 452–81, 469. Smyth offers an important corrective to this understanding of cutting, arguing that "every written word, and therefore every written sentence and written text, can only come into being through a process of selection: a process of eliminating or cutting out other possible words, letting them fall to the floor, and of grasping the word intended" (469). See also Shuger, "Laudian Feminism," who notes that earlier critics attributed the Story Books to Nicholas but argues that they should be understood as "the products of a multilevel, and largely female, collaborative authorship" (71).

5. Fowler's miscellany includes a Passion poem (see my Epilogue for a reading of this poem), the pastoral, epigraphs, elegies, and love poetry.

6. See Victoria Burke, "Women and Early Seventeenth-Century Manuscript Culture: Four Miscellanies," *Seventeenth Century* 12.2 (1997): 135–50; Helen Hackett, "Women and Catholic Manuscript Networks in Seventeenth-Century England: New Research on Constance Aston Fowler's Miscellany of Sacred and Secular Verse," *Renaissance Quarterly* 65.4 (2012): 1094–1124; Jenijoy La Belle, "A True Love's Knot: The Letters of Constance Fowler and

the Poems of Herbert Aston," *Journal of English and Germanic Philology* 79.1 (1980): 13–31; Mareile Pfannebecker, "'Love's Interest': Agency and Identity in a Seventeenth-Century Nun's Letters," *Literature Compass* 3.2 (2006): 149–58; Julie Sanders, "Tixall Revisited: The Coterie Writing of the Astons and the Thimelbys in Seventeenth-Century Staffordshire," *Staffordshire Studies* 12 (2000): 75–93; Victoria Van Hyning's unpublished Ph.D. thesis, "Cloistered Voices: English Nuns in Exile, 1550–1800" (2014); and Claire Walker, "'Doe not supose me a well mortifyed Nun dead to the world': Letter-Writing in Early Modern English Convents," in *Early Modern Women's Letter Writing, 1450–1700*, ed. James Daybell (Houndmills: Palgrave, 2001), 159–76.

7. As Hackett has demonstrated, the actual Southwell poems in Fowler's miscellany were added after the manuscript volume was bound. As a result, we cannot know whether the scribe (Hand B) of these and other explicitly religious poems in the collection was known to Fowler or whether the book was no longer in her possession (1111–14).

8. *The Poems of Andrew Marvell*, ed. Nigel Smith (Harlow: Pearson, 2007), 219, line 94. For responses to Astell, see Bridget Hill, "A Refuge from Men: The Idea of a Protestant Nunnery," *Past & Present* 117 (1987): 107–30.

9. For Southwell, see Arthur Marotti, "Southwell's Remains: Catholicism and Anti-Catholicism in Early Modern England," in *Texts and Cultural Change in Early Modern England*, ed. Cedric C. Brown and Arthur F. Marotti (New York: St. Martin's, 1997), 37–65; and Shell, *Catholicism*, 58–63. Shell notes that *Saint Peters Complaint* alone "ran through thirteen mainstream editions between 1595 and 1640, and two printed by clandestine Catholic presses" (61). For readings of Donne's ambiguities, see Brian Cummings, *The Literary Culture of the Reformation: Grammar and Grace* (Oxford: Oxford University Press, 2002), 365–417; and Molly Murray, *Poetics of Conversion*, 69–104.

10. Robert Southwell, *Saint Peters Complaint, With Other Poemes* (London: John Wolfe, 1595), A2r. For an analysis of Southwell as poetic theorist, see Shell, *Catholicism*, 63–77. For the sequence of poems in the Waldegrave manuscript (Stonyhurst MS A.v.27), see Peter Davidson and Anne Sweeney, eds., *Collected Poems*, by Robert Southwell (Manchester: Carcanet, 2007).

11. Shell, *Catholicism*, 63.

12. For readings of Southwell in this vein, see Shell, *Catholicism*; Marotti, "Southwell's Remains"; Cummings, *Literary Culture*; and Murray, *Poetics of Conversion*.

13. "Le guancie ch' adorna un dolce foco." Francesco Petrarca, *Petrarch's Lyric Poems: The Rime Sparse and Other Lyrics*, trans. and ed. Robert M. Durling (Cambridge, Mass. Harvard University Press, 1976), 252–53.

14. Southwell, *Saint Peters Complaint*, p. 35, line 1; cited parenthetically by line number.

15. Southwell, *Saint Peters Complaint*, A2r.

16. As James Kearney suggests in his reading of Luther, "Books, paper, ink—these are signs of the Fall, signs of the failure of human signification to be other than bodily, carnal" (*The Incarnate Text*, 24).

17. In a reading that explores how Southwell influenced Spenser's poetics, Jennifer Rust suggests that "Southwell seeks to re-inscribe the spiritualizing trajectory of Petrarchan erotic praise back into the religious context from which it was derived" (191). "Malengin and Mercila, Southwell and Spenser: The Poetics of Tears and the Politics of Martyrdom in *The Faerie Queene*, Book 5, Canto 9," in L. Gallagher, *Redrawing the Map*, 185–209.

18. Gary Kuchar offers a complementary reading of *Mary Magdalene's Funeral Tears*, suggesting that "The paradox of recusant melancholia as Southwell articulates it is Petrarchan in

structure insofar as the absence of the physical object results in a deepened spiritual relation with it." "Gender and Recusant Melancholia in *Mary Magdalene's Funeral Tears*," in *Catholic Culture in Early Modern England*, ed. Ronald Corthell, Frances E. Dolan, Christopher Highley, and Arthur F. Marotti (Notre Dame, Ind.: University of Notre Dame Press, 2007), 135–57, 149.

19. Robert Southwell, *Marie Magdalens Funeral Teares* (London: Gabriel Cawood, 1591), A3v.

20. Shell, *Catholicism*, 67; Southwell, *Marie Magdalens Funeral Teares*, A3r. Southwell's *Short Rule for a Good Life* was also written for a woman, and Susannah Monta has noted that "some manuscripts prepared for Catholic readers indicate that the treatise was thought particularly appropriate for women." "Anne Dacre Howard, Countess of Arundel, and Catholic Patronage," in *English Women, Religion, and Textual Production, 1500–1625*, ed. Micheline White (Farnham: Ashgate, 2011), 59–81, 68.

21. See Kuchar, "Gender and Recusant Melancholia," 139. For Arundel's association with the Brussels Benedictines, see the "Dorothea Arundell" entry in the *Who Were the Nuns?* database at http://wwtn.history.qmul.ac.uk.

22. British Library shelfmark 11623.aa.42: Robert Southwell, *Marie Magdalens Funerall Teares* (London: I.R. for W.L., 1602). For the biographical information on Sheldon, see the *Who Were the Nuns?*, http://wwtn.history.qmul.ac.uk.

23. Since family members share surnames, and those surnames change with marriage, I will refer to all letter writers by their given names.

24. For readings of Catholic assimilation, see Marotti's "Southwell's Remains" and Alexandra Walsham's *Church Papists*. I follow Helen Wilcox's attention to "the irrepressible intertextuality and rhetorical poise of the epistolary mode." See "'Free and Easy as ones discourse'?: Genre and Self-Expression in the Poems and Letters of Early Modern Englishwomen," in *Genre and Women's Life Writing in Early Modern England*, ed. Michelle M. Dowd, Julie A. Eckerle, and Laura Knoppers (Abingdon: Ashgate, 2007), 15–32, 24.

25. Sanders, 82. While Sanders has argued that the "female members of the family were invested in a deeper sense of the preservation of localized family work . . . looking little further than the county lines for its sphere of reference" (81), Helen Hackett makes a powerful case for the "outward-looking perspectives" of the circle and its "international outlook" ("Women and Catholic Manuscript Networks," 1103; 1102). Hackett traces the critical tendency to "emphasize the personal and domestic nature" of female writing in the Aston-Thimelby circle to the early nineteenth-century editions of the family papers published by descendent Arthur Clifford, whose "dynastic concerns meant that he was also interested in foregrounding the familial themes of the poems he selected and edited for publication" (1101).

26. For recent work on early modern letters, see James Daybell, ed., *Early Modern Women's Letter Writing, 1450–1700* (Houndmills: Palgrave, 2001); and Daybell, *The Material Letter: Manuscript Letters and the Culture and Practices of Letter-Writing in Early Modern England, 1580–1635* (Houndmills: Palgrave Macmillan, 2012).

27. Sanders, for example, explains that Fowler may adopt a persona in her letters by comparing her voice to a "first-person narrator in a fictional novel" and suggests her style is similar to "stream-of-consciousness" (84, 87). La Belle seems to be the origin of this type of reading: she claimed that Fowler was "practically writing a novel in her letters. . . . a historical foreshadowing of the eighteenth-century epistolary novel with very little plot and a great deal of sentiment and rhetoric" (14).

28. See, for example, Arthur Marotti, *Manuscript, Print and the English Renaissance Lyric* (Ithaca, N.Y.: Cornell University Press, 1995). Burke argues that "copying, transcribing, and

compiling, then, are often crucial aspects of manuscript writing. As we move away from our interest in the author as a monolithic figure, we can see men and women who compiled miscellanies as producing a type of writing which can give us insight into what they read, what they chose to record from their reading, how they recorded it—in short, how they participated in their culture" (135).

29. La Belle's work is a crucial exception.

30. Constance Aston Fowler to Herbert Aston, 17 August 1636, Aston Papers vol. 9, British Library, Additional MS 36452, fols. 21–22, fol. 22v; cited parenthetically by folio.

31. Hackett, "Women and Catholic Manuscript Networks," 1097–98. See also Paul Trolander and Zeynep Tenger, *Sociable Criticism in England: 1625–1725* (Newark: University of Delaware Press, 2007).

32. La Belle, 15.

33. La Belle, 16–17.

34. La Belle, 16.

35. Constance Aston Fowler to Herbert Aston, undated, Aston Papers vol. 9, British Library, Additional MS 36452, fols. 26–28, fol. 28r; cited parenthetically by folio.

36. Constance Aston Fowler to Herbert Aston, July 1639, Aston Papers vol. 9, British Library, Additional MS 36452, fols. 29–30, fols. 29v–30r.

37. As Sanders suggests, "Constance constructs for herself a central, indeed crucial, role in the furthering of Katherine and Herbert's love" (87).

38. Katherine Thimelby to Herbert Aston, undated, Aston Papers vol. 9, British Library, Additional MS 36452, fol. 33, fol. 33r.

39. The echo I trace here may be a result of reading one another's letters: Fowler sends her brother copies of Thimelby's letters to her (fol. 27r), and Thimelby instructs Aston to "let none se this but your deare sister"—implying that more extensive circulation was possible (fol. 35v).

40. Katherine Thimelby to Herbert Aston, 13 August [1638?], Aston Papers vol. 9, British Library, Additional MS 36452, fols. 34–35, fol. 34r; cited parenthetically by folio.

41. Deborah Aldrich-Watson, ed., *The Verse Miscellany of Constance Aston Fowler: A Diplomatic Edition* (Tempe, Ariz.: Renaissance English Text Society, 2000). For "exile" in an "accorsed clime" see the untitled poem on pp. 43–45, lines 7 and 2. For "D K on the Death of his Wife," see pp. 116–19. Unless otherwise noted, the poems I cite are transcribed by Fowler rather than Hand B. See Hackett for a detailed examination of the scribal history of the volume.

42. John Donne, *Poems* (London: John Marriot, 1633), 208.

43. Aldrich-Watson, *The Verse Miscellany of Constance Aston Fowler*, p. 117, line 42; p. 118, lines 95–97. Poem cited parenthetically by line number.

44. I agree with Burke and others who have suggested that "seventeenth-century studies might be better served by concentrating less on authorship and more on the issues around compilation, which is typically the primary activity in manuscript writing" (136), but would also argue for a more capacious understanding of authorship. See, for example, the work of Margaret J. M. Ezell, especially *Social Authorship and the Advent of Print* (Baltimore: Johns Hopkins University Press, 1999).

45. Aldrich-Watson, *The Verse Miscellany of Constance Aston Fowler*, 128–31; poem cited parenthetically by line number. Aldrich-Watson addresses the Donne references in the letters and miscellany in Deborah Aldrich Larson, "John Donne and the Astons," *Huntington Library Quarterly* 55.4 (1992): 635–41. Her focus is on the possible biographical connection be-

tween Donne and Walter Aston, and she argues that allusions to Donne may suggest that contemporary readers "were drawn to Donne's poetry at least as much for its relevance to his life as for its wit and toughness" (639). I would suggest instead that quotation (and revision) of Donne reveals the family's participation in contemporary poetics and engagement with the possible conflict between religious and poetic practice.

46. Burke suggests that "the Tixall group's engagement with Donne stretched from allusion and imitation to response" (139).

47. Winefrid Thimelby to Herbert Aston, October 4, Aston Papers vol. 9, British Library, Additional MS 36452, fol. 69, fol. 69v; cited parenthetically by folio. For slightly different transcriptions, see Victoria Van Hyning's edition in Bowden, *English Convents in Exile, 1600–1800*, 3:269; and Burke, 139.

48. These included letters from Constance Aston Fowler (fol. 48r), the younger Walter Aston (fol. 49), Eliza Southcott (fols. 50–51), and William Persall (fol. 52), and are followed in the British Library manuscript by "A perticular accompt of the most remarkable passages at the happy end of Mrs Ca: Aston & what past 7 dayes before with some generall reflections on the vertues & suffrings of her precedent life" (fol. 53r).

49. I refer to Winefrid by her religious name (her birth name was Mary Thimelby).

50. Victoria Van Hyning has questioned Claire Walker's contention that Winefrid Thimelby, prioress of the Augustinian convent at Louvain, "irrefutably breached clausura" in writing letters to her family (Walker, "Doe not supose me," 168); Van Hyning demonstrates that "the rate of her letter writing, the brevity of her letters, and their content, signals her conformity with house statutes and her life as a nun" ("Cloistered Voices"). I am grateful to Van Hyning for sharing excerpts from her unpublished Ph.D. thesis and allowing me to cite from her work on Thimelby.

51. Arthur Clifford discovered and edited the family papers in the nineteenth century, as *Tixall Letters*, 2 vols. (Edinburgh, 1815) and *Tixall Poetry* (Edinburgh: James Ballantyne, 1813). Clifford took liberties with the manuscripts, sometimes excising material from poems and letters. Van Hyning offers a trenchant analysis of his editing practices in her unpublished thesis.

52. Donne, *Poems* (London: John Marriot, 1633), 208–9; Donne, *Poems* (London: John Marriot, 1635), 14–15. In the *Poems*, "A Feaver" is not titled or otherwise marked "Dr Donne to his wife."

53. fol. 34v.

54. Marvell, pp. 216–41, lines 83, 87, 271–72; cited parenthetically by line number.

55. As Rosalie Colie has argued, "historical time is radically pleated" in Marvell's description of the dissolution. *"My Ecchoing Song": Andrew Marvell's Poetry of Criticism* (Princeton, N.J.: Princeton University Press, 1970), 254. Brian Patton suggests that "past and present are deliberately conflated, creating the appearance of a Fairfax essence that remains unchanged from generation to generation" in order to draw attention away from a history of disinheritance and Fairfax's own breaking of his property's entail. See "Preserving Property: History, Genealogy, and Inheritance in 'Upon Appleton House,'" *Renaissance Quarterly* 49.4 (1996): 824–39, 830. Patsy Griffin reads this episode as "part of a larger strategy to subvert the belief that those given monastic property came to disorder and dispossession" in "'Twas no *Religious House* till now': Marvell's 'Upon Appleton House,'" *SEL* 28.1 (1988): 61–76, 65. For the convent's history, see Claire Cross, "Yorkshire Nunneries in the Early Tudor Period," in *The Religious Orders in Pre-Reformation England*, ed. James G. Clark (Woodbridge: Boydell, 2002), 145–54.

56. For the relationship between religious change and the physical landscape, see Alexandra Walsham, *The Reformation of the Landscape: Religion, Identity, and Memory in Early Modern Britain and Ireland* (Oxford: Oxford University Press, 2011).

57. Kate Chedgzoy, for example, acknowledges the continued practice of English monasticism but argues that "For Marvell and his contemporaries, convents were inevitably *elsewhere*, the temporally distant products of a pre-Reformation culture, or a geographically dispersed aspect of the Counter-Reformation." " 'For *Virgin Buildings* Oft Brought Forth': Fantasies of Convent Sexuality," in *Female Communities, 1600–1800: Literary Visions and Cultural Realities*, ed. Rebecca D'Monté and Nicole Pohl (Houndmills: Palgrave Macmillan, 2000), 53–75, 62.

58. As Lynn Staley points out, Marvell "refers not to the Dissolution, a term commonly used to describe the dissolving of the monasteries, but to the 'demolishing', thus underlining the violence visited upon these virgin buildings." "Enclosed Spaces," in *Cultural Reformations: Medieval and Renaissance in Literary History*, ed. Brian Cummings and James Simpson (Oxford: Oxford University Press, 2010), 113–33, 131.

59. For a reading of Marvell's poem in relationship to Dodsworth's antiquarian pursuits, see Douglas Chambers, " 'To the Abbyss': Gothic as a Metaphor for the Argument About Art and Nature in 'Upon Appleton House,' " in *On the Celebrated and Neglected Poems of Andrew Marvell*, ed. Claude J. Summers and Ted-Larry Pebworth (Columbia: University of Missouri Press, 1992), 139–53, especially 143–49.

60. Anne Cotterill, "Marvell's Watery Maze: Digression and Discovery at Nun Appleton," *ELH* 69.1 (2002): 103–32, 112. Sarah Monette offers a similar reading, arguing that "the nun herself in these lines becomes a poet, 'weaving' her words and having indulged in efforts of composition prior to speaking" in "Speaking and Silent Women in Upon Appleton House," *SEL* 42.1 (2002): 155–71, 158.

61. Melissa E. Sanchez, " 'She Straightness on the Woods Bestows': Protestant Sexuality and English Empire in Marvell's 'Upon Appleton House,' " in *Atlantic Worlds in the Long Eighteenth Century: Seduction and Sentiment*, ed. Toni Bowers and Tita Chico (New York: Palgrave Macmillan, 2012), 81–96, 90.

62. James Holstun, " 'Will You Rent Our Ancient Love Asunder?': Lesbian Elegy in Donne, Marvell, and Milton," *ELH* 54.4 (1987): 835–67, 848; Elena Levy-Navarro, "History Straight and Narrow: Marvell, Mary Fairfax, and the Critique of Sexual and Historical Sequence," in *Postmodern Medievalisms*, ed. Richard Utz and Jesse G. Swan (Rochester, N.Y.: Boydell & Brewer, 2004), 181–92.

63. Derek Hirst and Steven Zwicker, "Andrew Marvell and the Toils of Patriarchy: Fatherhood, Longing, and the Body Politic," *ELH* 66 (1999): 629–54, 632.

64. Sanchez, 86.

65. Alison Shell, *Oral Culture and Catholicism in Early Modern England* (Cambridge: Cambridge University Press, 2007), 31.

66. While prayer might seem to be an individual act, "Catholic devotional writers usually claim that private or individual habits of prayer are also intrinsically corporate, that is, about the formation of holy communities." See Monta, "Uncommon Prayer?" 253.

67. See Susan Frye's account of the relationship between women's writing and needlework in *Pens and Needles: Women's Textualities in Early Modern England* (Philadelphia: University of Pennsylvania Press, 2010). For readings of the individual nun as a poet, see Monette; Cotterill; and Jonathan Crewe's "The Garden State: Marvell's Poetics of Enclosure,"

in *Enclosure Acts: Sexuality, Property, and Culture in Early Modern England*, ed. Richard Burt and John Michael Archer (Ithaca, N.Y.: Cornell University Press, 1994), 270–89.

68. The nun uses 37 first person plural, 4 first person singular, and 21 second person pronouns in twelve and a half stanzas.

69. Monette, 159.

70. Ibid.

71. In the seventeenth century, "gypsy" was used both to refer to "a member of a wandering race . . . which first appeared in England about the beginning of the 16th c. and was then believed to have come from Egypt" and as "a contemptuous term for a woman, as being cunning, deceitful, fickle, or the like." *OED*, 2nd ed., s.v. "gipsy | gypsy," definitions 1a and 2b.

72. I follow Marvell's use of "Maria" to refer to Mary Fairfax.

73. The speaker mentions both her mother and her father prior to the story of the convent: "Vere and Fairfax"—Thomas Fairfax and his wife, Anne Vere—first appear in the fifth stanza (36).

74. *OED*, 2nd ed., s.v. "precede, v.2," definitions 2 and 4.

75. Ibid., definition 1.

76. The Lady in John Milton's *A Masque at Ludlow Castle* offers another significant example: she, like Maria, is celebrated for her unblemished chastity, her acquiescence to patriarchal authority, and her resistance to the language of seduction lyrics. See Stephen Orgel, "The Case for Comus," *Representations* 81.1 (2003): 31–45.

77. In an irony that may have struck readers of the poem when it was printed in 1681, twenty-four years after Mary Fairfax married George Villiers, second duke of Buckingham, their union remained childless.

78. For a reading of the implicit violence of the "sacred bud" metaphor, see Monette, 166. Levy-Navarro suggests that the comparison to Thwaites "underscores the violence required to bring Maria in line with the sexual and patrilineal narrative of the Fairfax line" (186).

79. See the entry for "nunne" in A. H. Smith, *English Place-Name Elements*, 2 vols. (Cambridge: Cambridge University Press, 1956), 2: 52: "generally in allusion to the possessions of post-Conquest nunneries." Crewe has also noted this omission: "The nuns are said to dissolve like false enchanters, with no further place in the ongoing historical narrative, while the term 'nun' is deleted from 'Nun Appleton House'" (283).

80. See, for example, Wendy Wall, *The Imprint of Gender: Authorship and Publication in the English Renaissance* (Ithaca, N.Y.: Cornell University Press, 1993); and Jeff Masten, *Textual Intercourse: Collaboration, Authorship, and Sexualities in Renaissance Drama* (Cambridge: Cambridge University Press, 1997).

81. See, for example, Summit, *Lost Property*.

82. For female literary coteries, see Micheline White, "Women Writers and Literary-Religious Circles in the Elizabethan West Country: Anne Dowriche, Anne Lock Prowse, Anne Lock Moyle, Elizabeth Rous, and Ursula Fulford," *Modern Philology* 103.2 (2005): 187–214; and Julie Campbell, *Literary Circles and Gender in Early Modern Europe* (Aldershot: Ashgate, 2006).

83. Aemilia Lanyer's paratextual material surrounding *Salve Deus Rex Judaeorum*, including "The Description of Cookham," is an important exception: in her dedicatory verses and country house poem, Lanyer represents herself and her poetry as situated in a female community.

84. See my second chapter for an example of the strategic deployment of manuscript to represent collective literary practice. Poems 54 and 55 in Aldrich-Watson, *The Verse Miscellany*

of Constance Aston Fowler demonstrate the practice of poetic exchange between Aston and Shirley.

85. In an otherwise excellent reading of Cavendish's rethinking of the utopian economy, for example, Erin Lang Bonin suggests that the convent is "a space historically and geographically distant from Cavendish and her contemporaries," even while she acknowledges that "the institution harbored rich symbolic potential." "Margaret Cavendish's Dramatic Utopias and the Politics of Gender," *SEL* 40.2 (2000): 339–54, 347.

86. Cavendish traveled to Paris with Henrietta Maria in 1644, where she met William and married him in 1645. See Nicky Hallett, *The Senses in Religious Communities*, 13–15.

87. Margaret Cavendish, "A True Relation of My Birth, Breeding, and Life," in *Natures Pictures* (London: J. Martin and J. Allestrye, 1656), 390. Cavendish also describes how her mother "made her house her Cloyster, inclosing her self, as it were therein" (377).

88. Summit, *Lost Property*, 207.

89. Margaret Cavendish, *The Convent of Pleasure and Other Plays*, ed. Anne Shaver (Baltimore: Johns Hopkins University Press, 1999), 220; cited parenthetically by page number.

90. L. Owen, *The Running Register*, 116.

91. L. Owen, *The Unmasking*, 31–32.

92. Sara H. Mendelson, "Concocting the World's Olio: Margaret Cavendish and Continental Influence," in "Essays from the Fifth Biennial International Margaret Cavendish Conference," ed. Lisa Hopkins, Emma Rees, and Gweno Williams, special issue 14, *Early Modern Literary Studies* (May 2004): 1:1–34, http://purl.oclc.org/emls/si-14/mendconc.html, 18, 28.

93. Mendelson, 29. Erna Kelly suggests that "although it cannot be absolutely ascertained that Cavendish's playful use of convents, cloisters, martyrdom and vows shows a respect for, admiration of, or even attraction to some of Catholicism's principles, practices, and institutions or merely amusement with and/or disrespect toward them, it is clear that religion, as a means of preventing bad marriages and fostering good ones, is a privilege of the upper classes" (23). "Playing with Religion: Convents, Cloisters, Martyrdom, and Vows," in "Essays from the Fifth Biennial International Margaret Cavendish Conference," ed. Hopkins, Rees, and Williams, 4:1–24. See also Rebecca D'Monté's brief comparison to Mary Ward in "Mirroring Female Power: Separatist Spaces in the Plays of Margaret Cavendish, Duchess of Newcastle," in *Female Communities, 1600–1800: Literary Visions and Cultural Realities*, ed. Rebecca D'Monté and Nicole Pohl (Houndmills: Palgrave Macmillan, 2000), 93–110, 100.

94. Julie Crawford, "Convents and Pleasures: Margaret Cavendish and the Drama of Property," *Renaissance Drama* 32 (2003): 177–223, 183. Crawford is most interested in the convent as a site for "a politicized imaginative form of redress for women's tenuous relationship with property during the civil wars, interregnum, and early Restoration" (200).

95. Hallett, *The Senses in Religious Communities*, 13.

96. Ibid., 19; J. Crawford, "Convents and Pleasures," 203.

97. *OED*, 2nd ed., s.v. "sense," definition 4a.

98. See definition 7a.

99. Cavendish represents herself as unable to resist generic mixing in her "To the Reader" prefacing *Natures Pictures*: "some Poeticall tales or discourses, both in verse and prose; but most in prose, hath crowded in amongst the rest, I cannot say against my will, although my wil was forced by my Naturall Inclinations and affections to fancy" (C3v).

100. In addition to the genres referenced above, Bowden, *English Convents in Exile* includes convent chronicles, feast calendars, monastic rules, examinations, spiritual instructions, liturgies, martyrologies, visions, and financial records.

101. I am indebted to Katherine R. Kellett's compelling reading of *The Convent of Pleasure*, in which she argues that "For Cavendish, the convent exists discursively rather than materially." "Performance, Performativity, and Identity in Margaret Cavendish's *The Convent of Pleasure*," *SEL* 48.2 (2008): 419–42, 427.

102. Hero Chalmers, "The Politics of Feminine Retreat in Margaret Cavendish's *The Female Academy* and *The Convent of Pleasure*," *Women's Writing* 6.1 (1999): 81–94, 87. J. Crawford reads Cavendish's convent as "a royalist retreat that celebrates the values of an exiled court culture" ("Convents and Pleasures," 179).

103. Bonin, 350.

104. Mary Astell, *A Serious Proposal to the Ladies, for the Advancement of their true and greatest Interest* (London: R. Wilkin, 1694), 60–61. For a reading of Astell in relationship to the convents as educational models, see Nicole Pohl, "'In This Sacred Space': The Secular Convent in Late Seventeenth- and Eighteenth-Century Expository Literature," in D'Monté and Pohl, *Female Communities, 1600–1800*, 149–65.

EPILOGUE. FAILURES OF LITERARY HISTORY

Epigraph: Emily Dickinson, "One Crucifixion is Recorded Only," in *The Poems of Emily Dickinson: Variorum Edition*, ed. R. W. Franklin, 3 vols. (Cambridge, Mass.: Belknap Press of Harvard University Press, 1998), poem 670, lines 1–4; cited parenthetically by line number.

1. Ignatius Loyola, *The Spiritual Exercises*, quoted in Louis L. Martz, *The Poetry of Meditation: A Study in English Religious Literature of the Seventeenth Century* (New Haven, Conn.: Yale University Press, 1962), 27.

2. My readings of Passion poems are indebted to the work of scholars such as Arthur Marotti, Molly Murray, Richard Rambuss, and Alison Shell, who have drawn attention to how certain authors, poetic traditions, and confessional identities have been written out of literary history. Yet even their exceptional work has not yet accounted for how Catholic women helped shape the paths and perspectives of English literature—and how they were written out of that literature by authors like Milton. Arthur Marotti, *Religious Ideology*; Molly Murray, *The Poetics of Conversion*; Richard Rambuss, *Closet Devotions* (Durham, N.C.: Duke University Press, 1998); Alison Shell, *Catholicism*.

3. Philip J. Gallagher, "Milton's 'The Passion': Inspired Mediocrity," *Milton Quarterly* 11 (1977): 44–50, 45.

4. John Milton, *Milton's Selected Poetry and Prose*, ed. Jason P. Rosenblatt (New York: Norton, 2011), 21; cited parenthetically by line number.

5. Rambuss also explores how Milton's poem was published "as though it were to be the final lyric on a literally abandoned topic" but his focus in reading Milton in relationship to Crashaw, Donne, and Herbert is on a poetics of embodiment and "visceral displays of devotional affect . . . sighs and tears and shudders" (*Closet Devotions*, 134).

6. John Donne, *John Donne's Poetry*, ed. Arthur L. Clements (New York: Norton, 1992); cited parenthetically by line number.

7. Ignatius Loyola, *The Spiritual Exercises*, quoted in Martz, 27.

8. George Herbert, *The Temple* (Cambridge: Thomas Buck, 1633), 19–26; cited parenthetically by line number.

9. Deborah Aldrich-Watson, *The Verse Miscellany of Constance Aston Fowler*, 6–14; cited parenthetically by line number. The poem is in Fowler's hand.

10. Aldrich-Watson suggests that "On the Passion" "does not follow the meditative *Exercises* of St. Ignatius Loyola," but "contains some meditative elements" (6).

11. Michael Schoenfeldt, " 'That spectacle of too much weight': The Poetics of Sacrifice in Donne, Herbert, and Milton," *Journal of Medieval and Early Modern Studies* 31.3 (2001): 561–84, 563–64.

12. Schoenfeldt, 563. See also Debora Shuger, *The Renaissance Bible: Scholarship, Sacrifice, and Subjectivity* (Berkeley: University of California Press, 1994).

13. Schoenfeldt, 581.

14. Marshall Grossman, " 'In Pensive trance, and anguish, and ecstatic fit': Milton on the Passion," in *A Fine Tuning: Studies of the Religious Poetry of Herbert and Milton*, ed. Mary A. Maleski (Binghamton, N.Y.: Medieval and Renaissance Texts and Studies, 1989), 205–20, 212.

15. For tears poetry, see Shell, *Catholicism*, 56–104; and Gary Kuchar, *The Poetry of Religious Sorrow in Early Modern England* (Cambridge: Cambridge University Press, 2008).

16. Schoenfeldt, 580.

17. Rambuss, *Closet Devotions* and "Sacred Subjects and the Aversive Metaphysical Conceit: Crashaw, Serrano, Ofili," *ELH* 71 (2004): 497–530; Shell, *Catholicism*; and Murray, *The Poetics of Conversion*.

18. These characterizations are, ironically, reinscribed in the beginning of nearly every argument disputing them—certainly the most pervasive trope of Crashaw criticism and perhaps early modern criticism writ large.

19. Murray, 136.

20. Richard Rambuss, "Crashaw's Style," in L. Gallagher, *Redrawing the Map*, 132–58, 149.

21. Joseph R. Teller, "Why Crashaw Was Not Catholic: The Passion and Popular Protestant Devotion," *ELR* 43.2 (2013): 239–67, 242.

22. For "florid divagations," see Mario Praz, *The Flaming Heart: Essays on Crashaw, Machiavelli, and Other Studies in the Relations Between Italian and English Literature from Chaucer to T. S. Eliot* (Gloucester, Mass.: Peter Smith, 1966), 245. For "feminine perspectives," see Paul A. Parrish, " 'O Sweet Contest': Gender and Value in 'The Weeper,' " in *New Perspectives on the Life and Art of Richard Crashaw*, ed. John R. Roberts (Columbia: University of Missouri Press, 1990), 127–39, 127.

BIBLIOGRAPHY

Aldrich-Watson, Deborah, ed. *The Verse Miscellany of Constance Aston Fowler: A Diplomatic Edition*. Tempe, Ariz.: Renaissance English Text Society, 2000.

Anderson, Roberta. "'Well Disposed to the Affairs of Spain?' James VI & I and the Propagandists: 1618–1624." *Recusant History* 25.4 (2001): 613–35.

Arber, Edward. *A Transcript of the Registers of the Company of Stationers of London, 1554–1640 A.D.* 5 vols. London: privately printed, 1877.

The Arminian Nunnery. London: Thomas Underhill, 1641.

Articles into the Arches. Hampshire County Records Office. 44M69/F2/14/1, Bundles 1–2.

Astell, Mary. *A Serious Proposal to the Ladies, for the Advancement of their true and greatest Interest*. London: R. Wilkin, 1694.

Aston Papers. British Library. Additional MS 36452.

Aughertson, Kate. "Roaring Boys and Weeping Men: Radical Masculinity in Webster's *The Duchess of Malfi*." In *Literary Politics: The Politics of Literature and the Literature of Politics*, ed. Deborah Philips and Katy Shaw, 45–63. New York: Palgrave Macmillan, 2013.

Baines, Barbara. "Assaying the Power of Chastity in *Measure for Measure*." *SEL: Studies in English Literature, 1500–1900* 30.2 (1990): 283–301.

Baker, Augustine. "Concerning the Librarie of this howse." In *Vth Book of Collections*, Colwich Abbey. MS 9, 137–45.

———. *The Life and Death of Dame Gertrude More*. Ed. Ben Wekking. *Analecta Cartusiana* 119:19. Salzburg: Institut für Anglistik und Amerikanistik Universität Salzburg, 2002.

Barroll, Leeds. *Anna of Denmark, Queen of England: A Cultural Biography*. Philadelphia: University of Pennsylvania Press, 2000.

Beales, A. C. F. *Education Under Penalty: English Catholic Education from the Reformation to the Fall of James II: 1547–1689*. London: Athlone, 1963.

Beard, Thomas. *The Theatre of Gods Judgments*. London: Adam Islip, 1597.

Beauregard, David. "Shakespeare on Monastic Life: Nuns and Friars in *Measure for Measure*." In *Shakespeare and the Culture of Christianity in Early Modern England*, ed. Dennis Taylor and David Beauregard, 311–35. New York: Fordham University Press, 2003.

Beckwith, Sarah. *Shakespeare and the Grammar of Forgiveness*. Ithaca, N.Y.: Cornell University Press, 2011.

Bell, David N. *What Nuns Read: Books and Libraries in Medieval English Nunneries*. Kalamazoo, Mich.: Cistercian Publications, 1995.

Berry, Philippa. *Of Chastity and Power: Elizabethan Literature and the Unmarried Queen*. London: Routledge, 1989.

The Bible. Geneva: Rouland Hall, 1560.

Bicks, Caroline. "Staging the Jesuitess in *A Game at Chess*." *SEL: Studies in English Literature, 1500–1990* 49.2 (2009): 463–84.

Blom, Jos, and Frans Blom, eds. *Elizabeth Evelinge, II*. Vol. 5 of *The Early Modern Englishwoman: A Facsimile Library of Essential Works*. Series I, Printed Writings, 1500–1640: Part 3. Aldershot: Ashgate, 2002.

Bonin, Erin Lang. "Margaret Cavendish's Dramatic Utopias and the Politics of Gender." *SEL: Studies in English Literature 1500–1900* 40.2 (2000): 339–54.

Borlik, Todd. "'Greek Is Turned Turk': Catholic Nostalgia in *The Duchess of Malfi*." In Luckyj, *The Duchess of Malfi: A Critical Guide*, 136–52.

Bossy, John. *The English Catholic Community 1570–1850*. London: Darton, Longman & Todd, 1975.

Bowden, Caroline. "Books and Reading at Syon Abbey, Lisbon, in the Seventeenth Century." In Jones and Walsham, *Syon Abbey and Its Books*, 177–202.

———. "'A distribution of tyme': Reading and Writing Practices in the English Convents in Exile." *Tulsa Studies in Women's Literature* 31.1/2 (2012): 99–116.

———, ed. *English Convents in Exile, 1600–1800*. 6 vols. London: Pickering & Chatto, 2012–13.

Bowden, Caroline, and James E. Kelly, eds. *The English Convents in Exile, 1600–1800: Communities, Culture and Identity*. Farnham: Ashgate, 2013.

Britland, Karen. *Drama at the Courts of Queen Henrietta Maria*. Cambridge: Cambridge University Press, 2009.

Bruster, Douglas. "Shakespeare and the Composite Text." In Rasmussen, *Renaissance Literature and Its Formal Engagements*, 43–66.

Budick, Sanford. "Counter-Periodization and Chiasmus: The Case of Wordsworth and 'The Days of Dryden and Pope.'" In *The Challenge of Periodization: Old Paradigms and New Perspectives*, ed. Lawrence Besserman, 107–32. New York: Routledge, 1996.

Bullinger, Heinrich. *The Christian State of Matrimony*. London: John Awdeley, 1575.

Burke, Victoria. "Women and Early Seventeenth-Century Manuscript Culture: Four Miscellanies." *Seventeenth Century* 12.2 (1997): 135–50.

Burns, J. H., ed. *The Cambridge History of Political Thought, 1450–1700*. Cambridge: Cambridge University Press, 1991.

Burton, Robert. *The Anatomy of Melancholy*. Oxford: Henry Cripps, 1621.

Caldwell, Ellen. "Invasive Procedures in Webster's *The Duchess of Malfi*." In *Women, Violence, and English Renaissance Literature: Essays Honoring Paul Jorgensen*, ed. Linda Woodbridge and Sharon Beehler, 149–86. Tempe: Arizona Center for Medieval and Renaissance Studies, 2003.

Callaghan, Dympna. "*The Duchess of Malfi* and Early Modern Widows." In *Early Modern English Drama: A Critical Companion*, ed. Garrett A. Sullivan, Jr., Patrick Cheney, and Andrew Hadfield, 272–86. Oxford: Oxford University Press, 2006.

Calvin, John. *Sermons of M. John Calvine, upon the X Commandementes of the Lawe*. Trans. J. H. London: John Harison, 1579.

Campbell, Julie. *Literary Circles and Gender in Early Modern Europe*. Aldershot: Ashgate, 2006.

Cavendish, Margaret. *The Convent of Pleasure and Other Plays*. Ed. Anne Shaver. Baltimore: Johns Hopkins University Press, 1999.

———. *Natures Pictures*. London: J. Martin and J. Allestrye, 1656.

Chakravorty, Swapan. *Society and Politics in the Plays of Thomas Middleton*. Oxford: Clarendon, 1996.

Chalmers, Hero. "The Politics of Feminine Retreat in Margaret Cavendish's *The Female Academy* and *The Convent of Pleasure*." *Women's Writing* 6.1 (1999): 81–94.

Chambers, A. B. "Crooked Crosses in Donne and Crashaw." In *New Perspectives on the Life and Art of Richard Crashaw*, ed. John R. Roberts, 157–73. Columbia: University of Missouri Press, 1990.

Chambers, Douglas. "'To the Abbyss': Gothic as a Metaphor for the Argument About Art and Nature in 'Upon Appleton House.'" In *On the Celebrated and Neglected Poems of Andrew Marvell*, ed. Claude J. Summers and Ted-Larry Pebworth, 139–53. Columbia: University of Missouri Press, 1992.

Chedgzoy, Kate. "'For *Virgin Buildings* Oft Brought Forth': Fantasies of Convent Sexuality." In D'Monté and Pohl, *Female Communities, 1600–1800*, 53–75.

Cheney, Patrick. *Marlowe's Counterfeit Profession: Ovid, Spenser, Counter-Nationhood*. Toronto: University of Toronto Press, 1997.

Clark, J. P. H. "Augustine Baker, O.S.B.: Towards a Re-Assessment." *Studies in Spirituality* 14 (2004): 209–24.

Cleland, Katherine. "'Wanton loves, and yong desires': Clandestine Marriage in Marlowe's *Hero and Leander* and Chapman's Continuation." *Studies in Philology* 108.2 (2011): 215–37.

Clifford, Arthur, ed. *Tixall Letters*. 2 vols. Edinburgh, 1815.

———, ed. *Tixall Poetry*. Edinburgh: James Ballantyne, 1813.

Cogswell, Thomas. "Thomas Middleton and the Court, 1624: 'A Game at Chess' in Context." *Huntington Library Quarterly* 47.4 (1984): 273–88.

Cohen, Stephen. "Between Form and Culture: New Historicism and the Promise of a Historical Formalism." In Rasmussen, *Renaissance Literature and Its Formal Engagements*, 17–41.

Coles, Kimberly Anne. *Religion, Reform, and Women's Writing in Early Modern England*. Cambridge: Cambridge University Press, 2008.

Colie, Rosalie. *"My Ecchoing Song": Andrew Marvell's Poetry of Criticism*. Princeton, N.J.: Princeton University Press, 1970.

Constable, Barbara. *Considerations or Reflexions upon the Rule of the most glorious father St Benedict*. Downside Abbey. MS 82144/627, 1655.

Constitutions Compiled for the Better Observation of the Holie Rule of our Most Glorious Fa: and Patriarch S. Bennet. Archives Départmentales du Nord, Lille. Box 20H. MS 20 H 1.

Copley, Anthony. *A Fig for Fortune*. London: Richard Johnes, 1596.

Correll, Barbara. "Malvolio at Malfi: Managing Desire in Shakespeare and Webster." *Shakespeare Quarterly* 58.1 (2007): 65–92.

Cotterill, Anne. "Marvell's Watery Maze: Digression and Discovery at Nun Appleton." *ELH* 69.1 (2002): 103–32.

Cramer, Anselm. "'The Librairie of this Howse': Augustine Baker's Community and Their Books." In *"Stand up to Godwards": Essays in Mystical and Monastic Theology in Honour of the Reverend John Clark on His Sixty-Fifth Birthday*, ed. James Hogg, 103–10. *Analecta Cartusiana* 204. Salzburg: Institut für Anglistik und Amerikanistik Universität Salzburg, 2002.

Crawford, Julie. "Convents and Pleasures: Margaret Cavendish and the Drama of Property." *Renaissance Drama* 32 (2003): 177–223.

Crawford, Patricia. *Women and Religion in England 1500–1720*. London: Routledge, 1993.

Crewe, Jonathan. "The Garden State: Marvell's Poetics of Enclosure." In *Enclosure Acts: Sexuality, Property, and Culture in Early Modern England*, ed. Richard Burt and John Michael Archer, 270–89. Ithaca, N.Y.: Cornell University Press, 1994.

Cross, Claire. "Yorkshire Nunneries in the Early Tudor Period." In *The Religious Orders in Pre-Reformation England*, ed. James G. Clark, 145–54. Woodbridge: Boydell, 2002.

Cummings, Brian. *The Literary Culture of the Reformation: Grammar and Grace*. Oxford: Oxford University Press, 2002.

D'Monté, Rebecca. "Mirroring Female Power: Separatist Spaces in the Plays of Margaret Cavendish, Duchess of Newcastle." In D'Monté and Pohl, *Female Communities, 1600–1800*, 93–110.

D'Monté, Rebecca, and Nicole Pohl, eds. *Female Communities, 1600–1800: Literary Visions and Cultural Realities*. Houndmills: Palgrave Macmillan, 2000.

Dailey, Alice. *The English Martyr from Reformation to Revolution*. Notre Dame, Ind.: University of Notre Dame Press, 2012.

Davidson, Peter, and Anne Sweeney, eds. *Collected Poems*. By Robert Southwell. Manchester: Carcanet, 2007.

Daybell, James, ed. *Early Modern Women's Letter Writing, 1450–1700*. Houndmills: Palgrave, 2001.

———. *The Material Letter: Manuscript Letters and the Culture and Practices of Letter-Writing in Early Modern England, 1580–1635*. Houndmills: Palgrave Macmillan, 2012.

De Hamel, Christopher. "The Library: The Medieval Manuscripts of Syon Abbey, and Their Dispersal." In De Hamel, *Syon Abbey*, 48–133.

———. *Syon Abbey: The Library of the Bridgettine Nuns and Their Peregrinations After the Reformation*. Otley: Roxburghe Club, 1991.

Defense of Lady Mary Percy. British Library. Harley MS 4275.

Delsigne, Jill. "Reading Catholic Art in Edmund Spenser's Temple of Isis." *Studies in Philology* 109.3 (2012): 199–224.

Desmet, Christy. " 'Neither Maid, Widow, nor Wife': Rhetoric of the Woman Controversy in *Measure for Measure* and *The Duchess of Malfi*." In *In Another Country: Feminist Perspectives on Renaissance Drama*, ed. Dorothea Kehler and Susan Baker, 71–92. Metuchen, N.J.: Scarecrow Press, 1991.

Diehl, Huston. " 'Infinite Space': Representation and Reformation in *Measure for Measure*." *Shakespeare Quarterly* 49.4 (Winter 1998): 393–410.

———. *Staging Reform, Reforming the Stage: Protestantism and Popular Theater in Early Modern England*. Ithaca, N.Y.: Cornell University Press, 1997.

Digangi, Mario. "Pleasure and Danger: Measuring Female Sexuality in *Measure for Measure*." *ELH* 60.3 (1993): 589–609.

Dillon, Anne. *The Construction of Martyrdom in the English Catholic Community, 1535–1603*. Aldershot: Ashgate, 2002.

Doelman, James. "Claimed by Two Religions: The Elegy on Thomas Washington, 1623, and Middleton's *A Game at Chesse*." *Studies in Philology* 110.2 (2013): 318–49.

Dolan, Frances E. " 'Can this be certain?': The Duchess of Malfi's Secrets." In Luckyj, *The Duchess of Malfi: A Critical Guide*, 119–35.

———, ed. *Recusant Translators: Elizabeth Cary, Alexia Gray*. Vol. 13 of *The Early Modern Englishwoman: A Facsimile Library of Essential Works*. Series I, Printed Writings, 1500–1640: Part 2. Aldershot: Ashgate, 2000.

———. *Whores of Babylon: Catholicism, Gender, and Seventeenth-Century Print Culture.* Ithaca, N.Y.: Cornell University Press, 1999.

———. "Why Are Nuns Funny?" *Huntington Library Quarterly* 70.4 (2007): 509–35.

Donne, John. *John Donne's Poetry.* Ed. Arthur L. Clements. New York: Norton, 1992.

———. *Poems.* London: John Marriot, 1633.

———. *Poems.* London: John Marriot, 1635.

"Dorothea Arundell." In *Who Were the Nuns?* Accessed July 10, 2015. http://wwtn.history .qmul.ac.uk.

Dowd, Michelle M. "Delinquent Pedigrees: Revision, Lineage, and Spatial Rhetoric in *The Duchess of Malfi.*" *ELR* 39.3 (2009): 499–526.

Dractan, Carlos, trans. *Relacion que embiaron las religiosas del Monesterio de Sion de Inglaterra.* Madrid: P. Madrigal, 1594.

Drant, Thomas. *Two Sermons Preached.* London: John Daye, 1570.

Dubrow, Heather. *A Happier Eden: The Politics of Marriage in the Stuart Epithalamium.* Ithaca, N.Y.: Cornell University Press, 1990.

Duffy, Eamon. "The English Reformation After Revisionism." *Renaissance Quarterly* 59.3 (2006): 720–28.

———. *The Stripping of the Altars: Traditional Religion in England 1400–1580.* New Haven, Conn.: Yale University Press, 1992.

Dutton, Richard. *Mastering the Revels: The Regulation and Censorship of English Renaissance Drama.* Houndmills: Macmillan, 1991.

———. "Receiving Offence: *A Game at Chess* Again." In *Literature and Censorship in Renaissance England*, ed. Andrew Hadfield, 50–74. Houndmills: Palgrave, 2001.

Eaton, Sara. "Defacing the Feminine in Renaissance Tragedy." In *The Matter of Difference: Materialist Feminist Criticism of Shakespeare*, ed. Valerie Wayne, 181–98. Ithaca, N.Y.: Cornell University Press, 1991.

Edmondes Papers. British Library. Stowe MS 173.

Eggert, Katherine. "Spenser's Ravishment: Rape and Rapture in *The Faerie Queene.*" *Representations* 70 (2000): 1–26.

Elizabeth I. *Collected Works.* Ed. Leah S. Marcus, Janel Mueller, and Mary Beth Rose. Chicago: University of Chicago Press, 2000.

Ellison, James. "*Measure for Measure* and the Executions of Catholics in 1604." *ELR* 33.1 (2003): 44–87.

Erickson, Amy Louise. *Women and Property in Early Modern England.* London: Routledge, 1993.

Erne, Lukas. *Shakespeare and the Book Trade.* Cambridge: Cambridge University Press, 2013.

Espinosa, Ruben. *Masculinity and Marian Efficacy in Shakespeare's England.* Farnham: Ashgate, 2011.

Ezell, Margaret J. M. *Social Authorship and the Advent of Print.* Baltimore: Johns Hopkins University Press, 1999.

Farr, Dorothy M. *Thomas Middleton and the Drama of Realism: A Study of Some Representative Plays.* Edinburgh: Oliver & Boyd, 1973.

Featley, Daniel. *The Grand Sacrilege of the Church of Rome.* London: Robert Milbourne, 1630.

Felch, Susan M. "English Women's Devotional Writing: Surveying the Scene." *ANQ: A Quarterly Journal of Short Articles, Notes, and Reviews* 24.1/2 (2011): 118–30.

Ferguson, Margaret. *Dido's Daughters: Literacy, Gender, and Empire in Early Modern England and France.* Chicago: University of Chicago Press, 2003.

Findlay, Alison. *A Feminist Perspective on Renaissance Drama*. Oxford: Blackwell, 1999.

Fletcher, John Rory. *The Story of the English Bridgettines of Syon Abbey*. Devon: Syon Abbey, 1933.

Frye, Susan. *Elizabeth I: The Competition for Representation*. New York: Oxford University Press, 1993.

———. "Of Chastity and Rape: Edmund Spenser Confronts Elizabeth I in *The Faerie Queene*." In *Representing Rape in Medieval and Early Modern Literature*, ed. Elizabeth Robertson and Christine M. Rose, 353–79. New York: Palgrave, 2001.

———. *Pens and Needles: Women's Textualities in Early Modern England*. Philadelphia: University of Pennsylvania Press, 2010.

Gallagher, Lowell, ed. *Redrawing the Map of Early Modern English Catholicism*. Toronto: University of Toronto Press, 2012.

Gallagher, Philip J. "Milton's 'The Passion': Inspired Mediocrity." *Milton Quarterly* 11 (1977): 44–50.

Gascoigne, Catherine. "A Relation of the Lady Abesse her Spirituall Course." Colwich Abbey. MS 32.

Gascoigne, Margaret. *Devotions*. Colwich Abbey. MS 18.

Gee, John. *The Foot out of the Snare*. 3rd ed. London: Robert Milbourne, 1624.

———. *New Shreds of the Old Snare*. London: Robert Mylbourne, 1624.

Gertz, Genelle. "Barbara Constable's *Advice for Confessors* and the Tradition of Medieval Holy Women." In Bowden and Kelly, *The English Convents in Exile, 1600–1800*, 123–38.

Gillespie, Katharine. *Domesticity and Dissent in the Seventeenth Century: English Women Writers and the Public Sphere*. Cambridge: Cambridge University Press, 2004.

Gless, Darryl J. *"Measure for Measure," the Law, and the Convent*. Princeton, N.J.: Princeton University Press, 1979.

Goldberg, Jonathan. *The Seeds of Things: Theorizing Sexuality and Materiality in Renaissance Representations*. New York: Fordham University Press, 2009.

Goodrich, Jaime. "'Ensigne-Bearers of Saint Clare': Elizabeth Evelinge's Early Translations and the Restoration of English Franciscanism." In *English Women, Religion, and Textual Production, 1500–1625*, ed. Micheline White, 83–100. Farnham: Ashgate, 2011.

———. "Nuns and Community-Centered Writing: The Benedictine Rule and the Brussels Statutes." *Huntington Library Quarterly* 77.2 (2014): 287–303.

———. "Thomas More and Margaret More Roper: A Case for Rethinking Women's Participation in the Early Modern Public Sphere." *Sixteenth Century Journal* 39.4 (2008): 1021–40.

———. "Translating Lady Mary Percy: Authorship and Authority among the Brussels Benedictines." In Bowden and Kelly, *The English Convents in Exile, 1600–1800*, 109–22.

Goulart, Simon. *Admirable and Memorable Histories*. Trans. Edward Grimeston. London: George Eld, 1607.

Gray, Catharine. *Women Writers and Public Debate in Seventeenth-Century Britain*. New York: Palgrave Macmillan, 2007.

Greene, Roland. "Anne Lock's *Meditation*: Invention Versus Dilation and the Founding of Puritan Poetics." In *Form and Reform in Renaissance England: Essays in Honor of Barbara Kiefer Lewalski*, ed. Amy Boesky and Mary Thomas Crane, 153–70. Newark: University of Delaware Press, 2000.

———. *Five Words: Critical Semantics in the Age of Shakespeare and Cervantes*. Chicago: University of Chicago Press, 2013.

Griffey, Erin, ed. *Henrietta Maria: Piety, Politics and Patronage*. Aldershot: Ashgate, 2008.

Griffin, Patsy. "'Twas no *Religious House* till now': Marvell's 'Upon Appleton House'." *SEL: Studies in English Literature: 1500–1900* 28.1 (1988): 61–76.

Grossman, Marshall. "'In Pensive trance, and anguish, and ecstatic fit': Milton on the Passion." In *A Fine Tuning: Studies of the Religious Poetry of Herbert and Milton*, ed. Mary A. Maleski, 205–20. Binghamton, N.Y.: Medieval and Renaissance Texts and Studies, 1989.

Guy, J. A. "The Origins of the Petition of Right Reconsidered." *Historical Journal* 25.2 (1982): 289–312.

Haber, Judith. "'My Body Bestow upon My Women': The Space of the Feminine in *The Duchess of Malfi*." *Renaissance Drama* 28 (1999): 133–59.

———. "'True-loves blood': Narrative and Desire in *Hero and Leander*." *ELR* 28 (1998): 372–86.

Hackett, Helen. *Virgin Mother, Maiden Queen: Elizabeth I and the Cult of the Virgin Mary*. Houndmills: Macmillan, 1995.

———. "Women and Catholic Manuscript Networks in Seventeenth-Century England: New Research on Constance Aston Fowler's Miscellany of Sacred and Secular Verse." *Renaissance Quarterly* 65.4 (2012): 1094–1124.

Hadfield, Andrew. "Spenser and Religion—Yet Again." *SEL: Studies in English Literature, 1500–1900* 51.1 (2011): 21–46.

Haigh, Christopher. *English Reformations: Religion, Politics and Society Under the Tudors*. Oxford: Clarendon, 1993.

Hallett, Nicky. *The Senses in Religious Communities, 1600–1800*. Farnham: Ashgate, 2013.

———. "Shakespeare's Sisters: Anon and the Authors in Early Modern Convents." In Bowden and Kelly, *The English Convents in Exile, 1600–1800*, 139–55.

Hammill, Graham. "The Marlovian Sublime: Imagination and the Problem of Political Theology." In *The Return of Theory in Early Modern English Studies: Tarrying with the Subjunctive*, ed. Paul Cefalu and Bryan Reynolds, 143–66. New York: Palgrave Macmillan, 2011.

Hamrick, Stephen. *The Catholic Imaginary and the Cults of Elizabeth, 1558–1582*. Farnham: Ashgate, 2009.

Hastings, Henry. "12 Sep. 1576 The Earl of Huntington to the L. Treasurer." British Library. Harley MS 6992.

Hastrup, Kirsten. "The Semantics of Biology: Virginity." In *Defining Females: The Nature of Women in Society*, ed. Shirley Ardener, 49–65. New York: Wiley, 1978.

Heinemann, Margot C. "Drama and Opinion in the 1620s: Middleton and Massinger." In *Theatre and Government Under the Early Stuarts*, ed. J. R. Mulryne and Margaret Shewring, 237–65. Cambridge: Cambridge University Press, 1993.

———. "Middleton's *A Game at Chess*: Parliamentary-Puritans and Opposition Drama." *English Literary Renaissance* 5 (1975): 232–50.

———. *Puritanism and Theatre: Thomas Middleton and Opposition Drama Under the Early Stuarts*. Cambridge: Cambridge University Press, 1980.

Herbert, George. *The Temple*. Cambridge: Thomas Buck, 1633.

Heylyn, Peter. *Mikrokosmos*. Oxford: John Lichfield and William Turner, 1625.

Heywood, Lady Cecilia. "Records of the Abbey of Our Lady of Consolation at Cambrai, 1620–1793." In *Publications of the Catholic Record Society*. Vol. 13, *Miscellanea VIII*, ed. Joseph Gillow, 1–85. London: Ballantyne, Hanson, 1913.

Higgons, Theophilus. *The First Motive of T. H. Maister of Arts*. 1609.

Highley, Christopher. *Catholics Writing the Nation in Early Modern Britain and Ireland*. Oxford: Oxford University Press, 2008.

Hile, Rachel E. "The Limitations of Concord in the Thames-Medway Marriage Canto of *The Faerie Queene*." *Studies in Philology* 108.1 (2011): 70–85.

Hill, Bridget. "A Refuge from Men: The Idea of a Protestant Nunnery." *Past & Present* 117 (1987): 107–30.

Hinds, Hilary. *God's Englishwomen: Seventeenth-Century Radical Sectarian Writing and Feminist Criticism*. Manchester: Manchester University Press, 1996.

Hirst, Derek, and Steven Zwicker. "Andrew Marvell and the Toils of Patriarchy: Fatherhood, Longing, and the Body Politic." *ELH* 66 (1999): 629–54.

Hoby, Edward. *A Letter to Mr. T. H. Late Minister: Now Fugitive*. London: Ed. Blount and W. Barret, 1609.

Hogg, James, ed. *Answer to an Attack on the Nuns of Sion*. Analecta Cartusiana 244. Salzburg: Institut für Anglistik und Amerikanistik Universität Salzburg, 2006.

———, ed. *Studies in St. Birgitta and the Brigittine Order*. Analecta Cartusiana 35:19. Salzburg: Institut für Anglistik und Amerikanistik Universität Salzburg, 1993.

Holmes, David M. *The Art of Thomas Middleton: A Critical Study*. Oxford: Clarendon, 1970.

Holstun, James. "'Will You Rent Our Ancient Love Asunder?': Lesbian Elegy in Donne, Marvell, and Milton." *ELH* 54.4 (1987): 835–67.

Hopkins, Lisa. "With the Skin Inside: The Interiors of *The Duchess of Malfi*." In *Privacy, Domesticity, and Women in Early Modern England*, ed. Corinne S. Abate, 21–30. Aldershot: Ashgate, 2003.

Howard-Hill, T. H., ed. "Appendix I: Documents Relating to *A Game at Chess*." In Middleton, *A Game at Chess*, 192–213.

———. "Introduction." In Middleton, *A Game at Chess*, 1–59.

———. *Middleton's "Vulgar Pasquin": Essays on "A Game at Chess."* Newark: University of Delaware Press, 1995.

———. "Political Interpretations of Middleton's 'A Game at Chess' (1624)." *Yearbook of English Studies* 21 (1991): 274–85.

Hulse, Clark. "Dead Man's Treasure: The Cult of Thomas More." In *The Production of English Renaissance Culture*, ed. David Lee Miller, Sharon O'Dair, and Harold Weber, 190–225. Ithaca, N.Y.: Cornell University Press, 1994.

Hutchison, Ann M. "The Life and Good End of Sister Marie." *Birgittiana* 13 (2002): 33–89.

———. "Mary Champney: A Bridgettine Nun Under the Rule of Queen Elizabeth I." *Birgittiana* 13 (2002): 3–32.

———. "Syon Abbey Preserved: Some Historians of Syon." In Jones and Walsham, *Syon Abbey and Its Books*, 228–51.

An Intermediate Greek-English Lexicon. Oxford: Clarendon, 1997.

Jackson, Ken, and Arthur Marotti. "The Turn to Religion in Early Modern English Studies." *Criticism* 46.1 (2004): 167–90.

Janelle, Pierre, ed. *Obedience in Church & State: Three Political Tracts by Stephen Gardiner*. Cambridge: Cambridge University Press, 1930.

Jankowski, Theodora A. *Pure Resistance: Queer Virginity in Early Modern English Drama*. Philadelphia: University of Pennsylvania Press, 2000.

Jed, Stephanie H. *Chaste Thinking: The Rape of Lucretia and the Birth of Humanism*. Bloomington: Indiana University Press, 1989.

Jones, E. A., and Alexandra Walsham, eds. *Syon Abbey and Its Books: Reading, Writing and Religion c. 1400–1700*. Woodbridge: Boydell, 2010.

Kamaralli, Anna. "Writing About Motive: Isabella, the Duke and Moral Authority." *Shakespeare Survey* 58 (2005): 48–59.

Kearney, James. *The Incarnate Text: Imagining the Book in Reformation England*. Philadelphia: University of Pennsylvania Press, 2009.

Kegl, Rosemary. "'Those Terrible Aproches': Sexuality, Social Mobility, and Resisting the Courtliness of Puttenham's *The Arte of English Poesie*." *English Literary Renaissance* 20.2 (1990): 179–208.

Kellett, Katherine R. "Performance, Performativity, and Identity in Margaret Cavendish's *The Convent of Pleasure*." *SEL: Studies in English Literature 1500–1900* 48.2 (2008): 419–42.

Kelly, Erna. "Playing with Religion: Convents, Cloisters, Martyrdom, and Vows." In "Essays from the Fifth Biennial International Margaret Cavendish Conference," ed. Lisa Hopkins, Emma Rees, and Gweno Williams. Special issue 14, *Early Modern Literary Studies* (May 2004): 4:1–24.

Kelly, Kathleen Coyne, and Marina Leslie. "Introduction: The Epistemology of Virginity." In *Menacing Virgins: Representing Virginity in the Middle Ages and Renaissance*, ed. Kathleen Coyne Kelly and Marina Leslie, 15–25. Newark: University of Delaware Press, 1999.

Kerrigan, John C. "Action and Confession, Fate and Despair in the Violent Conclusion of *The Duchess of Malfi*." *Ben Jonson Journal* 8 (2001): 249–58.

Kingdom, Robert M. "Calvinism and Resistance Theory, 1550–1580." In Burns, *The Cambridge History of Political Thought*, 193–218.

Kinney, Arthur F. "Reading Marlowe's Lyric." In *Approaches to Teaching Shorter Elizabethan Poetry*, ed. Patrick Cheney and Anne Lake Prescott, 220–25. New York: Modern Language Association, 2000.

Kitch, Aaron. "The Golden Muse: Protestantism, Mercantilism, and the Uses of Ovid in Marlowe's *Hero and Leander*." *Religion and Literature* 38.3 (2006): 157–76.

Knapp, James A. "Penitential Ethics in *Measure for Measure*." In *Shakespeare and Religion: Early Modern and Postmodern Perspectives*, ed. Ken Jackson and Arthur F. Marotti, 256–85. Notre Dame, Ind.: University of Notre Dame Press, 2011.

Knoppers, Laura Lunger. *Politicizing Domesticity from Henrietta Maria to Milton's Eve*. Cambridge: Cambridge University Press, 2014.

Knowles, David. *Bare Ruined Choirs: The Dissolution of the English Monasteries*. Cambridge: Cambridge University Press, 1976.

Knox, T. F. et al., eds. *The First and Second Diaries of the English College, Douay*. London: David Nutt, 1878.

Korda, Natasha. *Shakespeare's Domestic Economies: Gender and Property in Early Modern England*. Philadelphia: University of Pennsylvania Press, 2002.

Kuchar, Gary. "Gender and Recusant Melancholia in *Mary Magdalene's Funeral Tears*." In *Catholic Culture in Early Modern England*, ed. Ronald Corthell, Frances E. Dolan, Christopher Highley, and Arthur F. Marotti, 135–57. Notre Dame, Ind.: University of Notre Dame Press, 2007.

———. *The Poetry of Religious Sorrow in Early Modern England*. Cambridge: Cambridge University Press, 2008.

La Belle, Jenijoy. "A True Love's Knot: The Letters of Constance Fowler and the Poems of Herbert Aston." *Journal of English and Germanic Philology* 79.1 (1980): 13–31.

Lake, Peter, and Michael Questier. "Margaret Clitherow, Catholic Nonconformity, Martyrology and the Politics of Religious Change in Elizabethan England." *Past & Present* 185
(November 2004): 43–90.

Lander, Jesse. *Inventing Polemic: Religion, Print, and Literary Culture in Early Modern England.*
Cambridge: Cambridge University Press, 2006.

Larson, Deborah Aldrich. "John Donne and the Astons." *Huntington Library Quarterly* 55.4
(1992): 635–41.

Latz, Dorothy. "Neglected Writings by Recusant Women." In *Neglected English Literature:
Recusant Writings of the 16th–17th Centuries,* ed. Dorothy L. Latz, 11–48. Salzburg: Institut für Anglistik und Amerikanistik, 1997.

Laven, Mary. *Virgins of Venice: Enclosed Lives and Broken Vows in the Renaissance Convent.*
London: Viking Penguin, 2002.

Lay, Jenna. "An English Nun's Authority: Early Modern Spiritual Controversy and the Manu-
scripts of Barbara Constable." In *Gender, Catholicism and Spirituality: Women and the
Roman Catholic Church in Britain and Europe, 1200–1900,* ed. Laurence Lux-Sterritt and
Carmen Mangion, 99–114. London: Palgrave Macmillan, 2010.

———. "Sander, Elizabeth (*d.* 1607)." In *Oxford Dictionary of National Biography.* Oxford:
Oxford University Press, 2004-. Article published May 2014. doi:10.1093/ref:odnb/105928.

Lehfeldt, Elizabeth A. *Religious Women in Golden Age Spain: The Permeable Cloister.* Aldershot: Ashgate, 2005.

Leinwand, Theodore B. "'Coniugium Interruptum' in Shakespeare and Webster." *ELH* 72.1
(2005): 239–57.

Leites, Edmund, ed. *Conscience and Casuistry in Early Modern Europe.* Cambridge: Cambridge University Press, 2002.

Leonard, Amy E. "Female Religious Orders." In *A Companion to the Reformation World,*
ed. R. Po-chia Hsia, 237–54. Malden, Mass.: Blackwell, 2004.

Leonard, John. "Marlowe's Doric Music: Lust and Aggression in Hero and Leander." *English
Literary Renaissance* 30.1 (2000): 55–76.

Lessius, Leonard, and Fuluius Androtius. *The Treasure of Vowed Chastity in secular persons.
Also the Widdowes Glasse.* Trans. I.W.P. 1621.

Levinson, Marjorie. "What Is New Formalism?" *PMLA* 122.2 (2007): 558–69.

Levy-Navarro, Elena. "History Straight and Narrow: Marvell, Mary Fairfax, and the Critique
of Sexual and Historical Sequence." In *Postmodern Medievalisms,* ed. Richard Utz and
Jesse G. Swan, 181–92. Rochester, N.Y.: Boydell & Brewer, 2004.

Lewalski, Barbara. *Protestant Poetics and the Seventeenth-Century Religious Lyric.* Princeton, N.J.: Princeton University Press, 1979.

Lezra, Jacques. "'The Lady Was a Litle Peruerse': The 'Gender' of Persuasion in Puttenham's
Arte of English Poesie." In *Engendering Men: The Question of Male Feminist Criticism,* ed.
Joseph A. Boone and Michael Cadden, 53–65. New York: Routledge, 1990.

"Licence from Queen Elizabeth to George Putenham." Hampshire County Records Office.
44M69/M6/7/24.

The Life and Good End of Sister Marie. British Library. Additional MS 18650.

Limon, Jerzy. *Dangerous Matter: English Drama and Politics in 1623/24.* Cambridge: Cambridge University Press, 1986.

Loe, William. *A Stil Voice, to the Three Thrice-honourable Estates of Parliament.* London: John
Teage, 1621.

Loftis, John. *Renaissance Drama in England & Spain: Topical Allusion and History Plays.* Princeton, N.J.: Princeton University Press, 1987.

Loughnane, Rory. "The Artificial Figures and Staging Remembrance in Webster's *The Duchess of Malfi.*" In *Arts of Remembrance in Early Modern England: Memorial Cultures of the Post-Reformation*, ed. Andrew Gordon and Thomas Rist, 211–27. Farnham: Ashgate, 2013.

Lowe, K. J. P. *Nuns' Chronicles and Convent Culture in Renaissance and Counter-Reformation Italy.* Cambridge: Cambridge University Press, 2003.

Lublin, Robert I. *Costuming the Shakespearean Stage: Visual Codes of Representation in Early Modern Theatre and Culture.* Farnham: Ashgate, 2011.

Luckyj, Christina, ed. *The Duchess of Malfi: A Critical Guide.* London: Continuum, 2011.

———. *A Winter's Snake: Dramatic Form in the Tragedies of John Webster.* Athens: University of Georgia Press, 1989.

Lupton, Julia Reinhard. *Afterlives of the Saints: Hagiography, Typology, and Renaissance Literature.* Stanford, Calif.: Stanford University Press, 1996.

Lux-Sterritt, Laurence. *Redefining Female Religious Life: French Ursulines and English Ladies in Seventeenth-Century Catholicism.* Aldershot: Ashgate, 2005.

Magedanz, Stacy. "Public Justice and Private Mercy in *Measure for Measure.*" *SEL: Studies in English Literature, 1500–1900* 44.2 (2004): 317–32.

Marcus, Leah. "The Duchess's Marriage in Contemporary Contexts." In Luckyj, *The Duchess of Malfi: A Critical Guide*, 106–18.

Marlowe, Christopher. *The Complete Poems and Translations.* Ed. Stephen Orgel. New York: Penguin, 2007.

———. *Hero and Leander.* London: Edward Blount, 1596.

———. *Hero and Leander: A Facsimile of the First Edition, London 1598.* New York: Johnson Reprint, 1972.

Marlowe, Christopher, and George Chapman. *Hero and Leander.* London: Paul Linley, 1598.

Marotti, Arthur F. "Alienating Catholics in Early Modern England: Recusant Women, Jesuits and Ideological Fantasies." In Marotti, *Catholicism and Anti-Catholicism*, 1–34.

———, ed. *Catholicism and Anti-Catholicism in Early Modern English Texts.* Houndmills: Macmillan, 1999.

———, ed. *Gertrude More.* Vol. 3 of *The Early Modern Englishwoman: A Facsimile Library of Essential Works.* Series II, Printed Writings, 1641–1700: Part 4. Farnham: Ashgate, 2009.

———. *Manuscript, Print and the English Renaissance Lyric.* Ithaca, N.Y.: Cornell University Press, 1995.

———. *Religious Ideology and Cultural Fantasy: Catholic and Anti-Catholic Discourses in Early Modern England.* Notre Dame, Ind.: University of Notre Dame Press, 2005.

———. "Southwell's Remains: Catholicism and Anti-Catholicism in Early Modern England." In *Texts and Cultural Change in Early Modern England*, ed. Cedric C. Brown and Arthur F. Marotti, 37–65. New York: St. Martin's, 1997.

Martz, Louis L. *The Poetry of Meditation: A Study in English Religious Literature of the Seventeenth Century.* New Haven, Conn.: Yale University Press, 1962.

Marvell, Andrew. *The Poems of Andrew Marvell.* Ed. Nigel Smith. Harlow: Pearson, 2007.

Masten, Jeff. *Textual Intercourse: Collaboration, Authorship, and Sexualities in Renaissance Drama.* Cambridge: Cambridge University Press, 1997.

Matchinske, Megan. *Writing, Gender and State in Early Modern England: Identity Formation and the Female Subject.* Cambridge: Cambridge University Press, 1998.

May, Steven W. "George Puttenham's Lewd and Illicit Career." *Texas Studies in Literature and Language* 50.2 (2008): 143–76.

Mazzola, Elizabeth. "Who's She When She's at Home?: 'Manifest Housekeepers', Jealous Queens, and the Artistry of Mary Stuart." *Exemplaria* 15.2 (2003): 385–417.

McCann, Justin. "Introduction." In Peter Salvin and Serenus Cressy, *The Life of Father Augustine Baker, O.S.B. (1575–1641)*, ed. Justin McCann, xxiii–xxviii. Salzburg English & American Studies 20. Salzburg: Institut für Anglistik und Amerikanistik, 1997.

McFeely, Maureen Connolly. "'This day my sister should the cloister enter': The Convent as Refuge in *Measure for Measure*." In *Subjects on the World's Stage: Essays on British Literature of the Middle Ages and the Renaissance*, ed. David G. Allen and Robert A. White, 200–216. Newark: University of Delaware Press, 1995.

McManus, Claire. *Women on the Renaissance Stage: Anna of Denmark and Female Masquing in the Stuart Court (1590–1619)*. Manchester: Manchester University Press, 2002.

Mendelson, Sara H. "Concocting the World's Olio: Margaret Cavendish and Continental Influence." In "Essays from the Fifth Biennial International Margaret Cavendish Conference," ed. Lisa Hopkins, Emma Rees, and Gweno Williams. Special issue 14, *Early Modern Literary Studies* (May 2004): 11–34. http://purl.oclc.org/emls/si-14/mendconc.html.

Middleton, Thomas. *A Game at Chess*. Ed. T. H. Howard-Hill. Revels Plays. Manchester: Manchester University Press, 1993.

———. *Thomas Middleton: The Collected Works*. Ed. Gary Taylor and John Lavagnino. Oxford: Oxford University Press, 2007.

Mikesell, Margaret Lael. "Catholic and Protestant Widows in *The Duchess of Malfi*." *Renaissance and Reformation/Renaissance et Réforme* 7.4 (1983): 265–79.

Miles, Rosalind. *The Problem of "Measure for Measure": A Historical Investigation*. London: Vision Press, 1976.

Milton, John. *Milton's Selected Poetry and Prose*. Ed. Jason P. Rosenblatt. New York: Norton, 2011.

Monette, Sarah. "Speaking and Silent Women in 'Upon Appleton House'." *SEL: Studies in English Literature, 1500–1900* 42.1 (2002): 155–71.

Monta, Susannah Brietz. "Anne Dacre Howard, Countess of Arundel, and Catholic Patronage." In *English Women, Religion, and Textual Production, 1500–1625*, ed. Micheline White, 59–81. Farnham: Ashgate, 2011.

———. "Uncommon Prayer? Robert Southwell's *Short Rule for a Good Life* and Catholic Domestic Devotion in Post-Reformation England." In L. Gallagher, *Redrawing the Map*, 245–71.

More, Cresacre. *The Life and Death of Sir Thomas Moore*. 1631.

More, Gertrude. "The Sixt Confession D.G." Colwich Abbey. MS 22.

———. *The Spiritual Exercises of the Most Vertuous and Religious D. Gertrude More*. Paris: Lewis de la Fosse, 1658.

More, Thomas. *The Workes of Sir Thomas More Knyght*. London: John Cawod, John Waly, and Richarde Tottell, 1557.

Munday, Anthony, trans. *The Masque of the League and the Spanyard discovered*. London: I. Charlewoode, 1592.

Murphy, Jessica C. "'Of the sicke virgin': Britomart, Greensickness, and the Man in the Mirror." *Spenser Studies* 25 (2010): 109–27.

Murray, Molly. *The Poetics of Conversion in Early Modern English Literature: Verse and Change from Donne to Dryden*. Cambridge: Cambridge University Press, 2009.

Mush, John. "A True Report of the Life and Martyrdom of Mrs. Margaret Clitherow." In *The Troubles of Our Catholic Forefathers, Related by Themselves*, ed. John Morris, 3:360–440. London: Burns and Oates, 1877.

The New Testament of Jesus Christ. Rhemes: John Fogny, 1582.

Norman, Marion. "Dame Gertrude More and the English Mystical Tradition." *Recusant History* 13.3 (1976): 196–211.

North, Marcy. *The Anonymous Renaissance: Cultures of Discretion in Tudor-Stuart England*. Chicago: University of Chicago Press, 2003.

Oakley, Francis. "Christian Obedience and Authority, 1520–1550." In Burns, *The Cambridge History of Political Thought*, 159–92.

Orgel, Stephen. "The Case for Comus." *Representations* 81.1 (2003): 31–45.

———. "Mr. Who He?" *London Review of Books*, 8 August 2002. Reprinted in *A Companion to Shakespeare's Sonnets*, ed. Michael Schoenfeldt, 137–44. Oxford: Blackwell, 2007.

———. "Musaeus in English." *George Herbert Journal* 29.1/2 (2005/2006): 67–75.

Owen, Hywel Wyn, and Luke Bell. "The Upholland Anthology: An Augustine Baker Manuscript." *Downside Review* 107 (1989): 274–92.

Owen, Lewis. *The Running Register: Recording a True Relation for the State of the English Colledges, Seminaries and Cloysters in all Forraine Parts*. London: Robert Milbourne, 1626.

———. *The Unmasking of All Popish Monks, Friers, and Jesuits*. London: J. H. for George Gibs, 1628.

Owens, Margaret E. "John Webster, Tussaud Laureate: The Waxworks in *The Duchess of Malfi*." *ELH* 79.4 (2012): 851–77.

Oxford English Dictionary. 2nd ed. Oxford: Oxford University Press, 2013–15.

Painter, William. *The Second Tome of the Palace of Pleasure*. London: Henry Bynneman, 1567.

"Papers Relating to the English Jesuits." British Library. Additional MS 21203.

Parker, Patricia. *Inescapable Romance: Studies in the Poetics of a Mode*. Princeton, N.J.: Princeton University Press, 1979.

———. *Literary Fat Ladies: Rhetoric, Gender, Property*. London: Methuen, 1987.

Parrish, Paul A. "'O Sweet Contest': Gender and Value in 'The Weeper.'" In *New Perspectives on the Life and Art of Richard Crashaw*, ed. John R. Roberts, 127–39. Columbia: University of Missouri Press, 1990.

Pasquarella, Vincenzo. "The Implications of Tucker Brooke's Transposition in *Hero and Leander* by Christopher Marlowe." *Studies in Philology* 105.4 (2008): 520–32.

Patton, Brian. "Preserving Property: History, Genealogy, and Inheritance in 'Upon Appleton House.'" *Renaissance Quarterly* 49.4 (1996): 824–39.

Perry, Curtis, and Melissa Walter. "Staging Secret Interiors: *The Duchess of Malfi* as Inns of Court and Anticourt Drama." In Luckyj, *The Duchess of Malfi*, 87–105.

Perry, Elizabeth. "Petitioning for Patronage: An Illuminated Tale of Exile from Syon Abbey, Lisbon." In Bowden and Kelly, *The English Convents in Exile, 1600–1800*, 159–74.

Persons, Robert. *Relacion de Algunos Martyrios, que de nuevo han hecho los hereges en Inglaterra, y de otras cosas tocantes a neustra santa y catolica Religion*. Madrid: Pedro Madrigal, 1590.

Peters, Christine. "Religion, Household-State Authority, and the Defense of 'Collapsed Ladies' in Early Jacobean England." *Sixteenth Century Journal* 45.3 (2014): 631–57.

Petrarca, Francesco. *Petrarch's Lyric Poems: The Rime Sparse and Other Lyrics*. Trans. and ed. Robert M. Durling. Cambridge, Mass.: Harvard University Press, 1976.

Pfannebecker, Mareile. "'Love's Interest': Agency and Identity in a Seventeenth-Century Nun's Letters." *Literature Compass* 3.2 (2006): 149–58.

Pohl, Nicole. "'In this Sacred Space': The Secular Convent in Late Seventeenth- and Eighteenth-Century Expository Literature." In D'Monté and Pohl, eds., *Female Communities, 1600–1800*, 149–65.

Praz, Mario. *The Flaming Heart: Essays on Crashaw, Machiavelli, and Other Studies in the Relations Between Italian and English Literature from Chaucer to T. S. Eliot*. Gloucester, Mass.: Peter Smith, 1966.

Prynne, William. *Philanax Protestant*. London, 1663.

Puttenham, George. *The Art of English Poesy*. Ed. Frank Whigham and Wayne A. Rebhorn. Ithaca, N.Y.: Cornell University Press, 2007.

Questier, Michael. *Catholicism and Community in Early Modern England: Politics, Aristocratic Patronage and Religion, c. 1550–1640*. Cambridge: Cambridge University Press, 2006.

———. *Conversion, Politics and Religion in England, 1580–1625*. Cambridge: Cambridge University Press, 1996.

Raber, Karen, ed. *Elizabeth Cary*. Farnham: Ashgate, 2009.

Rambuss, Richard. *Closet Devotions*. Durham, N.C.: Duke University Press, 1998.

———. "Crashaw's Style." In L. Gallagher, *Redrawing the Map*, 132–58.

———. "Sacred Subjects and the Aversive Metaphysical Conceit: Crashaw, Serrano, Ofili." *ELH* 71 (2004): 497–530.

Rasmussen, Mark David. "Introduction: New Formalisms?" In Rasmussen, *Renaissance Literature and Its Formal Engagements*, 1–14.

———, ed. *Renaissance Literature and Its Formal Engagements*. New York: Palgrave, 2002.

Rastell, John. *An Exposition of Certaine Difficult and Obscure Words, and Termes of the Lawes of this Realme*. London: Richard Tottell, 1579.

Reigle, Kimberly. "Staging the Convent as Resistance in *The Jew of Malta* and *Measure for Measure*." *Comparative Drama* 46.4 (2012): 497–516.

Rex, Richard. "The Crisis of Obedience: God's Word and Henry's Reformation." *Historical Journal* 39.4 (1996): 863–94.

Reynolds, John. *Vox Coeli*. London, 1624.

Rhodes, J. T., ed. *Catalogue des livres provenant des religieuses angloises de Cambray: Book List of the English Benedictine Nuns of Cambrai c. 1739*. Analecta Cartusiana 119:32. Salzburg: Institut für Anglistik und Amerikanistik Universität Salzburg, 2013.

Rist, Thomas. *Revenge Tragedy and the Drama of Commemoration in Reforming England*. Aldershot: Ashgate, 2008.

Roberts, Sasha. "Feminist Criticism and the New Formalism: Early Modern Women and Literary Engagement." In *The Impact of Feminism in English Renaissance Studies*, ed. Dympna Callaghan, 67–91. New York: Palgrave Macmillan, 2007.

———. *Reading Shakespeare's Poems in Early Modern England*. Houndmills: Palgrave Macmillan, 2003.

———. "Shakespeare 'creepes into the womens closets about bedtime': Women Reading in a Room of Their Own." In *Renaissance Configurations: Voices/Bodies/Spaces, 1580–1690*, ed. Gordon McMullan, 30–63. Houndmills: Palgrave, 2001.

Robinson, John Martin. "Introduction." In De Hamel, *Syon Abbey*, 3–10.

Robinson, Thomas. *The Anatomy of the English Nunnery at Lisbon*. London: Robert Mylbourne and Philemon Stephens, 1622.

Roper, Margaret More, trans. *A Devout Treatise upon the Pater Noster*. By Desiderius Erasmus. London: Thomas Berthelet, (1526?).

Rowlands, Marie B. "Recusant Women 1560–1640." In *Women in English Society 1500–1800*, ed. Mary Prior, 112–35. London: Methuen, 1985.

Rust, Jennifer. "Malengin and Mercila, Southwell and Spenser: The Poetics of Tears and the Politics of Martyrdom in *The Faerie Queene*, Book 5, Canto 9." In L. Gallagher, *Redrawing the Map*, 185–209.

Salmon, J. H. M. "Catholic Resistance Theory, Ultramontanism, and the Royalist Response, 1580–1620." In Burns, *The Cambridge History of Political Thought*, 219–53.

Sanchez, Melissa E. " 'She Straightness on the Woods Bestows': Protestant Sexuality and English Empire in Marvell's 'Upon Appleton House.' " In *Atlantic Worlds in the Long Eighteenth Century: Seduction and Sentiment*, ed. Toni Bowers and Tita Chico, 81–96. New York: Palgrave Macmillan, 2012.

Sanders, Julie. "Tixall Revisited: The Coterie Writing of the Astons and the Thimelbys in Seventeenth-Century Staffordshire." *Staffordshire Studies* 12 (2000): 75–93.

Schoenfeldt, Michael. " 'That spectacle of too much weight': The Poetics of Sacrifice in Donne, Herbert, and Milton." *Journal of Medieval and Early Modern Studies* 31.3 (2001): 561–84.

Schwarz, Kathryn. *What You Will: Gender, Contract, and Shakespearean Social Space*. Philadelphia: University of Pennsylvania Press, 2011.

———. "The Wrong Question: Thinking Through Virginity." *differences* 13.2 (2002): 1–34.

Scott-Baumann, Elizabeth. *Forms of Engagement: Women, Poetry, and Culture 1640–1680*. Oxford: Oxford University Press, 2013.

Scott, Thomas. *Vox Populi or Newes from Spayne*. London, 1620.

Shagan, Ethan. *Popular Politics and the English Reformation*. Cambridge: Cambridge University Press, 2003.

Shakespeare, William. *The Riverside Shakespeare*. Ed. G. Blakemore Evans and J. J. M. Tobin. Boston: Houghton Mifflin, 1997.

Shell, Alison. *Catholicism, Controversy and the English Literary Imagination, 1558–1660*. Cambridge: Cambridge University Press, 1999.

———. *Oral Culture and Catholicism in Early Modern England*. Cambridge: Cambridge University Press, 2007.

Sherman, Jane. "The Pawns' Allegory in Middleton's *A Game at Chesse*." *Review of English Studies* 29 (1978): 147–59.

Shuger, Debora. "Laudian Feminism and the Household Republic of Little Gidding." *Journal of Medieval and Early Modern Studies* 44.1 (2014): 69–94.

———. *Political Theologies in Shakespeare's England: The Sacred and the State in "Measure for Measure."* New York: Palgrave, 2001.

———. *The Renaissance Bible: Scholarship, Sacrifice, and Subjectivity*. Berkeley: University of California Press, 1994.

Slater, Michael. "Spenser's Poetics of 'Transfixion' in the Allegory of Chastity." *SEL: Studies in English Literature, 1500–1900* 54.1 (2014): 41–58.

Slights, Jessica, and Michael Morgan Holmes. "Isabella's Order: Religious Acts and Personal Desires in *Measure for Measure*." *Studies in Philology* 95.3 (1998): 263–92.

Smith, A. H. *English Place-Name Elements*. 2 vols. Cambridge: Cambridge University Press, 1956.

Smyth, Adam. "'Shreds of holinesse': George Herbert, Little Gidding, and Cutting Up Texts in Early Modern England." *ELR* 42.3 (2012): 452–81.

Southwell, Robert. *Marie Magdalens Funeral Teares*. London: Gabriel Cawood, 1591.

———. *Marie Magdalens Funerall Teares*. London: I.R. for W.L., 1602. British Library, 11623. aa.42.

———. *Saint Peters Complaint, With Other Poemes*. London: John Wolfe, 1595.

Spenser, Edmund. *The Faerie Qveene*. Ed. A. C. Hamilton. London: Longman, 1977.

Sperling, Jutta Gisela. *Convents and the Body Politic in Late Renaissance Venice*. Chicago: University of Chicago Press, 1999.

Staley, Lynn. "Enclosed Spaces." In *Cultural Reformations: Medieval and Renaissance in Literary History*, ed. Brian Cummings and James Simpson, 113–33. Oxford: Oxford University Press, 2010.

The Statutes at Large. London: Bonham Norton and John Bill, 1618.

Stevenson, Jane, and Peter Davidson. *Early Modern Women Poets: An Anthology*. Oxford: Oxford University Press, 2001.

Stewart, Susan. *Poetry and the Fate of the Senses*. Chicago: University of Chicago Press, 2002.

Strasser, Ulrike. *State of Virginity: Gender, Religion, and Politics in an Early Modern Catholic State*. Ann Arbor: University of Michigan Press, 2004.

Stretton, Tim. "Misogyny and Male Honour in the Life of George Puttenham, Elizabethan 'Princepleaser.'" In *Worth and Repute: Valuing Gender in Late Medieval and Early Modern Europe; Essays in Honour of Barbara Todd*, ed. Kim Kippen and Lori Woods, 337–63. Toronto: Centre for Reformation and Renaissance Studies, 2011.

Strong, Roy. *The Cult of Elizabeth: Elizabethan Portraiture and Pageantry*. London: Thames and Hudson, 1977.

Summit, Jennifer. *Lost Property: The Woman Writer and English Literary History, 1380–1589*. Chicago: University of Chicago Press, 2000.

Suzuki, Mihoko. "Daughters of Coke: Women's Legal Discourse in England, 1642–1689." In *Challenging Orthodoxies: The Social and Cultural Worlds of Early Modern Women; Essays Presented to Hilda L. Smith*, ed. Sigrun Haude and Melinda S. Zook, 165–91. Farnham: Ashgate/Gower, 2014.

Taylor, Gary. *Castration: An Abbreviated History of Western Manhood*. New York: Routledge, 2000.

———. "Forms of Opposition: Shakespeare and Middleton." *ELR* 24.2 (1994): 283–314.

———. "Historicism, Presentism and Time: Middleton's *The Spanish Gypsy* and *A Game at Chess*." *SEDERI: Journal of the Spanish Society for English Renaissance Studies* 18 (2008): 147–70.

Teller, Joseph R. "Why Crashaw Was Not Catholic: The Passion and Popular Protestant Devotion." *ELR* 43.2 (2013): 239–67.

Tennenhouse, Leonard. *Power on Display*. New York: Methuen, 1986.

Teskey, Gordon. *Allegory and Violence*. Ithaca, N.Y.: Cornell University Press, 1996.

Travitsky, Betty S. "The Puzzling Letters of Sister Elizabeth Sa[u]nder[s]." In *Textual Conversations in the Renaissance: Ethics, Authors, Technologies*, ed. Zachary Lesser and Benedict S. Robinson, 131–45. Aldershot: Ashgate, 2006.

Tricomi, Albert H. *Anticourt Drama in England, 1603–1642*. Charlottesville: University Press of Virginia, 1989.

Trolander, Paul, and Zeynep Tenger. *Sociable Criticism in England: 1625–1725*. Newark: University of Delaware Press, 2007.

Van Hyning, Victoria. "Cloistered Voices: English Nuns in Exile, 1550–1800." Ph.D. thesis, University of Sheffield, 2014.

———. "Expressing Selfhood in the Convent: Anonymous Chronicling and Subsumed Autobiography." *British Catholic History* 32.2 (2014): 219–34.

Vaughan, William. *The Golden Fleece*. London: Francis Williams, 1626.

Verstegan, Richard. *Theatrum Crudelitatum Hæreticorum Nostri Temporis*. Antwerpe: Adrian Hubert, 1587.

Virgil. *The Aeneid*. Trans. Robert Fitzgerald. London: Harvill, 1984.

Walker, Claire. "Combining Martha and Mary: Gender and Work in Seventeenth-Century English Cloisters." *Sixteenth Century Journal* 30.2 (Summer 1999): 397–418.

———. "Continuity and Isolation: The Bridgettines in the Sixteenth and Seventeenth Centuries." In Jones and Walsham, *Syon Abbey and Its Books*, 155–76.

———. "'Doe not supose me a well mortifyed Nun dead to the world': Letter-Writing in Early Modern English Convents." In Daybell, *Early Modern Women's Letter Writing, 1450–1700*, 159–76.

———. *Gender and Politics in Early Modern Europe: English Convents in France and the Low Countries*. New York: Palgrave Macmillan, 2003.

———. "Spiritual Property: The English Benedictine Nuns of Cambrai and the Dispute over the Baker Manuscripts." In *Women, Property, and the Letters of the Law in Early Modern England*, ed. Nancy E. Wright, Margaret W. Ferguson, and A. R. Buck, 237–55. Toronto: University of Toronto Press, 2004.

Wall, Wendy. *The Imprint of Gender: Authorship and Publication in the English Renaissance*. Ithaca, N.Y.: Cornell University Press, 1993.

———. "Just a Spoonful of Sugar: Syrup and Domesticity in Early Modern England." *Modern Philology* 104.2 (2006): 149–72.

Wallace, David. *Strong Women: Life, Text, and Territory, 1347–1645*. Oxford: Oxford University Press, 2011.

Walsham, Alexandra. *Church Papists: Catholicism, Conformity and Confessional Polemic in Early Modern England*. London: Royal Historical Society, 1993.

———. *The Reformation of the Landscape: Religion, Identity, and Memory in Early Modern Britain and Ireland*. Oxford: Oxford University Press, 2011.

Warren, Nancy Bradley. *The Embodied Word: Female Spiritualities, Contested Orthodoxies, and English Religious Cultures, 1350–1700*. Notre Dame, Ind.: University of Notre Dame Press, 2010.

———. *Women of God and Arms: Female Spirituality and Political Conflict, 1380–1600*. Philadelphia: University of Pennsylvania Press, 2005.

Weaver, Elissa B. *Convent Theatre in Early Modern Italy: Spiritual Fun and Learning for Women*. Cambridge: Cambridge University Press, 2007.

Webster, John. *The Duchess of Malfi*. Ed. René Weis. Oxford: Oxford University Press, 1996.

Whetstone, George. *An Heptameron of Civill Discourses*. London: Richard Jones, 1582.

Whigham, Frank. *Seizures of the Will in Early Modern English Drama*. Cambridge: Cambridge University Press, 1996.

Whigham, Frank, and Wayne A. Rebhorn. "Introduction." In Puttenham, *The Art of English Poesy*, 1–72.

White, Micheline. "Women Writers and Literary-Religious Circles in the Elizabethan West Country: Anne Dowriche, Anne Lock Prowse, Anne Lock Moyle, Elizabeth Rous, and Ursula Fulford." *Modern Philology* 103.2 (2005): 187–214.

Wilcox, Helen. "'Free and Easy as ones discourse'?: Genre and Self-Expression in the Poems and Letters of Early Modern Englishwomen." In *Genre and Women's Life Writing in Early Modern England*, ed. Michelle M. Dowd, Julie A. Eckerle, and Laura Knoppers, 15–32. Abingdon: Ashgate, 2007.

Williams, John. *A Vindication of the History of the Gunpowder-Treason*. London: Richard Chiswell, 1681.

Wilson-Okamura, David Scott. "Belphoebe and Gloriana." *ELR* 39.1 (2009): 47–73.

Wolfe, Heather. "Dame Barbara Constable: Catholic Antiquarian, Advisor, and Closet Missionary." In *Catholic Culture in Early Modern England*, ed. Ronald Corthell, Frances E. Dolan, Christopher Highley, and Arthur F. Marotti, 158–88. Notre Dame, Ind.: University of Notre Dame Press, 2007.

———, ed. *The Literary Career and Legacy of Elizabeth Cary, 1613–1680*. New York: Palgrave Macmillan, 2007.

———. "Reading Bells and Loose Papers: Reading and Writing Practices of the English Benedictine Nuns of Cambrai and Paris." In *Early Modern Women's Manuscript Writing*, ed. Victoria E. Burke and Jonathan Gibson, 135–56. Aldershot: Ashgate, 2004.

Wooding, Lucy. *Rethinking Catholicism in Reformation England*. Oxford: Oxford University Press, 2000.

Yachnin, Paul. "*A Game at Chess*: Thomas Middleton's 'Praise of Folly.'" *Modern Language Quarterly: A Journal of Literary History* 48.2 (1987): 107–23.

Yates, Julian. "Parasitic Geographies: Manifesting Catholic Identity in Early Modern England." In Marotti, *Catholicism and Anti-Catholicism*, 63–84.

Yepes, Diego de. *Historia particular de la persecucion de Inglaterra*. Madrid: Luis Sanchez, 1599.

Zurcher, Andrew. "Deficiency and Supplement: Perfecting the Prosthetic Text." *SEL: Studies in English Literature, 1500–1900* 52.1 (2012): 143–64.

INDEX

ACKNOWLEDGMENTS

This book would not exist without the many individuals and communities who have facilitated my work, and I am delighted to have the opportunity to recognize their contributions. I have been especially lucky in my mentors: Stephen Orgel has been a champion of the project since its earliest stages, and his guidance and support have been essential to its development. Roland Greene's intellectual generosity has enriched my career in innumerable ways, and his rigorous readings of earlier versions helped to shape the final form of the book. Jennifer Summit's feedback allowed me to hone my arguments, and James Holstun remains my model for engaged scholarship and teaching. I have also had the good fortune to learn from Terry Castle, Denise Gigante, Seth Lerer, Patricia Parker, and the late J. Martin Evans, all of whom helped to cultivate the ideas behind this project.

At Lehigh University, I have benefited from generous and supportive colleagues, including Lyndon Dominique, Suzanne Edwards, Betsy Fifer, Scott Paul Gordon, Dawn Keetley, Barry Kroll, Barbara Pavlock, James Peterson, and Barbara Traister. Mary Foltz's enthusiasm for this project helped sustain my own, and Kate Crassons read the entire manuscript and offered excellent advice on how to improve it; I am glad to have them both as interlocutors and friends. At the University of Texas at Austin, Frank Whigham and Wayne Rebhorn invited me to participate in the 2010 Texas Institute for Literary and Textual Studies summer symposium on "Literature and Religious Conflict," at which they and other symposium participants offered valuable feedback on an early version of the third chapter.

I have learned a great deal in conversations with other scholars working on nuns, including Jaime Goodrich, Nicky Hallett, Carmen Mangion, Laurence Lux-Sterritt, and Victoria Van Hyning. I am particularly grateful to Caroline Bowden, whose generous mentorship and exceptional editorial work have made so much possible. Frances Dolan, Brad Gregory, Arthur Marotti, David Wallace, and Nancy Bradley Warren offered encouragement at various stages of the project's development, and discussions with friends such as J. K. Barret, Lee Konstantinou, Noah Millstone, Michael Ursell, Ryan Zurowski, and Jolene Hubbs helped to refine my thinking along the way. Jolene not only read the completed manuscript, but also many half-finished bits at nearly every step in the process; she is a brilliant colleague and beloved friend, and I take full responsibility for any infelicitous adjectives or adverbs that remain.

The generosity and rigor with which two anonymous readers approached my manuscript helped me to clarify my ideas and better articulate my intervention; this is a stronger book as a result of their thoughtful advice. Working with Jerry Singerman of Penn Press has been a joy: his kindness and professionalism have made the publication process far smoother than I had imagined possible.

Early archival work for this project was supported by fellowships from Stanford University, the Institute of Historical Research, the Huntington Library, and the Renaissance Society of America. I was able to complete the book with the support of a National Endowment for the Humanities Summer Stipend, a Faculty Research Grant at Lehigh University, and the generous pre-tenure summer funding offered by Lehigh's College of Arts and Sciences. I am especially grateful to the staff at the many libraries and archives where I worked, including the Arundel Castle Archives, Beinecke Library, Bibliothèque Mazarine, Bodleian Library, British Library, Hampshire County Records Office, Harry Ransom Center, Huntington Library, Lille Archives Départementales du Nord, Stanford's Green Library, and the University of Exeter Special Collections. My research on the English convents was facilitated by the hospitality and knowledge of Sister Christina Kenworthy-Browne and the late Sister Gregory Kirkus at Bar Convent, Sister Margaret Truran at Stanbrook Abbey, Dom David Foster at Downside Abbey, and Sister Benedict Rowell at Colwich Abbey. Special thanks go to the librarians at Lehigh, including Lois Black, Ilhan Citak, Heather Simoneau, and the very patient individuals handling interlibrary loan. Part of Chapter 2 previously appeared, in a different form, as "The Literary Lives of Nuns: Crafting Identities Through Exile" in *The English Convents in Exile, 1600–1800: Communities, Culture and Identity*, ed. Caroline Bowden and James E. Kelly (Farnham: Ashgate, 2013), 71–86, and I thank the publishers for their permission to reprint.

I would not be in this profession were it not for the students I have the privilege to teach, and from whom I learn so much. While it is impossible to record all of those who have enriched my life and career, I would like to take special notice of Michael Albright, Luke Barnhart, Kimberly Campbell, Alicia Clark-Barnes, Kelsey Lee, Sava Marinkovic, Emily Rau, Jacob Silber, Sarah Tischbein, Matthew Werkheiser, Rachel Whittemore, and especially Jacob Stern. For helping to make Bethlehem a home, I thank my friends Jessica Aberle, Colleen Martell, Brad Rogers, and particularly David Fine, whose conversation and friendship illuminate so much. Domenic Breininger saw me through the final stages of the book's completion, and offered clarifying respite from it.

My deepest gratitude goes to my two families. It is impossible to adequately express what the friendship of Amanda Betts, Sandra and Garret Lau, and Kate Racculia means to me, especially as our circle has been augmented by the joyful addition of Elena and Zoey. Thank you for everything. Kate read every word of this book more times than either of us should count, and she remains my first, last, and best reader; none of this, etc. My godmother Pamela White, brother Devon Lay, sister-in-law Lauren, nieces Madelyn and Gabriella, and parents Jody Duggan-Lay and Stephen Lay have been unfailing in their love, support, and enthusiasm. This book is for them and in memory of my grandmother, Edna Livingston Duggan, whose ferocious intellect and religious politics are at the root of my interest in this topic—an influence she never would have imagined but I hope would have appreciated.